Foreign Legions
of the
Third Reich

by
David Littlejohn
M.A., A.L.A.

Vol. 3: Albania, Czechoslovakia, Greece, Hungary and Yugoslavia

R. JAMES BENDER PUBLISHING
P.O. Box 23456, San Jose, Calif. 95153 [408] 225-5777

INTRODUCTION

2775755

This third volume of "Foreign Legions" deals with Central and Southern Europe. It also contains a substantial "Addendum" made possible by the large amount of additional material, especially relating to Belgium, which has become available since publication.

The author would like to express his gratitude to all those readers of the first two volumes of this series who, as invited, wrote in with further information and/or corrections. He would wish to extend this invitation to the present volume as well. Any supplementary facts or corrections would be very welcome. In this connection particularly appreciated would be further information on the youth movements mentioned (with view to possible future publication on this subject).

It may be observed that much of the material on the medals and decorations of Slovakia and Croatia has already appeared in the author's "Orders, Decorations, Medals and Badges of the Third Reich" Vol. 2 (Bender, 1973), but as this is now out of print, it was considered appropriate to include this material here along with some additional facts. Quite a sizeable section has been devoted to the orders, decorations and medals of Hungary. This has been done because, as medal collectors will be aware, no comprehensive study of the awards of the Horthy period in Hungary has ever appeared in English. This is an attempt to remedy this sad deficiency.

The fourth, and final, volume in this series will deal with the "Ostvolk" - the multifarious array of eastern volunteers in the German forces, along with those from the Baltic states, Finland and Romania.

ACKNOWLEDGEMENTS

The author gratefully acknowledges the help afforded by the following:

VerKuilen Ager, Chris Ailsby, Brian Ambrose, Albert Barrows, Stan Cook, Václav Duchač, Adrian Forman, Peter Groch, Paul Jarvis, Prof. Y. Jelinck, Pierre P. Lambert-Dudeffand, Mike McAdams, Dr. André Mathias, Václav Měřička, Andrew Mollo, Claude Morin, George Petersen, Marcel Roubiček, Otto Spronk, W.P.B.R. Saris, Hugh P. Taylor, Pierre C.T. Verheye, Jan Vincx, Adrian Weale, César van Wiele.

A special word of thanks is due to John Trenka and Zoltán V. Kőrössy, who contributed many of the photographs which appear in the "Hungary" section as well as supplying information to go with them.

3

TABLE OF CONTENTS

ALBANIA

Italy conquered and occupied Albania in March 1939 (six months *before* the out-break of the Second World War). After the Axis victory over Yugoslavia in 1941, the frontiers of Albania were extended at Yugoslavia's expense to include the province of Kossovo with its mixed Serb and Moslem population. When Italy quit the war, Germany took over the "protection" of Albania. Hitler ordained that it was to be "treated generously" (this was due mainly to his desire to maintain good relations with the Islamic world - Albania's population being largely Moslem).

Himmler argued that with their traditional hatred of the Christian Serbs, the Albanians could be counted on to make fierce anti-resistance fighters. Following this line of reasoning, he authorized the setting up, in April 1944, of an all-Albanian division of the Waffen S.S. For this new formation he selected the name Skanderbeg in recognition of Albania's most celebrated warrior-hero (Iskander Beg) who, in the mid-15th century, had driven the Turkish invaders out of Albania.

Although nominally "Albanian," the new division drew many of its recruits from the former Yugoslav region of Kossovo. Volunteers came forward in insufficient numbers (about 9,000 volunteered of whom only 6,500 were passed as medically fit), and it became necessary to pad the new division with men drafted from other S.S. units. The cadre personnel were German or *Volksdeutsche*. By August the division, now known as the *21 Waffen-Gebirgs Division der S.S. "Skanderbeg,"* was deemed fit to be sent into action against the Partisans (the only duty for which it had been trained). Its performance was lamentable. Within two months there had been close to 3,500 desertions! To compensate for these losses, Himmler was obliged to draft in some 3,800 officers, petty officers, and ratings of the Kriegsmarine currently "unemployed" in various parts of the Aegean. Even this was not enough to save it from disintegration. By early 1945 the 21st Division was in such sorry shape that Himmler decided to stand it down and use what reliable personnel remained to form a "Battle Group" *(Kampfgruppe)* - a conveniently vague term which could signify anything from several thousand men to a few score! Eventually the "Skanderbeg" faithful were incorporated into the "Prinz Eugen" Division as part of its 14th Regiment which was then accorded the somewhat dubious honor of bearing the name "Skanderbeg." The involuntary "volunteers" from the Kriegsmarine appear to have ended up in another scratch Waffen S.S. division (the 32nd Volunteer Infantry Division) hastily thrown together in the closing stages of the war.

Collar patch with runes. Worn only by officers.

Plain black collar patch. Worn by non-commissioned ranks.

Special collar patch with the helmet of Skanderbeg. This was tried out but was withdrawn on the grounds that it was unrecognizable from any distance.

Albanian double headed eagle worn on left arm by all ranks of the division (an example in the Forman Collection).

Silver-grey thread on black Skanderbeg cuff title.

The "Skanderbeg" Division had a special collar patch designed for it. This took the form of the goat's head helmet of Iskander Beg. No doubt this patriotic symbol was highly appropriate but it was also, unfortunately, quite unrecognizable at any distance! The result was that it was never adopted (although it was certainly manufactured and the S.S. "map" continued to feature it long after its official abandonment!) In place of this special patch, officers wore the standard S.S. runes, and other ranks simply a plain black patch. On the left upper arm the black double headed eagle of Albania was worn on a red shield with a black backing. As a mountain division, its members were entitled to wear the S.S. type edelweiss on the right upper arm and on the side of the cap. A black and silver "Bevo" cuff title SKANDERBEG was authorized. It may have been carried over to the "Prinz Eugen" when the "Skanderbeg" veterans were transferred to the 14th Regiment of that division (this, however, is uncertain).

A conical fez, or skull cap, in white lamb's wool (traditional Albanian headgear) with the S.S. eagle and death's head on the front was authorized for wear by Moslem members of the division.

German made belt buckle with Skanderbeg helmet. This may, or may not, have been intended for the Skanderbeg Division.

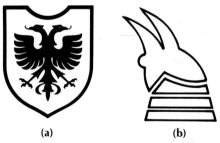

(a)   (b)

(a) The official vehicle sign of the division; (b) an alternative, but unconfirmed vehicle sign (based on the Skanderbeg helmet).

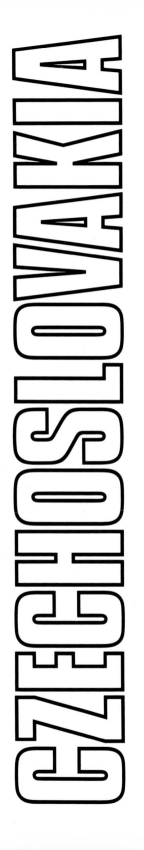

CZECHOSLOVAKIA

CZECHOSLOVAKIA

The Treaty of Versailles which reconstituted Europe after the First World War brought several new states into being - among these, Czechoslovakia. This was created out of four former regions of the defunct Austro-Hungarian Empire: Bohemia-Moravia, Slovakia, Carpethian Ruthenia, and parts of Silesia. The Czechs, Slovaks, and Moravians are Slav peoples, but considerable bodies of ethnic Germans were left within the bounds of the new state. These minorities were not always happy to accept their changed status and their reluctance turned to militancy with the rise of Hitler in neighboring Germany. Discontent was deliberately fostered as a part of long-term Nazi strategy. Without doubt, the German propagandists from the Reich found fertile soil among the expatriate Teutons of Czechoslovakia.

In 1910, a Pan-Austrian Workers Party had been formed in Vienna. Before the end of the First World War, it had been renamed the German National-Socialist Workers Party (D.N.S.A.P.). A Czech section of this party was created in November 1918. Despite the close similarity of their party labels, the D.N.S.A.P. and Hitler's N.S.D.A.P. were not directly connected although sharing many of the same pan-Germanic, anti-Slav, and anti-Semitic sentiments. By 1929 the D.N.S.A.P. had some 200,000 supporters among German-speaking Czech citizens.

Even innocent sounding bodies like the German Gymnastic Association *(Deutsche Turnverband)* acted as vehicles for the dissemination of Hitlerite ideas among the German community. This influence was particularly strong along the border regions of Bohemia and Germany (known as the Sudetenland where Germans formed a high percentage of the population). Tension between the Czech state and its German subjects increased and led to the suppression of overtly Nazi parties and political "sports clubs." In October 1933 the D.N.S.A.P. went into voluntary dissolution (one day before the official decree ordering it to do so came into effect). In the same year a *Sudetendeutsche Heimatfront* (Sudeten German Home Front, or S.H.F.) was formed under Konrad Henlein, leader of the *Deutsche Turnverband* in the Sudetenland. In order to conform with Czech regulations relating to political movements, the "Front" changed its name to "Party (Sudetendeutsche Partei, or S.d.P.) the following year. Uniform as such had been banned by the Czech authorities since 1931, but the wearing of a brassard was permitted, and "rank" within the S.d.P. was indicated by a scheme of bars and chevrons, etc., worn behind the Party's lapel badge.

Throughout the mid-30s, the S.d.P. stepped up its activities, encouraged and financed by various Nazi agencies in the Reich. Hitler's occupation of Austria in March 1938 left the Czechs in an even more precarious position. Western Czechoslovakia was now enclosed on both flanks by "jaws" of Nazi controlled territory, and the government was well aware that the type of subversion that had preceded the invasion of Austria was now being practiced by Hitler's henchmen within their own state. Prior to the Anschluss, a so-called "Austrian Legion" had been formed by the S.S. and S.A. from among pro-Nazi exiles from Austria. This clandestine "Legion" had been transformed into regular S.S. and S.A. units after Austria had been incorporated into the Greater German Reich, but its organizational structure (in Germany) had remained intact. This was now put to use as the basis for a Sudeten German Legion (Sudetendeutsche Legion) raised along exactly similar lines. Like the Austrian Legion, the Sudeten Legion was not, in reality, a single entity, but the generic term for a variety of units, some S.A., some Allgemeine S.S., a few Waffen S.S. (known at this point in time as S.S.-Verfügungstruppen). The S.A. units were styled S.A. Hilfswerk Nord-West (H.N.W.), roughly, "S.A. Auxiliary Formation North-West." As a sub-division of S.A. Gruppe Hochland, its members were entitled to wear an edelweiss badge on the side of their kepis. On their reddish-brown collar patches (right side) they may have had the metal letters HNW (or simply NW). There were around 8,000 men in this particular S.A. formation. Those of a higher physical standard and proven political dedication (perhaps some 1,500) were accepted into the Allgemeine S.S. Of these latter, about 500 were adjudged fit to be admitted into the S.S.-VT Standarte "Sudetenland" recently formed at Munich (Dachau). Later this regiment was incorporated into the S.S. Standarte 2 "Deutschland," thus, finally, to become part of the celebrated "Das Reich" Division.

Within the Sudetenland itself, Henlein had formed a strong arm group of the S.d.P. known as the Freiwilliger Schutzdienst (Volunteer Defense Service), or F.S., ostensibly to provide "physical training and furnish voluntary aid in the case of accidents and natural disasters," but in reality a para-military training unit. The local S.d.P. leader at Eger let the cat out of the bag when he spoke of it as, "a body of soldiers on duty at all times."

From July 1938 onwards, the German army ran weekly, five-day courses (Monday to Saturday) at Neuhammer, near Breslau, for F.S. men who secretly slipped out of, and back into, Czechoslovakia under the guise of holiday-makers or travelling businessmen. In Germany they were furnished with a make-shift uniform (mainly German army) and instructed in the arts of rifle shooting and demolition of static defenses - clearly in preparation for sabotage of the Czech frontier installations. Each course comprised some 50 trainees who, at its conclusion, took an oath of loyalty to Hitler. **13**

In September 1938, the Sudeten Legion had its name changed to *Sudetendeutsches Freikorps.* Units were set up along the Czech border, and it appeared that an armed insurrection might break out at any moment. This was prevented only by the shameful "Munich Agreement," by which Britain and France (without consulting, or even informing, the Czechs) turned over the entire Sudetenland to Hitler. On October 1st of the same year, Czechoslovakia ceded more than a third of her territory (including her most vital frontier defenses) to Germany. With the result that only six months later, on 14 March 1939, when the Germans moved in to take over the remainder of Czechoslovakia, the government was powerless to resist. From that day on the Czech state as a political entity ceased to exist. The Sudetenland was incorporated into the Reich as *Gau Sudetenland,* Bohemia and Moravia were declared to be a German "Protectorate," while Slovakia became, in theory, an independent state - in practice, a German puppet.

SUDETENLAND

The Sudetenland was formally incorporated into the Greater German Reich in January 1939. The headquarters of the new *Reichsgau* was at Reichenberg; its leader, Gauleiter Konrad Henlein - his reward from a grateful Führer for his part in the destruction of Czechoslovakia.

Konrad Henlein in uniform.

Type of belt buckle worn by Henlein and Freikorps members.

After the absorption of the Sudetenland into Germany proper, the S.d.P. no longer had a function to fulfill and was, consequently, dissolved. All the Nazi organizational structure was introduced. Until such time as standard N.S.D.A.P. uniforms were available, some S.d.P. leaders wore a sort of provisional uniform consisting of tunic, trousers, and peaked cap. On the band of the cap was a ribbon in the Sudeten colors: black/red/black, and on the peak an elongated swastika very similar to that later adopted by the Flemish Germanis S.S. (see Vol. 2 of the present series). A semi-uniform of white shirt, black tie, and black breeches was sometimes worn by S.d.P. members both before and after the take-over of the Sudetenland (despite the Czech government's prescription of "political uniform").

An S.A. *Gruppe Sudeten* was established in September 1938 drawing its strength mainly from the now disbanded *Freikorps*. Although Prague was not, of course, included in the Sudetenland, S.A. *Standarte 52* (a regiment of *S.A. Gruppe Sudeten*) was quartered in that city (again made up largely of ex-*Freikorps* men).

Decoration of Honor for Gau Sudetenland. Instituted as late as January 1944. All gilt except for the black-red-black (Sudeten colors) at base of wreath.

Three versions of the Achievement Badge of the German Gymnastic Association in the Sudetenland (in fact, a political organization).

(a)   (b)   (c)

Lapel badges: (a) S.H.F. (Sudeten Heimat Front)
              (b) S.d.P. (Sudetendeutsche Partei) Ladies type
              (c) S.d.P. male party member

(all the above are silver on red.

S.d.P. lapel badges of rank. There are, in fact, 14
ranks since each of the above can be in gold or
in silver. The author apologizes for the fact that
the first of the above (the type with oak leaves)
was wrongly identified in his "Orders, Decorations and Medals of the Third Reich," Vol. 2 as
being the "Badge of Honor of the S.d.P."

Karl Hermann Frank wears the first version illustrated above with oak leaves.

16

The last gathering of the S.d.P. flags at Reichenberg, 5 November 1938.

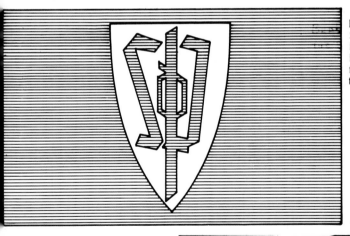

Brassard (and flag) of the S.d.P. Sudeten deutsche Partei (Sudeten German Party) which existed before the German occupation of Czechoslovakia.

Flag of the S.d.P. after the German occupation of Bohemia-Moravia. This flag was also used later by the Kuratorium. This design was also sometimes seen as a brassard (photos show, for example, K.H. Frank wearing one). Black and red are the colors of Bohemia.

Metal belt buckle with runic F.S. Said to be for the Freikorps Sudetenland but probably never issued. A box containing a large number of these was dug up in Czechoslovakia in 1979.

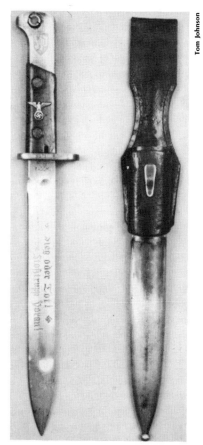

Tom Johnson

Bayonet of the Assault troop (Stosstrupp) of the S.d.P. or Freikorps Sudetenland. Blade says *Sieg oder Tot* (Victory or death), and *Stosstrupp voran* (Assault troops, advance). Note S.d.P. badge and S.A. type eagle and swastika on hilt of bayonet.

Belt buckle of the S.d.P.

Members of the Freiwilliger Schutzdienst perform military style drill with spades. Although not actually in uniform, they deliberately dressed alike. It would take only a change of dress to convert this squad into German R.A.D.!

BOHEMIA-MORAVIA

In March 1939, a "Protectorate" of Bohemia and Moravia was established. Although, for all practical purposes a satellite of Germany, it was permitted its own civilian administration under a Czech president, Dr. Emil Hácha. All political parties were banned except the "official" National Solidarity *(Národni Souručenstvi)* Movement (N.S.) which declared itself in favor of the setting up of a corporatist state on fascist lines. By May 1939 over 98% of the male population of the Protectorate had been enrolled in the N.S., but its very size made it unwieldy, and its protestations of loyalty were never trusted by the Germans. Theoretically, the supreme authority was the *Reichsprotektor,* a post held by career diplomat Constantin von Neurath from 1938 to 1943, but in truth, real power was vested in his deputy. The most celebrated incumbent of this office was Reinhard Heydrich (appointed in September 1941 to succeed K. H. Frank). When, in June 1942, Heydrich was assassinated by the Czech resistance, his place was taken by Police General Kurt Daluege. In August 1943 there was a revision of the administrative structure of the Protectorate. The largely nominal office of *Reichsprotektor* was given to Wilhelm Frick (Nazi Germany's Minister of the Interior), and a new post of German Minister of State in the Protectorate of Bohemia-Moravia was created. Karl Hermann Frank (predecessor to Heydrich as Deputy *Reichsprotektor)* was given this post and invested with virtually dictatorial powers. He remained in it until the end of the war (after which, along with Daluege, he was hanged as a war criminal).

Although, in theory, all political parties, other than the N.S. were banned, a number of overtly fascist organizations were allowed to continue in existence. They were:

(a) The National Fascist Community *(Národni Obec Fašistická)* formed by General Rudolf Gajda in 1920 and owing its inspiration to Mussolini rather than Hitler.

Membership badge of the Národni Obec Fašistická (about twice actual size).

(b) Czech National Solidarity Movement "The Flag" (C.N.S.T. *"Vlajka"*). It had a membership of around 13,000 (less than 0.2 percent of the population) and, like the above, was modeled more on Italian than German fascism.

Two versions of the membership badge (not actual size) of the C.N.S.T. Vlajka Movement *(Česky Národni Souručenstvi Vlajka).*

Two membership badges of the Národni Sourčenstvi. The ladies' version is the same as for adult males except that it is on a gilt, horizontal brooch pin. The motto "Vlasti Zdar" means "All for the Fatherland."

Adult males   **Youth**

(c) Fascist Action Committee *(Fasisticke Akčni Komité)*

(d) Movement for National Restoration *(Akce Národni Obrody).* This was not so much a political party as a grouping of anti-Semites.

(e) Czech Federation for Collaboration with the Germans *(Cesky svaz pro Spolupraći s Němci)* founded by Jan Fousek shortly after the outbreak of war.

Gold and silver honor badges for members of the Czech Federation for Collaboration with Germany.

(f) The Activists. A group of out-and-out collaborators founded by Colonel Emanuel Moravec (formerly of the Czech General Staff) in the summer of 1940.

None of these groups was of any great importance in itself, but as the war progressed, the leaders of some of these factions began to infiltrate the Czech civil administration and displace officials whose "loyalty" was regarded as suspect. For example, Jan Fousek was, in May 1941, placed in charge of the N.S. His first action was to dismiss 1,573 prominent members of the party as politically untrustworthy. Fousek then compelled all N.S. office holders to take an oath of unconditional loyalty to Hitler. Colonel Moravec of the Activists became a cabinet minister (in January 1942) as Secretary for Education. Later he was appointed to the Office of Public Enlightenment (the Czechs borrowed this euphemism for "Propaganda" from the Germans!). When the *Kuratorium für Jugenderzeihung* (see below) was formed, Moravec was appointed its General Leader.

(a)

(a) Lapel badge of the D.N.S.A.P. (German National-Socialist Workers Party). Despite the close similarity of name, this was *not* directly related to Hitler's N.S.D.A.P. (although sharing many of its aims).

(b)

Peter Groch

(b) A well-made lapel badge, but very probably only a commemorative piece relating to the occupation of the Sudetenland in 1938 rather than an award (certainly not the equivalent of the Golden Party Badge).

(c)

C. Ailsby Collection

(c) Lapel badge of the DeutscheTurnerbund with date "1919" (the date on which this "Gymnastic Association" was founded in Czechoslovakia).

(d)

V. Duchac

(d) Lapel badge worn by German civilian employees in the Protectorate.

Honor Shield of Duke Wencelas. With and without wreath, below is the miniature with wreath. Black eagle with red "flames" on silver.

With the break-up of Czechoslovakia, the former Czech army was disbanded, but in October 1939, President Hácha asked the Germans for permission to raise an armed force to assist the police in the maintenance of internal order and security in the Protectorate. The Germans agreed. They stipulated, however, that this Government army *(Regierungstruppe, or Vládni Vojsko)* must not exceed 8,000. In practice, it fell short of this figure. It had about 7,000 members of whom 280 were officers (including no fewer than 40 generals!). In addition, there were some 350 uniformed civilian administrators, 15 of whom held a rank equivalent to that of army general. The result was a somewhat top heavy force! Artillery and automatic weapons were not allowed. The *Regierungstruppe* had only Model 98/24 Mauser rifles (ex-Czech army), bayonets, and, for officers and senior NCOs, 7.65mm calibre revolvers. Sabers, later replaced by daggers (ex-Czech Air Force), could be carried by commissioned ranks on ceremonial duties or on leave. Cavalry units were envisaged, but the horses ear-marked for these were appropriated by the Wehrmacht at the start of the Russian campaign.

The government army had three rather grandly named "Inspectorates" - Prague, Brno, and Hradec Krolové - each with four battalions (subdivided into four companies each). Almost all the personnel were former officers or NCOs of the Czech army. Few soldiers can have had so peaceful a life! Duties consisted either in ceremonials or "guarding" property and installations which, in fact, were never at any time in danger of attack! Only in the latter stages of the war did the government troops see anything approaching active service. In May 1944, 11 of its 12 battalions were moved to Northern Italy, leaving only the 1st Battalion for guard duty in Prague. In Partisan-infested Italy, the Czechs were used only in the passive role of building defensive installations *(Stellungsbau)*. About ten percent promptly deserted to the enemy! In the autumn of 1944, the remainder were brought back to the Protectorate. By this time, the four-year engagement for which most had enrolled had expired. Few wished to sign on for a further four. Before the end of the year, the government army had disintegrated. What little was left took the side of the resistance in the last days of the war.

The only "decoration" which could be awarded to the *Regierungstruppe* was an Achievement Badge *(Leistungsabzeichen)*, instituted about July 1944 "for repeated acts of assistance to the German forces." It was in three classes (bronze, silver, and

Achievement Badge (Leistungsabzeichen)
awarded to the "Government Army" in
bronze, silver, or gilt.

gilt), but judging from its extreme rarity, the Czechs must have given their German masters little cause to award it!

Unlike their Slovak brothers, the Czechs did not take an active part in the campaign against Russia. A Czech League against Bolshevism (*Česká Liga proti Bolševismu*) was formed, but it did little more than hold meetings and mount anti-Soviet exhibitions. It is true that one slightly demented ex-brigadier of the former Czech army did try repeatedly to persuade the Germans that he could raise a "St. Wenceslas Division" from among his pro-German compatriots who would be happy to serve side-by-side with their Wermacht comrades. The Germans were not convinced. When, in the last desperate weeks of the war, they agreed to allow him to try, he succeeded in raising only 13 volunteers!

UNIFORMS OF THE *REGIERUNGSTRUPPE*

All ranks wore a grass green tunic buttoned to the neck (senior officers occasionally wore an open neck with white shirt and black tie) and grass green trousers with black shoes. Officers could wear breeches and black top boots, NCOs black German-style Jack boots. Shoulder straps were piped in yellow. Senior NCOs (sergeant and up-wards) had yellow lace down the center of their shoulder straps. The battalion number (in Arabic numerals) was worn on both shoulders, in gilt metal for officers, in white metal for others. Staff officers wore the number of their military district, or Inspectorate, in Roman numerals. Rank was indicated by the combination of the shoulder strap style with the number of stars worn on the collar. These were five-pointed and attached directly to the collar (not to a collar patch). Junior NCOs wore white metal stars, senior NCOs silver, officers gilt. As an alternative to stars, officers occasionally wore rosettes. Headgear for all ranks was either a Czech army style forage cap or peaked cap. On duty an ex-Czech army Mod. 1935 steel helmet (painted green) was worn, on the left side was a transfer, or decal, with a white lion rampant (emblem of Bohemia). The forage cap badge was simply crossed swords; later this was replaced by

Government Army Rank Insignia (Enlisted Ranks)

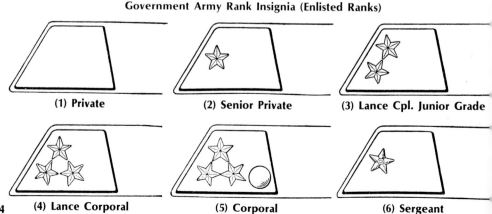

| (1) Private | (2) Senior Private | (3) Lance Cpl. Junior Grade |
| (4) Lance Corporal | (5) Corporal | (6) Sergeant |

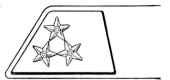

(7) Staff Sergeant

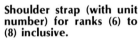

(8) Sergeant Major

Shoulder strap (with unit number) for ranks (1) to (5) inclusive.

Shoulder strap (with unit number) for ranks (6) to (8) inclusive.

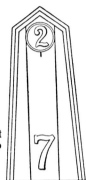

Andrew Mollo

Two soldiers of the government army, a corporal and sergeant. Note badge over right breast.

25

Cloth breast badge

a shield with the arms of Bohemia-Moravia. The peaked cap badge was also originally crossed swords surmounted by a rosette of white/red/blue (blue being the outer color), but later this was changed to a wreath of linden leaves with crossed swords superimposed. The piping on both types of headgear was yellow. Cap badges were gold for officers, white metal for others. On the peaked cap the chin strap was gold braid for officers, silver braid for senior NCOs, and brown leather for others.

All ranks could wear a double-breasted greatcoat with two rows of six buttons down each side. Belts were brown for officers, black for other ranks.

Cap badge for non-commissioned ranks (not actual size).

Government Army Rank Insignia (Officers)

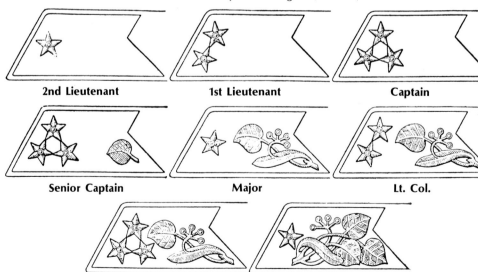

2nd Lieutenant   1st Lieutenant   Captain

Senior Captain   Major   Lt. Col.

Colonel   General 3rd Class

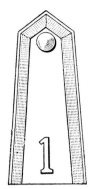
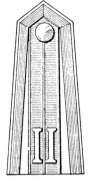
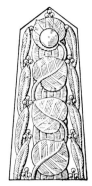

Shoulder straps for (left to right) Subaltern ranks (with battalion number), Staff Officer (with Military District Roman numeral), General.

Rosette as an alternative to star for officer's collar patch.

NOTE:
The ranks of General 2nd Class and General 1st Class existed in theory but no officer reached either of these grades.

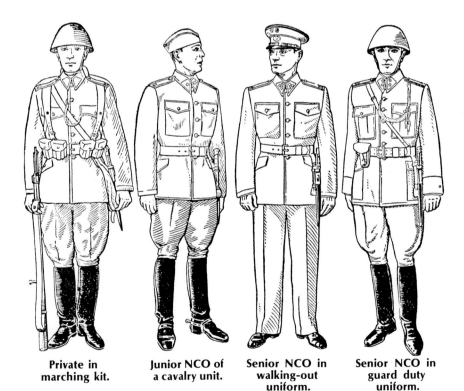

Private in marching kit.

Junior NCO of a cavalry unit.

Senior NCO in walking-out uniform.

Senior NCO in guard duty uniform.

Senior NCO in
walking-out
uniform with sword.

General in
undress uniform
with greatcoat.

General in
parade uniform.

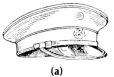

(a)

(c)

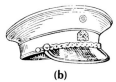

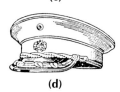

(b)

(d)

Peaked caps for:
(a) Junior NCOs and men
(b) Senior NCOs
(c) Officers (other than Generals
(d) Generals.

Officer in marching kit.

Military Official with rank equivalent to Captain in walking-out uniform with greatcoat.

Officer in guard duty uniform.

Forage cap for non-commissioned ranks.

Officers' cap badge, 1st design

Officers' cap badge, 2nd design

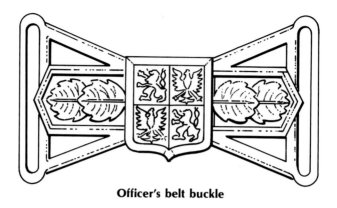

Officer's belt buckle

On-duty guards wore a lanyard and aigulette which varied according to rank as follows:

Red lanyard with brass aigulette: junior NCOs and men

Silver lanyard with white metal aigulette: senior NCOs

Gold lanyard with gold aigulette: officers.

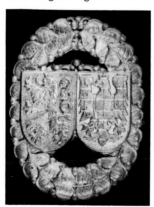

Badge for Marksman's lanyard of the "Government Army." (Shields with the arms of Bohemia and Moravia within an oval wreath of linden leaves. The whole in grey metal.)

In 1943 a badge which had no function other than ornamentation was introduced for wearing above the right breast pocket (symbolically, perhaps, since this was where the Wehrmacht wore its well-known eagle-and-swastika device). It took the form of a red shield with the lion rampant of Bohemia. The shield is flanked on both sides by "wings" of two linden leaves on a red background, piped in blue, then white. This badge is known to exist in a gold thread, silver thread, and white cotton version - presumably for officer, senior NCOs, and men, respectively.

Officers' and military officials' shoulder strap badges:

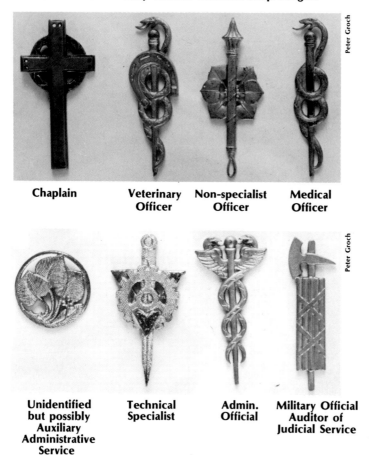

Peter Groch

Chaplain	Veterinary Officer	Non-specialist Officer	Medical Officer

Unidentified but possibly Auxiliary Administrative Service	Technical Specialist	Admin. Official	Military Official Auditor of Judicial Service

Bandmaster collar patch (golden lyre)

GENDARMERIE AND OTHER POLICE FORMATIONS

The Protectorate *Gendarmerie* was, in the main, simply the previous Czech *Gendarmerie* carried over into the new regime with only a very slight modification of insignia. As an auxiliary to the Gendarmerie, a *Bereitschaftspolizei* (Alert Police - literally "Readiness Police") was raised by voluntary enlistment during 1943. Its function was to fulfill the role of "other ranks" to the Gendarmerie - all of whom were either commissioned officers or senior NCOs. Both Gendarmerie and Alert Police wore a light grey uniform. Gendarmerie officers wore peaked caps, tunics, and trousers with, in bad weather, capes (also grey but with a dark collar). The cap badge was the Protectorate coat of arms upon a square set at a 45 degree angle, surrounded by a wreath of linden leaves. The old Czech Gendarmerie helmet continued to be worn by NCOs - officers did not wear this type of headgear, only a peaked cap. On the front of the helmet was a large metal badge incorporating the arms of the Protectorate.

The old Czech Gendarmerie helmet is shown being worn.

Cap badge of the Gendarmerie.

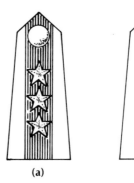

(a)   (b)

Shoulder straps (a) for officers and (b) for NCOs. Each can be with one, two, or three stars according to rank.

All ranks had red collar patches and red down the center of the shoulder strap upon which rank was indicated by either one, two, or three stars (officers had five-pointed stars, NCOs three-pointed). Stars were white metal for NCOs and junior officers, gilt for senior officers. Belts, gaiters, shoes, etc., were brown leather. Breeches were worn on duty, trousers and shoes off duty. Senior officers had twin red stripes down the outer seams of their trousers.

The Gendarmerie was equipped only with very light weapons, some of these, like the short saber, symbolic rather than practical. Officers could carry a 7.65mm pistol; NCOs had a 1895 model Mannlicher carbine (with a bayonet).

The Alert Police wore a similar grey uniform to that of the Gendarmerie but with trousers, not breeches. They had a red band round a peaked cap which was rather similar in appearance to the old Czarist army type. On their red shoulder straps rank was indicated by one, two, three, or four white metal "buttons." The cap badge was the same as for the Gendarmerie. Again, only light weapons were carried.

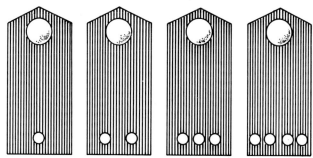

Shoulder straps with rank "buttons," one, two, three, or four in silver.

The Traffic Police wore a dark blue uniform with ranks indicated by stars on the collar patch (but in 1944 changed to the same scheme of ranks as the Gendarmerie). The Water Police had light blue in place of red as the center color of the shoulder strap. The Excise Guard wore the same style of uniform as the Gendarmerie but in light green with dark green collar patches. The cap badge was the same for all branches of the Protectorate Police.

An indigenous *Luftschutz* was raised by selective conscription in 1943. This served both as a Civil Defense force and as an auxiliary to the German Flak artillery. The uniform for non-commissioned ranks consisted of a brown tunic and brown breeches with dark blue puttees (this may have come from French army stores) and a greenish-grey forage cap with the crossed swords badge of the government army. Officers wore an open-necked greenish-grey tunic with rank indicated by one, two, or three stars on both collars. All ranks wore the Protectorate coat of arms (in full color) on the left upper arm. On duty German blue-grey Luftwaffe steel helmets were worn with the Protectorate badge on the left side. Civilians employed as messengers wore a dark blue brassard with *Alarm-Verbindungsdienst* (Emergency Communication, or Liaison,

Service) with, below this, its Czech equivalent, *Poplachová Spojovací služba*. This service was attached to, but not part of, the *Luftschutz*.

There was also an Air Raid Clearance Service *(Aufräumungsdienst)* whose members wore a red brassard with this German word above its Czech equivalent. This service was later incorporated into the *Luftschutz*.

A Harvest Guard, the equivalent of the *Gardes Champêtres* in France, existed in Czechoslovakia before the war and continued, under German tutelage, during the Protectorate. It was not uniformed. Members wore only an oval badge which features the Protectorate lion with, at the top, the German words *Beeidete Wache* and its Czech equivalent, *Přísežná Stráž* (Harvest Guard) below.

Peter Groch Collection

Badge of the Beeidete Wache (Harvest Guard) of the Protectorate. The above is actual size. It was based on a rather similar pre-war Czech badge.

In the autumn of 1944, the Red Army was beginning to close in on Czechoslovakia, and the Germans started to press Czech (and other) civilians into service as defense construction workers. A line of fortifications was hastily thrown up along the frontier in northeastern Moravia. Czechs employed on this task wore a dark blue arm band

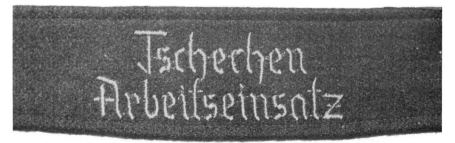

Cuff band "Czech Labor Action" (yellow on dark blue) worn by Czech citizens employed by the Germans in the construction of defensive fortifications as the Red Army approached Czechoslovakia.

Foreigners Labor Action cuff band worn by nonCzech citizens engaged on the same task (yellow on dark blue).

with *Tschechen-Arbeitseinsatz* (Czech Labor Action) in yellow, other civilians had an arm band with *Ausländereinsatz* (Foreigners Labor Action). As a reward for those who did particularly well, a special badge of honor was instituted. It is a bronze shield with the Protectorate eagle and swastika above a scroll upon which is *Für Arbeit zum Schutze der Heimat* (For work on the defense of the Homeland) with, beneath, its equivalent in the Czech language. Behind the scroll is a spade crossed with a pick.

Badge of Honor for Work on Home Defense. Date of institution uncertain, but late in the war. Bronze pin-back shield.

THE KURATORIUM FOR YOUTH TRAINING

As a counterpart to the Hitler Youth,* the German authorities set up in May 1942 a Czech Youth Movement known (in German) as the *Kuratorium für Jugenderziehung in Böhmen und Mähren* (The Curatorship for Youth Training in Bohemia and Moravia). Under the supervision of Hitler Youth officers, Czech boys and girls between the ages of 10 and 21 had to perform "service duty." In 1944 and official announcement stated that there were 300,000 boys in the *Kuratorium*. Officers wore a blue-grey tunic with deep turned-up cuffs, silver buttons, silver piping round the collar, black breeches, and top boots. On a Hitler Youth type peaked cap the so-called

*German boys and girls in the Protectorate had their own Hitler Youth units which wore standard H.J. uniform.

Officer's cap badge

Officers wore a blue-grey tunic with the collar piped in silver. Black breeches were worn with black top boots. The belt was in black leather with the Kuratorium eagle on a round metal buckle. Metal cap badge as above.

**Minister
Emanuel Moravec**

Wenzel-Adler (Eagle of Duke Wencelas) was worn above a white/red/blue cockade (blue being the outer color). This same eagle with, on its wings, the heraldic shields of Bohemia and Moravia (in full color) was worn on a white background on a red/white/red brassard (i.e. a brassard in the same basic colors as that of the Hitler Youth). The *Kuratorium* was divided into two age groups, 10 to 15, and 16 to 21 years. The younger boys wore a blue-grey shirt without shoulder straps, open at the neck with a neckerchief, belt and cross-stray, black or brown short trousers, white stockings, and black shoes. The older boys wore white shirts with black ties, black trousers, black shoes, and a belt without a cross-strap. This was known as the "emergency uniform" - presumably the Germans planned a more elaborate uniform for "after the war." Both age groups wore the *Wenzel-Adler* brassard (as described above). But due to wartime shortages, even the "emergency uniform" proved too difficult to provide, and a variety of dress was, in practice, worn. Swastika flags were carried. These differed slightly from the normal type in that the central white circle is outline in black - this was, in fact, the flag of the former S.d.P.   Leader of the *Kuratorium* was Emanuel Moravec, a former lecturer at the Czech Military Academy, and currently Minister of Education in the Portectorate government. He had a son in the Waffen S.S.

Brassard of the Kuratorium für Jugenderziehung in Böhmen u. Mähren. Red with white inset edges. Black eagle with arms of Bohemia and Moravia in color. This may have been adapted from the N.S. Sudetenbund brassard.

Alternative version of the above. Brassard is now colored red/white/red in the style of that of the Hitler Youth.   **37**

Emanuel Moravec, leader of the Kuratorium between an unidentified S.S. officer and an officer of the Hitler Youth.

The *Wenzel-Adler* (presumably in a metal version) was awarded annually to the fifteen best members of the *Kuratorium* from each *Bezirk* (District). This eagle also featured on another award of the Protectorate - the "Shield of Honor of the Protectorate of Bohemia and Moravia with the Eagle of Duke Wenceslas" *(Ehrenschild des Protektorates des Böhmen und Mähren mit dem Herzog-Wenzel-Adler)*. This decoration was instituted by K.H. Frank on 6 June 1943, the first anniversary of the assassination of Reinhard Heydrich. Duke Wenceslas (or Wenceslaus) of Bohemia lived from 908 to 929 A.D. and made a treaty of friendship with the Saxon King Henry I ("Henry the Fowler," who later became Holy Roman Emperor and was one of Himmler's idols),

Karl Hermann Frank awards the first "Shield of Honor of the Protectorate" on 18 June 1944.

Recruiting label urging Czech youth to join the Kuratorium.

which placed Bohemia under German protection.* He was, therefore, to the Germans, the symbol of Czech-German collaboration (he paid the price for this collaboration by being murdered by his own brother - a fact which German propaganda tended to gloss over). The Honor Shield of Duke Wencelas is in three grades: a shield without a wreath at the base, a shield with a silver wreath at the base, a shield with a gold wreath at the base. Any of these could be worn as a miniature on a stick-pin.

*For these corrections to the information given in my "Orders, Decorations, Medals and Badges of the Third Reich" Vol. 2, pages 87-88, I am indebted to Mr. Václav Měřička of Prague.

SLOVAKIA

On 18 March 1939, after the German occupation of Bohemia and Moravia, what was left of Czechoslovakia became the, theoretically, Independent State of Slovakia under Prime Minister (later President) Josef Tiso. In reality, Slovakia was, and remained, a vassal of Germany. Under the so-called Treaty of Protection by which Hitler took Slovakia under his "care," the Slovaks were required to forego an independent foreign policy and follow Germany's lead. This took them, a few months later, into war.

Ever since the formation of Czechoslovakia in 1918, some Slovaks had worked for the break-up of the state and the creation of an autonomous Slovakia. The most important faction in this respect was the Slovak Peoples Party of Father Hlinka (*Hlinková Slovenská L'Udová Strana,* or H.S.L'S) formed as early as 1918 by a Roman Catholic priest, Father Andrej Hlinka. It was originally Catholic and chauvenistic rather than fascist. It acquired its Nazi tone only after Hlinka's death in August 1938 by which time the Slovak autonomists had come to regard Hitler rather than God as the person most likely to bring about the miracle of Slovak independence!

The H.S.L'S had, early on, formed its own black-shirted action squads, known as the *Rodobrana* (Home Defense) modeled on Mussolini's Blackshirts (Hitler had not at this stage - 1922 - appeared on the political scene). On the left breast of their black shirts members of the *Rodobrana* wore a silver double-armed cross. This emblem represents the twin patron Apostles of the Slavs - Saints Cyril and Methodius. When set upon a three-peaked mountain, it is the national emblem of Slovakia and, as such, features on many of the insignia of the period.

The *Rodobrana* was subjected to a good deal of police harassment and eventually was outlawed. In July 1938 a new Party militia, the Hlinka Guard, was formed. This guard was to play a sinister role in the later history of Slovakia. It might be compared to the S.S. in Germany, although, due to internal squabbles among its leaders, it never achieved the status or influence of that organization.

By an order of 5 September 1939, membership of the Hlinka Guard was made compulsory for all males between the ages of 18 and 60 years, while membership of its youth branch (The Hlinka Youth) was obligatory for young persons between the ages of six and 17 years. But this sweeping decree proved so unpopular (not to say impractical) that a new statute was drawn up on 21 December 1939 which allowed enlistment to be purely voluntary. The guard was now organized as follows:

Hlinka Guard 1st Class (men in the 20 to 35 age group)

Hlinka Guard 2nd Class (men in the 36 to 60 age group)

Hlinka Transport Guard, H.D.G. *(Hlinková Dopravna Garda)*

Hlinka Academic Guard, A.H.G. *(Akademická Hlinková Garda)*

Hlinka Guard Abroad, Z.H.G. *(Zahraničná Hlinková Garda)*

Hlinka Guard Elite Storm-Troop (P.O.H.G.)

President Tiso is greeted by an S.S. guard of honor on his arrival in Berlin.

In addition to the above, there was the Hlinka Youth *(Hlinková Mládež)* "a voluntary organization for boys and girls of the Roman Catholic faith, of aryan descent, in sound health, and without a criminal record." They were sub-divided as follows:

Vlčatá (Wolf Cubs): boys from six to ten years

Orli (Eagles): boys from 11 to 16 years

Junáci (Young Lads: boys from 17 to 20 years

Víly (Pixies): girls from six to ten years

Tatranky (Tatrian maidens): girls from 11 to 15 years

Devy (Maidens): girls from 16 to 20 years

The Hlinka Youth manual for 1943 refers to a "dagger of honor," and several medals but does not, unfortunately, illustrate any of these. Boys wore a Hitler Youth type of uniform with brown shirt, dark shorts, and a black forage cap with a round badge in the form of a Slovak double cross upon a stylized eagle. The girls uniform appears to have been a dark skirt and white blouse with a neckerchief (rather like the B.d.M. uniform) with the Slovak double cross above the left breast pocket.

41

Cap badge of the Hlinka Guard,
cloth version (white cotton eagle
with red fasces and red Slovak
Cross in blue circle), all on black.
(Example in a private collection.)

Slovakian Dr. Tuka wears a metal version of the above Hlinka Guard cap badge during
a visit to Berlin on 24 November 1940. To his left is German Foreign Minister von
Ribbentrop.

Lapel badge of the Hlinka Peoples Party of Slovakia (Slovak cross above H.S.L'S., standing for Hlinková Slovenská L'Udová Strana)

Commemorative badge (gilt metal) worn on left breast pocket by former members of the Rodobrana, now part of the Hlinka Guard.

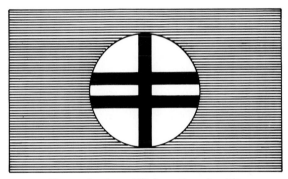

Flag of the Hlinka Guard. Blue cross on white circle on red field.

Unidentified cloth badge. Probably only a trial item never actually issued.

Belt buckle for ceremonial belt of Hlinka Guard officer. The motto "Nazpat cesta nemozna na straz" means "To go back is impossible, be on your guard."

Two officers of the Hlinka Transport Guard. Note ceremonial dress belt.

Officers of the Hlinka Guard. Note officer on right carries a dagger.

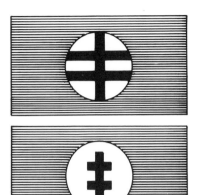

Two versions of the brassard of the Hlinka Guard (blue cross on white circle, red background).

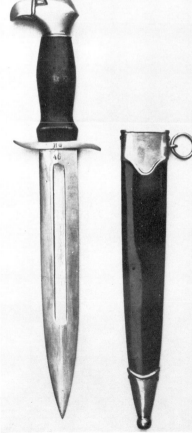

Dagger of the Hlinka Guard. This dagger has been the subject of several mis-identifications, it is definitely *not* "Eastern Peoples" or "Spanish," but is one of some four variants made at the Brno Arsenal for the Hlinka Guard during the Second World War. Some versions have an inscription on the blade which in translation reads "Never retreat," others have a narrower blade than is shown in the accompanying photo. Others still have a lanyard ring on the pommel and there are alternative types of metal in which the dagger is finished.

It does not appear (from photos) that all Hlinka Guard officers carried a dagger, possibly it was regarded as a distinction to be earned (or possibly just not enough were produced in the time!)

45

Officer of the Hlinka Transport Guard

Detail of cap cockade in Slovak national colors and wreath of linden leaves.

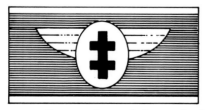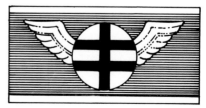

Two versions of brassard of the Hlinka Transport Guard.

Emblem of the Hlinka Transport
Guard

Hlinka Guard (also Hlinka Youth)
bronze cap badge.

Hlinka Guard. Cloth version of cap
badge (white cotton).

Josef Kirschbaum, the
commander of the
Hlinka Academic Guard.

Armed members of the Hlinka Guard wearing ex-Czech army steel helmets. (The collar patches as worn in this photo were later dropped.)

Boys of the Vlčatá (Wolf Cubs) of the Hlinka Youth on parade through a town in Slovakia.

Parade of the Girls section of the Hlinka Youth. Note that girl on the extreme right is in a German B.d.M. uniform. Girls wear the Hlinka emblem above left breast pocket, but on upper arm (except for the officer, extreme left).

Hlinka emblem worn on left upper arm by male Hlinka Youth, and above left breast pocket by female Hlinka Youth.

VK. Ager

Members of the Hlinka Youth on friendly terms with members of the Hitler Youth. Note the tassel worn on the side of the forage caps of the Hlinka Youths.

49

Member of the Hlinka Youth (center) with, left, a Hungarian boy and right, a German boy. It might appear that the Hlinka Youth is wearing a badge on his collar, but this is, in fact, the cap badge of the boy behind who is resting his hand, with his cap in it, on the shoulder of his comrade in front.

Civil lapel badge of the Hlinka Youth. Red double cross on white within a blue circle on which, in yellow, Hlinková Mladez (Hlinka Youth).

The basic Guardist uniform was black - in fact, ex-Allgemeine S.S. uniforms supplied by the Germans. Rank was indicated on the collar patch and by a narrow shoulder strap (in the manner of the old Austro-Hungarian army). Shirts could be black or white, worn with a black tie. Officers had black breeches and top boots, "Sam Browne" belts, and cross-straps. Daggers were not normally carried, but photos show some officers with them - possibly presentation awards. Headgear could be either the ex-Czech army "pork pie" type of forage cap or a peaked cap in the German style. On the left upper arm all members of the guard wore a red brassard with the double cross of Slovakia in blue on a white background (sometimes circular, sometimes oval). The Transport Guard had the addition of white "wings" on either side of this center piece. The design of the brassard varied; there appears to have been no "standard" or "issue" type.

On the peaked cap an eagle, rather like the German type, was worn above, for the Academic Guard, a metal fasces, and for all others a wreath of linden leaves enclosing the national cockade, a red/blue/white rosette (white being the outer color).

50

Dr. Tuka arriving in Berlin on 24 November 1940. Note the dagger being worn.

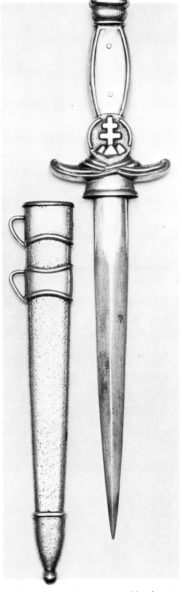

Slovak army dagger, but also worn by senior diplomatic officials (see photo above).

Veterans of the original *Rodobrana* wore, on the left breast pocket, a metal badge in the form of a Slovak cross within a wreath of thorns (symbolic of their suffering under the erstwhile Republic).

The Hlinka Guard Elite Storm Troop *(Pohotovostne Oddiely Hlinkovej Gardy)* or P.O.H.G., was a specially selected unit of the fittest and most dedicated young Guardists formed in May 1941 and sent to Germany for instruction by the S.S. For much of the war, the P.O.H.G. was held as a sort of special reserve, but after the Slovak national revolt in the autumn of 1944 when the Germans had to step in and restore order, the P.O.H.G. was given a fresh lease on life, armed by the S.S., and accorded a leading role in crushing the revolt. Insufficient volunteers could be found at this late date to bring the existing P.O.H.G. up to effective strength as a fighting unit, with the result that men from other Slovak military, or para-military, formations had to be drafted. By these means the P.O.H.G. was brought up to a strength of around 3,500 men.

Estimates of the strength of the Hlinka Guard as a whole vary considerably. In 1939 there were said to be 27,682 Guardists 1st Class, and 19,703 Guardists 2nd Class. At its maximum the Guard may have had around 100,000 members, but as German fortunes declined, so did enthusiasm for the Guard. By 1943 it may have shrunk to as few as 3,-000. Only the fanatics of the P.O.H.G. remained loyal to the end, and even here, as we have seen, it was impossible to raise a respectable number by purely voluntary means.

THE VOLKSDEUTSCHE

Rather more devoted to Hitler's cause were, of course, those citizens of Slovakia who were of German stock (the *Volksdeutsche*). Most of the racial Germans of pre-war Czecloslovakia had lived in the Czech areas, but there were also pockets of ethnic Germans scattered throughout Slovakia. Of the three million citizens of Slovakia, 128,-347 were registered as Germans.

The pro-Nazi *Volksdeutsche* of Slovakia had, before the break-up of the Czechoslovak Republic, belonged to the Carpathian German Party *(Karpatendeutsche Partei,* or K.d.P.), which was the Slovak branch of Heinlein's S.d.P., but on 9 October 1938 the K.d.P. became the *Deutsche Partei* (D.P.). Its former monogram lapel badge was replaced by a black swastika on a red outlined white shield. The *Volksdeutsche* of Slovakia were disappointed that the Führer did not annex Slovakia and declare it to be a German colony, but Hitler had no wish to prejudice good relations with Slovakia for the sake of its less than 5 percent German population. Despite this disappointment, the D.P. consciously and, with the unconcealed aid of various agencies within Germany, set about building itself into a facsimile of the N.S.D.A.P.

As the K.d.P., the party had had only 27,585 registered members, but as the D.P. it had (by March 1939) more than doubled this figure - about 20 percent of its membership being women. The D.P. was divided into seven districts *(Kreise),* administered by some 3,800 "political leaders." In November 1940, and *Arbeitsfront der Volksdeutschen* (A.d.V.) - a Labor Front for the *Volksdeutsche* was established as a counterpart to the D.A.F. in the Reich; leaders for it were trained in Germany. The D.P.'s *Deutsche Jugend* (German Youth) was its equivalent of the Hitler Youth. An embryonic Labor Service, the *Deutscher Aufbau Dienst,* or D.A.D., carried out building projects such as the construction of a new sports stadium in Bratislava, the Slovak capital. The D.P.'s equivalent of the Allgemeine S.S. was the *Freiwillige Schutzstaffel* (Volunteer Defense Squad, or F.S.). Its uniform was virtually the same as its German counterpart except that the S.S. eagle held in its claws, not a wreathed swastika, but a shield with a swastika on it (similar to the D.P. lapel pin). It is interesting to note the

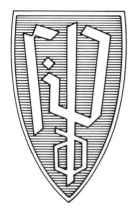

Badge of the K.d.P. (Karpaten deutsche Partei) Carpathian German Party for Volksdeutsche in pre-war Slovakia.

In 1939 the K.d.P. became simply the D.P. (Deutsche Partei) and adopted the above as its badge (a black swastika on a white shield with a red border).

"evolution" of this badge. Originally the eagle was of a "non-political" sort (unlike with the S.S., German army, or N.S.D.A.P. types) and held in its claws a shield with the Slovak emblem. Later the eagle became the S.S. type but still the shield was Slovak; finally, all pretense having been dropped, the S.S. eagle held in its claws the badge described above - a swastika on a shield.

F.S. eagle. 1st design. "Non-political" eagle with shield of Slovakia.

F.S. eagle. 2nd design. S.S. type eagle with shield of Slovakia.

F.S. eagle. 3rd design. S.S. type eagle with Nazi shield.

A member of the F.S. wearing the 2nd design eagle.

Arm badge of the F.S.
(white cotton on black)

Belt buckle of the F.S.
Motto is "Honor, Blood
and Soil."

Stick pin of the German Labor Service (Deutscher Aufbau Dienst or
D.A.D.) in Slovakia. Said to have
been given in bronze, silver, or gilt,
according to merit of work done or
number of hours put in as a volunteer

Soldiers in the German-speaking battalion of the Slovak army. Man nearest camera wears the "shield" type of brassard, others wear the normal round center type.

Just as the Allgemeine S.S. in Germany developed within its ranks an Action Troop (the *Verfügungstruppen,* the forerunner of the Waffen S.S.), so the F.S. burgeoned its own active corps, the *Einsatztruppen,* or *E.T.,* which was armed, trained, and provided with uniforms by the S.S. in the Ostmark (Austria). In March 1940 the F.S. numbered 5,622 spread throughout 127 different units in the country. By 1942 this had risen to 7,-500 with its own flying, motorized, and "cavalry" sub-units. The F.S. played a minor role in operations against Poland in September 1939 (as did the Hlinka Guard). Although encouraged to volunteer for the Waffen S.S., only some 750 F.S. or E.T. lads had, by the spring of 1942, done so, and those who did join up found themselves distributed piecemeal along its several divisions. By the summer of 1942, however, with Germany's manpower shortage becoming critical as the result of fearful losses on the Eastern front, the *S.S. Ersatzkommando Südost* (S.S. Replacement Command South East) decided, in July of that year, to introduce conscription for all Slovak *Volksdeutsche* males between the ages of 18 and 40 years. This move was strongly resisted by the *Volksgruppenführer* Franz Karmasin who feared that his most reliable followers might be filched from him and the administrative posts which they vacated filled by Slovaks.

A compromise was reached: recruitment would be entrusted to Karmasin who would encourage all physically fit men up to the age of 35 to "do their bit" by joining the Waffen S.S., but compulsion, as such, would not be applied. Karmasin would be allowed the final decision as to who was, or was not, essential at home. This solution seems to have produced reasonably good results. Between 70 and 80 percent of men in that age group presented themselves at the recruiting stations. No exact figures are available, but between 1,000 and 2,000 Slovak *Volksdeutsche* were passed as fit for the Waffen S.S. Although this would have been sufficient to form at least one regiment,

Members of the Freiwillige Schutzstaffel of the German Racial Group in Slovakia receive a badge of honor (of some sort - possibly for a sports competition). Note the "shield" type of brassard.

the volunteers were simply distributed to whatever division required replacements. Some were sent to anti-partisan formations, a few ended up as concentration camp guards. In January 1944, the voluntary principle was abandoned and conscription applied. In June of the same year, even the *Volksdeutsche* in the Slovak armed forces were compulsorily transferred to the Waffen S.S. An arm shield with *"Slowakei"* (German spelling) exists. It is almost certain that this was *not* worn by anyone in the Waffen S.S. since *individual* volunteers never wore nationality emblems (such devices were worn only where a whole unit consisted either very largely or entirely of volunteers of the same ethnic origin).

Freiwillige Schutzstaffel parade through a Slovak town.

Rally of members of the Hlinka Guard and Volksdeutsche officials.

Lapel badge of the Deutsche Jugend (D.J.), the equivalent of the Hitler Youth in Slovakia. This same design was also used as the cap badge of the D.J.

Carpathian-German Decoration. A silver swastika and silver oak leaves with the silver and red K.d.P. badge in the center.

By the end of 1944, most of the young manhood of the D.P. had been absorbed into military service of some sort on Germany's behalf. Lads from the *Deutsche Jugend* were being sent to the Military Toughening-up Camps run jointly by the Hitler Youth and the Waffen S.S. The very young and the elderly were organized into an armed *Heimatschutz* (Home Defense) whose creation was announced over Bratislava radio on 28 August 1944. This was the equivalent of the *Volkssturm* in Germany and was compulsory for all males between the ages of 16 and 60 years. Those who were under the age of 40 were regarded as automatically belonging to the Waffen S.S. By this time the whole of Slovakia was under direct German rule. Most of the *Heimatschutz* were employed in guarding their locality against partisan attack, some, however, were used to assist the Germans in their round-ups and deportations of Slovak Jews - something which continued almost to the very end of the war.

THE ARMED FORCES OF SLOVAKIA

The Slovak army took an active part in the war. During the brief campaign against Poland in September 1939, some 115,000 Slovak reservists were called up, and three divisions and a so-called "Swift Group" were created. They formed part of General List's 14th (German) Army. Once the Polish campaign was over, most of the Slovak reservists were demobilized, but after Hitler's attack on Russia on 22 June 1941, there was a second general mobilization. Two divisions and a new "Swift Group" (the term might best be translated as motorized light infantry group) were activated. The total strength of these three formations was 1,346 officers and 40,393 other

Slovak infantrymen marching in formation.

ranks. They joined the 17th German Army which formed part of Army Group South. By August 1941, the Slovaks had suffered losses of 106 killed, 188 wounded, and 30 missing. The bulk of their expeditionary corps was brought home, leaving only about 18,-000 still on front-line service. From these still-active units, two new divisions were created:

(a) The Swift Division (*Schnelle Division* in German, or *Rýchla Diviźia* in Czech). This was the resurrected "Swift Group" under new command.

(b) The Security Division (*Sicherheits Division* or *Záistna Diviźia*) which consisted of three battalions and was used mainly on anti-partison operations in the German rear.

The Swift Division comprised two infantry and one artillery regiment plus a *Panzer* battalion. The Security Division had a total of 8,475 officers and men. Unlike its sister division, it was almost without mechanical transport. On its strength were 601 farm carts and 2,577 horses! The Swift Division took part in the fighting in the Crimea, but during the enforced airborne evacuation from the Kuban which followed this campaign, it lost all its heavy equipment. Bereft of transport, it was reformed as the 1st (Slovak) Infantry Division.

Desertions became frequent: 1,300 members of the Security Division went over to the Soviet Partisans whom they were supposed to be fighting, while an entire regiment from the 1st (Slovak) Infantry Division laid down its arms and joined the enemy. In September 1943, the Slovak High Command begged Hitler to be allowed to withdraw its forces from Russia. Hitler refused. He demanded instead that the Slovaks *increase* their commitment of troops. In the end, the most that he would allow was that the Slovaks be transferred to a quieter front. Both divisions were pulled out of the line and amalgamated as a single unit under the designation Technical Brigade. Brought up to divisional strength at home, it was then sent, as the Technical Division, to northern Italy where it was put to work building defenses.

The two officers who, in turn, commanded the *Schnelle Division,* Josef Turanec and Augustin Malár, were both awarded the Knight's Cross of the Iron Cross by Hitler. The Slovak government, for its part, created a multitude of decorations and war badges which it lavished on its soldiers; indeed, *all* members of Slovakia's armed forces received, in a grade commensurate with their rank, a decoration known as the "War Victory Cross" (on 14 March 1944).

Josef Turanec   Augustin Malár

The national uprising of the autumn of 1944 brought about the virtual collapse of the Slovak army. Apart from the Technical Division in Italy, all that remained were a few companies of ex-regulars (that is to say, former regular soldiers of the pre-war Czech army). They were reformed as the *Domobrana* (Home Defense, or Home Army) and became the Slovak equivalent of the *Heimatschutz.*

Slovakia also had a small Air Force consisting (in 1940) of three fighter squadrons, three reconnaissance squadrons, one technical wing, and one reserve wing. The Air Force, like the army, played a small part in the Polish campaign in the autumn of 1939 and was again in action after Hitler's invasion of the Soviet Union. It sent two of its three fighter squadrons to Russia (equipped with ex-Czech Air Force Avia B-534 fighters), along with one reconnaissance squadron of Letov S-328 biplanes. The Slovak aircraft were hopelessly obsolete and their crews inadequately trained. The two fighter squadrons were pulled out of service in October 1941 and sent to Germany for re-equipping and further training. They returned in the summer of '42 as a single squadron (No. 14) equipped with Messerschmitt 109-E fighters to serve as part of *Luftflotte* 4 (which was the air support of Army Group South).

After suffering heavy losses in the course of the air battles above the Crimea in the autumn of 1943, the Luftwaffe replaced the 109-Es of No. 14 (Slovak) Fighter Squadron with the improved 109-G. The antiquated Letov S-328s were replaced by Hienkel 111 bombers.

Shortly after the Slovak land forces were withdrawn from Russia, the Slovak Air Force requested permission to bring back its flying units. By early 1944 the Slovak aircrews were returned to their homeland where they assisted the Luftwaffe in the defense of Slovak airspace.

The total strength of the Slovak Air Force was only around 4,000 officers and men, and at no given time were there more than about eighty Slovak aircraft in serviceable condition. As its insignia the Slovak Air Force used a Balkan Cross, similar to that of the Luftwaffe except that it was blue and with, in the center, a large red disk. The cross was outlined in white, thus combining the red/white/blue national colors of Slovakia. During the Polish campaign Slovak aircraft flew under German colors but with a white outlined, blue Slovak double cross on a red circle as their tail marking.

UNIFORMS OF THE SLOVAK ARMED FORCES

The Slovak army and Air Force (there was, of course, no navy!) wore the same uniform. It was basically the khaki garb of the pre-war Czech army with the characteristic "pork pie" forage cap or, for dress occasions, a peaked cap.

(a)   (b)   (c)   (d)   (e)

Officers: (a) Major on the General Staff. Working dress. Khaki tunic and trousers. (b) 1st Lieutenant in the Cavalry. "Walking out" dress - khaki tunic, maroon breeches, black top boots, white shirt, white gloves. (c) 1st Lieutenant in Motor Transport Corps in parade dress. Khaki tunic and trousers, white shirt, white gloves, gold braid belt, and gold aigulette. (d) Captain in air force. Khaki tunic, breeches and shirt, black tie. Service dress. (e) Colonel in the Flak artillery in parade dress. All officer ranks have gold buttons and have dark cuffs (either dark brown or dark green). (f) Captain in Medical branch in all white summer uniform (cap band is dark green). (g) Captain on the General Staff in parade dress. Very dark green tunic and breeches, white shirt and black tie, gold braid belt, and gold aigulette.

All officers were entitled to carry a dagger. It is the same for both army and air force, except that the army type has a white hilt and a silver sheath and was worn with a gold troddel. The air force type has a gold hilt and part of the sheath is also gold, but it was worn without the troddel. Officers sometimes wore ceremonial swords.

(f)   (g)   61

Top row (left to right). Cadet NCO in khaki service dress; Cadet NCO in active service kit; Sergeant of the Cavalry in walking out dress (khaki tunic and maroon breeches); Sergeant of the Air Force in walking out dress (white shirt and black tie). Lower row: bayonet and troddel (silver for officers, silver and red for NCOs, brown for other ranks); peaked and forage caps, sports vest with red band and gold emblem on black inverted tirangle; buttons with crossed swords emblem (gold, silver, brown according to grade). Infantryman and Pioneer (or assault engineer) infantryman, both in active service dress.

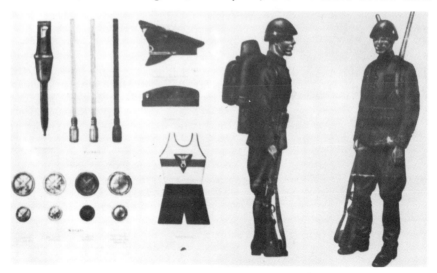

Rank was indicated on both collars, the branch of the service being denoted by the color of the collar patch. A white uniform could be worn in summer (by officers only). Cavalry units had maroon colored breeches. On active duty the tunic was buttoned to the neck, but for "walking out" or parade dress, officers could wear an open neck tunic with a white shirt and black tie. As their parade dress, all ranks of the Air Force wore a dark, open neck, blue

tunic and trousers.

On active duty, ex-Czech army steel helmets were worn which had, on the left side, the Slovak double cross in white. The *Volksdeutsche* of Slovakia were allowed to serve in their own German-speaking units. By an agreement between the Slovak and the German governments, ethnic Germans could transfer at will from the Slovak to the German forces without loss of citizenship. It would appear that not all were anxious to do so despite the exhortations of their *Volksgruppenführer* since, even as late as June 1944, there was still one *Volksdeutsche* infantry battalion and one *Volksdeutsche* artillery battery within the Slovak army. In July 1944, all *Volksdeutsche* in the Slovak forces were compulsorily remustered into the Waffen S.S. The *Volskdeutsche* in the Slovak army wore on the left upper arm a swastika brassard and, as their collar badge, a swastika on a shield.

Fisher Collection

Peaked cap of a general in the Slovak army. Dark brown with green *Waffenfarbe*. Gold bullion eagle, wreath and swords. Gold visor cord. Black leather peak.

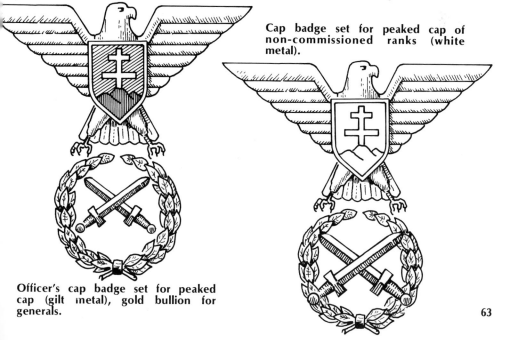

Cap badge set for peaked cap of non-commissioned ranks (white metal).

Officer's cap badge set for peaked cap (gilt metal), gold bullion for generals.

63

Cap badge for forage cap. In gilt for officers, in white metal for non-commissioned ranks.

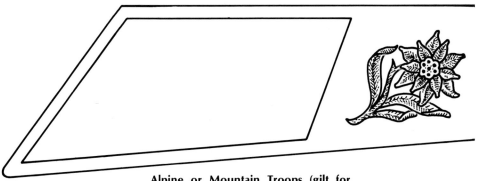

Alpine or Mountain Troops (gilt for officers, silver for others).

The collar badges (left and right) are gilt for officers, white metal for NCO ranks.

Regimental number worn on collars.

Collar shield for racial German (Volksdeutsch) units of the Slovak army.

Collar badge for Guards Regiments.

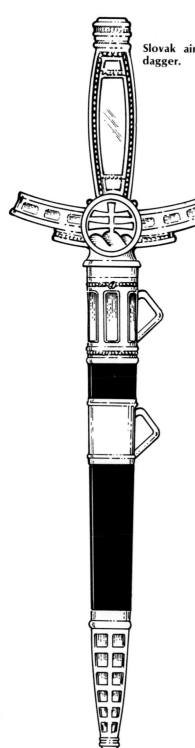

Slovak air force dagger.

Graduate's badge of the General Staff College.

Graduate's badge of the Admin. (or Commissariat) School

65

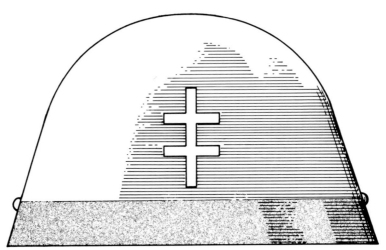

Slovak army steel helmet.

ARMY AND AIR FORCE RANK INSIGNIA (Worn on Both Collars)
(Below: silver stars)

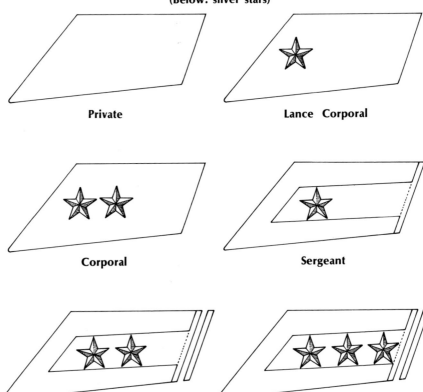

Private

Lance Corporal

Corporal

Sergeant

Staff Sergeant

Sergeant Major

(2nd Lieutenant-Colonel: gold stars. General ranks: silver stars)

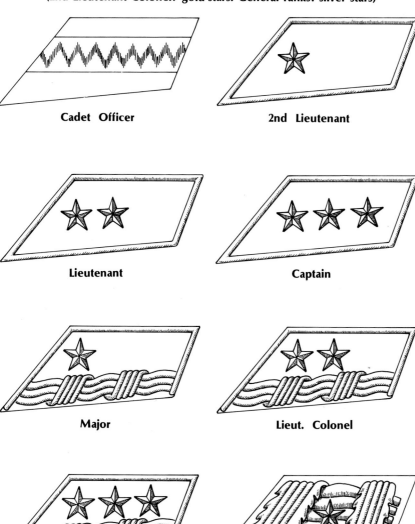

Cadet Officer

2nd Lieutenant

Lieutenant

Captain

Major

Lieut. Colonel

Colonel

Brigadier General

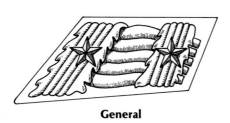

General

The branch of service colors of the Slovak armed forces were:

General Staff ⎱
Infantry ⎰ carmine
Artillery: red
Cavalry: yellow
Air Force: light blue
Medical: dark blue

Engineers: black
Armored Units: pink
Transport: light brown
Signals: dark brown
Legal Dept.: dark green
Cartographic Dept.: light green

Officer's belt buckle

Non-commissioned ranks belt buckle

SLOVAK ARMY TRADE BADGES
(Worn on Left Upper Arm)

Signals
(red on brown)

Machine Gunner
(red on brown)

Armored Reconnaissance
(yellow on brown)

Mortar Crews
(red on brown)

Mountain Artillery
(red on brown)

Mounted Infantry
(red on brown)

Transport Units
(red on brown)

Boat-Pontoon Engineers
(green on brown)

Machinists
(green on brown)

Bandsmen
(yellow on brown)

Carpenters
(green on brown)

Headquarters Staff
(white/green/red)

Cyclist

Pioneers (Infantry)

Searchlight Crews

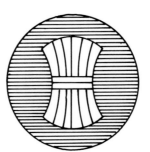

Antiaircraft
Battery Personnel

Supply Units
Commissariat

Radio Operator
(red flash on white, upper,
and brown, lower, half circle)

Expert Motorist. This is one of a series of proficiency
badges most of which (although not this one) date back
to the pre-war Czech army.

Authorized certificate for Light Machine Gun
Proficiency Badge (for wearing as a miniature on
civilian clothes).

LABOR BATTALIONS

Males of an age or a physical grading which rendered them unsuitable for normal military service could be conscripted into the Labor Battalions of the Slovak army. These wore the same uniform as the army but were distinguished by having dark brown cuffs and collars and a trade, or speciality, badge on the left breast pocket. The Labor Battalions also had their own rank insignia. The Company Commander wore an embroidered rosette on both collars (all the officers above this grade were Slovak army). Technical instructors had two metal buttons on their inverted triangular collar patches. A Forman 1st Grade had two silver stripes around collar and cuffs, a Forman 2nd Grade, a single silver stripe in these places.

Special all-Jewish Labor units were formed, with their own distinctive headgear - a sailor's cap (from the now disbanded Czech Danube Fleet). This had a dark blue cap ribbon. The Jews had the dark brown cuffs replaced by dark blue ribbons placed in the form of a St. Andrew's cross on the lower parts of both sleeves. They had no rank insignia, all their officers and NCOs being non-Jewish personnel from the army. Initially there were two of these all-Jewish units, but after the invasion of Russia they were merged as a single battalion and sent to the Ukraine as a bridge building formation. Later the battalion was brought back to Slovakia to work on airfield construction. It was then given a dark blue uniform (their former khaki dyed this color). By 1942 the less physically fit members of the Jewish battalion were being weeded out and dispatched to the death camps along with other Slovak Jews. What was left of the battalion was renamed a Civil Forced Labor Brigade and turned over to the tender mercies of the Hlinka Guard.

There was also a Labor Battalion made up of Slovak gypsies.

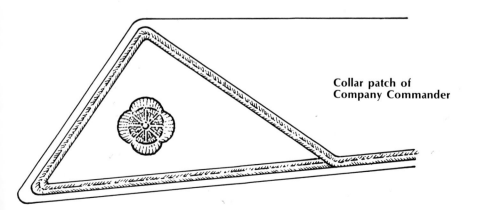

Collar patch of Company Commander

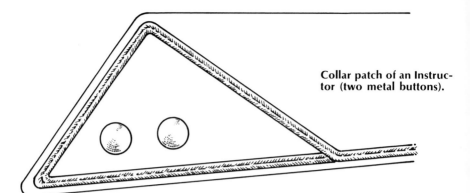

Collar patch of an Instructor (two metal buttons).

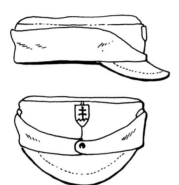

Forage cap for "Aryans."

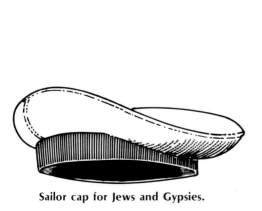

Sailor cap for Jews and Gypsies.

Private. Dark brown collar and cuffs. Trade or speciality badge on left breast pocket.

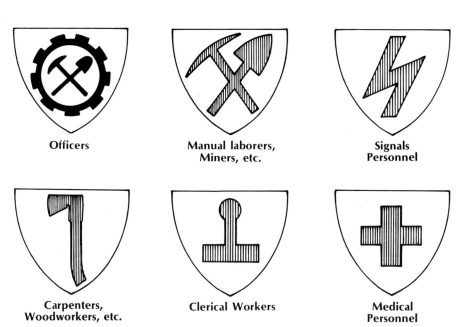

Officers

Manual laborers, Miners, etc.

Signals Personnel

Carpenters, Woodworkers, etc.

Clerical Workers

Medical Personnel

The above are only a few of the several emblems worn in the Labor Battalions.

Tunic and sailor cap worn by the Jewish Battalions of the Slovak army. This was the first design.

Pilot/Observer badge. Gilt eagle and silver wreath for day fighter and day bomber pilots. All-gilt for night flying pilots; silver eagle and wreath for observers (day); silver eagle and gilt wreath for night flying observers.

Air Gunner's badge. One color only: silver.

Flight Engineer's badge. For officers the propeller is silver, the wreath gilt; for others the whole badge is silver.

Insignia worn on the tail of Slovak aircraft taking part in the campaign against Poland in 1939. The other markings (wing and fuselage) were German.

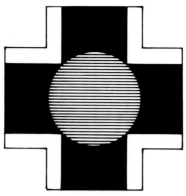

Wing, fuselage, and tail marking for
Slovak Air Force units operating on
the Russian front.

Slovak pilots being awarded certificates of proficiency. Note
the daggers being worn.

SLOVAK GENDARMERIE

Gendarmerie cap badge

Junior non-commissioned ranks (one, two, or three stars)

Senior non-commissioned ranks (one, two, or three stars). Silver "bar" at rear of patch.

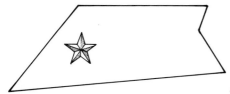

Warrant Officer grades (one, two, or three stars). Silver edging on two sides.

Commissioned grades (one, two, or three stars). Silver edging on all sides.

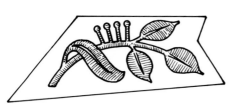

Generals. Silver wire linden leaves.

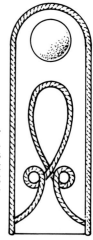

Shoulder strap for officer grades. Warrant officers have the same but without the piping round the strap itself. (Silver wire).

Officers of the Slovak Gendarmerie with an officer of the Hlinka Academic Guard (second from right, pointing). Uniform is very similar to that of the Slovak Army, but note different type of cap badge and different shape of collar patch.

SLOVAKIA: ORDERS, DECORATIONS, AND MEDALS

ORDER OF PRINCE PRIBINA

The senior order of the State of Slovakia, the Order of Prince Pribina, was instituted on 8 May 1940 and named in memory of the first ruler of an independent Slovakia (in the 9th century A.D.) It is in six grades as follows:

(a) Special Grade: a collar with breast star and sash.

(b) Grand Cross: a breast star, sash, and sash "badge."

(c) Grand Officer: Neck decoration, breast star but without a sash.

(d) Commander: neck decoration only.

(e) Officer: unknown, but possibly a pin-back cross.

(f) Knight: a cross from a ribbon.

The basic emblem of the Order is a circular medallion with the profile of Prince Pribina from which emanates rays in the form of a cross; between their arms are three blue enamel "hills," from the center one of which rises the Slovak double cross. Any grade could be "with swords"; in which case the normal bound twigs (or fasces) which form the suspension are replaced by a circular wreath of linden leaves with crossed swords (excactly like the "swords" to the Order of the Slovakian Cross).

The ribbon for all grades (and sash) is coral red with a narrow blue central stripe - this stripe being always one-seventh of the total width of the ribbon (or sash) which, of course, varied in width with the grade.

The Special Grade collar was awarded to King Carol and Crown Prince Michael of Romania, King Boris of Bulgaria, and German Foreign Minister von Ribbentrop. An award of the Grand Cross was made to Himmler in March 1943.

Sash and sash badge of the Grand Cross.

**Grand
Cross**

**Commander
grade (civil)**

ORDER (AND MEDAL) OF THE SLOVAKIAN CROSS

Instituted in May 1940, the Order of the Slovakian Cross in in seven
classes:

Collar of the Order
Grand Cross
Grand Officer
Commander
Officer
Knight
Medal

As from 4 November 1942, "swords" could be added to any grade.

Grand Cross with swords

Medal of the Order of the Slovakian Cross. It is in three grades: bronze, silver, and gold. When the award was "with swords," the cluster of linden leaves on the suspension loop was replaced by crossed swords on a small circular wreath (as with the War Victory Cross Order 5th Class with Swords). The motto of the Order, *Verni sebe svorne napred* means "True to yourselves, go forward."

"With swords" suspension for the medal of the Order.

The Grand Cross with swords is pictured. The ribbon (and sash) of the Order and Medal is black with two narrow light blue stripes (slightly inset from either edge).

"WAR VICTORY CROSS" ORDER

The so-called "War Victory Cross" Order, which was instituted on 11 September 1939, ranks third in precedence among Slovak honors (the Order of Prince Pribina and the Order of the Slovakian Cross coming before it). Originally in only four grades, it was later expanded to seven (including the Medal of the Order). The basic emblem is the double cross of Slovakia with its arms ornamented with linden leaves.

The class structure was:

Grand Cross: an eight-pointed silver breast star upon which a gilt outlined red Slovak cross and a cross worn at the throat from a ribbon.

1st Class: a neck decoration in the form of a red enamel Slovak cross with gold rays between its arms. The cross is outlined in gilt.

2nd Class: as above, but the rays are silver instead of gold.

3rd Class: a pin-back blue enamel cross with a silver frame and silver rays, worn on left breast.

4th Class: a bronze Slovak cross without rays worn from a ribbon.

5th, 6th, and 7th Classes: round medals in, respectively, gold, silver, and bronze, worn from a ribbon.

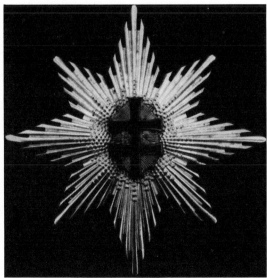

Grand Cross

2nd Class neck decoration with original ribbon (blue with woven linden leaves, edged in white/red/white).

3rd Class without swords.

**1st Class
without swords**

Any grade of the order or medal could be "with swords." These were added along the arms of the breast star, or placed between the two horizontal arms of the 1st, 2nd, and 3rd Classes. On the 4th class they feature on the ribbon. The 4th Class has an enamelled metal Slovak eagle attached to the ribbon; with "with swords," the eagle holds gilt crossed swords in its talons, when without swords, it holds a fasces. It may be noted that the 4th Class with swords has a white enamel center (not brown as is the case when without swords).

The Medal of the Order has as its obverse design the Slovak cross with rays between the arms, the reverse has linden leaves and *Za Zasluhy* (For Merit). When the medal is "with swords," the suspension is a circular wreath of linden leaves with superimposed, crossed swords. When the medal is without swords, the suspension is a bar of linden leaves attached to the medal by a V, similar to the V on the Bravery Medal.

The ribbon of the medal and neck decorations is red with two yellow center stripes. The ribbon of the 4th Class, however, is a very elaborate one - basically red with a sort of "folk art" ornamentation of "dots" of red, yellow, white, and blue between vertical white stripes at either edge.

The original ribbon for the 1st Class neck decoration was coral red with woven linden leaves in yellow; that of the original 2nd Class neck decoration was blue with woven linden leaves and inset edges striped in white/red/white (the white being much narrower than the red).

In March 1944, *all* members of the armed forces of Slovakia who had served without a break for the past four years were awarded a War Victory decoration in a grade commensurate with their rank (the 6th and 7th classes went to non-commissioned ranks, the 5th to subalterns, the 4th to majors and lieutenant colonels, and so on, up to generals). In all, 3,769 awards of the Order (and Medal) were made during the Second World War, of these 437 were made to Germans and 142 to Romanians.

4th Class without swords

4th Class with swords

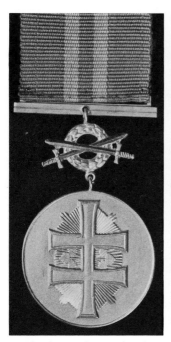

| 5th Class with swords (obverse) | 5th Class without swords (obverse) | 5th Class without swords (reverse) |

Metal emblem for 5th, 6th, or 7th classes without swords.

BRAVERY MEDAL

On 8 May 1939, the Slovak government instituted a gold medal for "heroic deeds in the struggle for the independence of the Slovak people."

On 11 September 1939 (i.e. after the outbreak of war), a bronze and a silver class was added and this medal could now be awarded for bravery in the field.

The gold medal has a red ribbon with a narrow blue central stripe flanked by white. The silver medal has a blue ribbon with a narrow red central stripe flanked by white. The bronze medal has a yellow ribbon with a narrow green central stripe flanked by white.

The reverse of the medal shows the arms of Slovakia above palm leaves tied at the base by a ribbon or scroll.

When the award was for merit rather than for bravery, a "bar" could be added to the ribbon. This bar takes the form of a circular wreath of linden leaves from which flies a ribbon bearing the words *Za Zasluhy* (For Merit).

3rd Class (obverse)   3rd Class (Reverse)

"For Merit" bar (the
actual size is 19mm)

COMMEMORATIVE MEDAL FOR THE DEFENSE OF SLOVAKIA

A bronze shield-shaped medal was awarded for two minor incidents in 1939. The obverse of this medal is the same for both, but one has on the reverse the wording: *Za obranu Slovenska v Marci 1939* (For the defense of Slovakia in March 1939), the second has the *Za obranu Slovenska Javorina/Orava*. The first commemorates some scuffles with the forces of Hungary when that country was allowed (by Hitler) to occupy part of Slovakia (the Sobrance District) in March 1939.

The second reverse commemorates actions on Slovakia's frontier with Poland at the start of the Second World War (in the Javorina-Orava region).

Both versions of this medal have the same ribbon - blue with a narrow white central stripe and white/red edges (red being the outer color).

"Bars" could be added to the ribbon. A bar with JAVORINA could be added to the ribbon of the first issue medal. There is also a bar with III/IX 1939 (probably for frontier defense up to the outbreak of the Second World War, and a bar with simply IX 1939, presumably for actions in the brief campaign against Poland (in which Slovakia participated).

Obverse

Medal with "Javorina" bar (bronze).

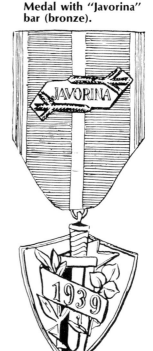

CROSS OF MERIT FOR THE DEFENSE OF THE STATE

Instituted in 1939 in two classes: a silver cross and a bronze cross. This decoration was awarded by the Ministry of Defense to civilians who had made outstanding contributions to the work of Slovakia's armed forces. There were no further awards after December 1942, by which time only 20 of the silver crosses had been bestowed and possibly less than 100 of the bronze crosses.

The ribbon is red with a blue central stripe, flanked by white on either side. The cross itself is white enamel; it is the outer frame which is either silver or bronze (according to its class).

Cross of Merit for the
Defense of the State.

MERIT MEDAL FOR THE SUPPRESSION OF THE NATIONAL INSURRECTION

To reward courage and loyalty during the popular uprising against his regime in the autumn of 1944, President Tiso instituted a special medal in six grades: (a) large medal (36mm) in bronze, silver, and gold; and (b) small medal (30mm) in bronze, silver, and gold. The ribbon for all grades is the same. It is 30mm wide with six sets of alternate red/white/blue stripes (red being to the left). The obverse shows a profile of Dr. Tiso with his name and *I. Prezident Republiky* (1st President of the Republic). The reverse has the motto *Za Boha, Za Narod* (For God and For the Nation) around the Slovak emblem with linden leaves at the base.

Merit Medal for the
Suppression of the
National Insurrection.

RED CROSS DECORATION

A decoration in three grades was instituted by the Slovak Red Cross, possibly about 1943. The grading is:

1st Class: a cross worn at the throat. This is a red enamel Latin cross with silver-gilt "frame" and silver-gilt laurel leaves between the arms. In the center is a red cross on white within a blue circle. The ribbon is blue with white/red/white edges.

2nd Class: the same type of cross as above but worn on the left breast from a ribbon whose colors are the reverse of the 1st Class, i.d., a blue ribbon with white/blue/white edges.

3rd Class: the same as the 2nd Class but blue enamel arms. It was worn from the same type of ribbon as the 2nd Class (on left breast).

2nd Class decoration. On the reverse is (in Czech): "Slovak Red Cross. Cross of Merit of the 2nd Grade" and a number.

Badge of Honor for service in the Crimea, 1943-1944.

Commemorative badge of the "Schnelle Division" on the Russian front.

Tank crew badge. For officers in silver (with colored shield); for others, all bronze.

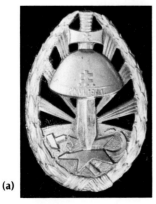

(a)

(b)

Badge of Honor for service on the Eastern front
(a) design as issued (b) original, unissued, design

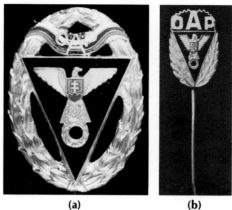

(a)   (b)

**Military Sports badge. (a) Full size; (b) as a
miniature stick pin**

Labor Service Sports badge

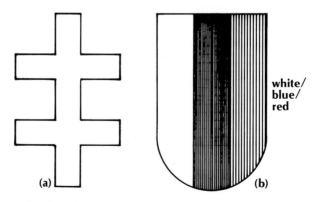

white/
blue/
red

(a)   (b)

**Slovak Military Vehicle (and tank) markings
(a) 1940-1942   (b) 1942-1945**

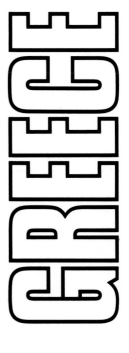

GREECE

GREECE

Mussolini, jealous of Hitler's triumphs of the spring and summer of 1940, determined to stage a spectacular military conquest of his own. For this reason alone (he had no outstanding quarrel with the country), he invaded Greece from Italian-occupied Albania on 28 October 1940. The anticipated easy victory failed to materialize, and by the winter the Greeks had actually passed over to the offensive and were pushing the Italians back. The fate of Greece was, however, sealed when, after destroying Yugoslavia in April 1941, Hitler turned his armies on that country. The Germans brought the campaign to a speedy conclusion, and from April 1941 until October 1944, Greece was an Axis-occupied land.

The Ionian Islands were annexed by Italy, Eastern Macadonia and Thrace were awarded to Bulgaria, and the remainder of the country was divided into German, Italian, and Bulgarian zones of occupation. The Germans held Athens and Thessalonika and, after a celebrated battle, also the island of Crete.

The Greek king, George II, fled the country before the arrival of the Axis forces, and a puppet government was set up in his place. Resistance movements in Greece, as in neighboring Yugoslavia, were split between the communist and the non-communist, and although they dissipated much of their respective strengths in fighting one another, they did, individually, succeed in causing the Axis forces a great deal of trouble. Particularly vulnerable were the lines of communication running through the country which were vital to the conduct of Rommel's campaign in North Africa.

To counteract this insurrgency, the Germans (always the dominant force in the occupation partnership) recruited Special Security Battalions (*Ellinika Tagmata Asphaleias*) which were nominally under the control of the Greek government, rather like the *Milice Francaise* of Vichy France (see Volume 1). These "governmental" forces continued to wear Greek army uniform: khaki, and of a style very similar to that of the pre-war British army. The Royal Crown was, however, dropped from its insignia on the grounds that the king had "abdicated" on quitting Greece in April 1941.

The Higher S.S. and Police Leader in Greece set up a so-called Volunteer Gendarmerie (in Greek, *Ethelontiki Chorophylaki*) which was independent of the govern-

Flag presentation to one of the Special Security Battalions recruited to fight the Greek resistance.

Preceded by two buglers, Colonel Poulos leads his *Poulos Verband.* Although he wears Greek army uniform, the rest of his unit wore German uniform.

ment's Security Battalions, and wore German uniform (a mixture of German Police and army), with, on the left upper arm, a facsimile of the Greek flag. Units with this

German-sponsored force were often named after their individual commander. For example, one notorious battalion was referred to as the *Poulos Verband* from Colonel Poulos, a regular Greek army officer who commanded it. Although the unit as a whole was garbed in German uniform, Poulos himself continued to wear his Greek army uniform.

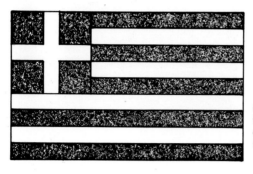

Greek national flag as worn on the left upper arm by members of the Volunteer Gendarmerie (on their German uniforms).

Greece, like all other occupied lands, had, of course, its own home-grown fascists. Before the war an extreme right-wing and "patriotic" movement, the E.O.N. *(Ethniki Organosis Neolaeas* - National Youth Organization) had been formed by Alexandro Kanellopoulos. It was subdivided into two age groups:

Scaponfs (Pioneers): young people of 10 to 13 years

Phalangites (Falangists): young people of 14 to 25 years.

The E.O.N. wore a blue uniform of forage cap, blouse-type shirt, and ski trousers with a white tie, white spats, and a white belt. The shoulder straps and the flaps of the breast pockets were piped in blue/white. (Blue and white are the national colors of Greece). The E.O.N. emblem was a Greek double headed axe not unlike the *francisque* of Petain's France within a wreath of laurel leaves surmounted by a crown. Oddly enough, this crown did not disappear with the supposed "abdication" of the king as it did from army insignia. The E.O.N. flag was a white cross on blue (like the upper left quarter of the Greek national flag) with, in the center, the axe head within a wreath of green laurels.

E.O.N. badge worn on front of the forage cap.

Bugler and drummer of the E.O.N. Blue uniform with white tie.

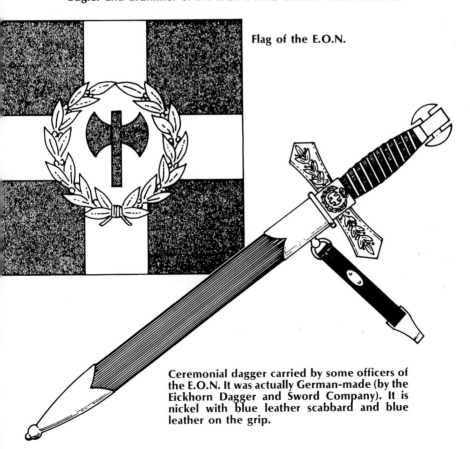

Flag of the E.O.N.

Ceremonial dagger carried by some officers of the E.O.N. It was actually German-made (by the Eickhorn Dagger and Sword Company). It is nickel with blue leather scabbard and blue leather on the grip.

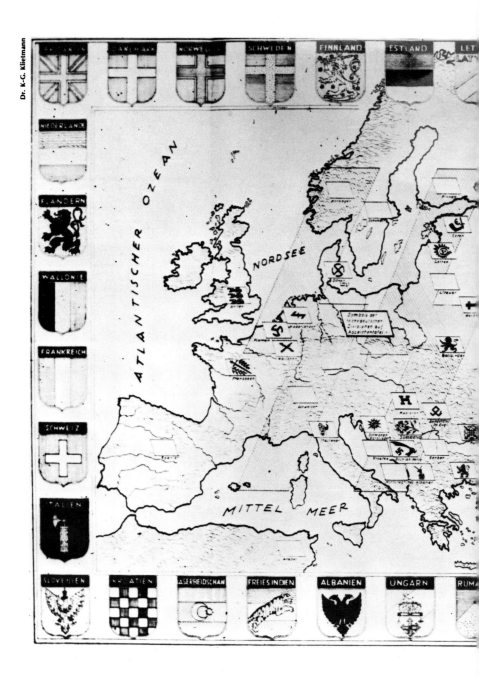

The celebrated "S.S. map" of February 1945, to which frequent reference is made in this and other volumes of this series. It purports to show all the arm shields and collar patches of the non-German volunteers in the Waffen S.S. Many of these are confirmed as having actually been worn, some appear to have existed but not worn, others belong to the realm of fantasy - for example, the arm shields of Switzerland and Sweden. By the time this map had been produced, many of the areas shown as being under German occupation had, in fact, been liberated!

HUNGARY

After the war of 1914-1918, the old Austro-Hungarian Empire went into a state of voluntary liquidation; a process given legal sanction by a series of treaties more or less forcibly imposed upon the defeated by the victors of that war. Under the Treaty of Trianon (in 1920) Hungary lost three-fifths of its former territory and two-thirds of its former population.* This loss of what Hungary regarded as her rightful domains (in fact, the ceded areas were ethnically very mixed) induced a deep sense of grievance. It appeared that Hitler was the only hope of redress. In this the Hungarians were not disappointed. The German Leader did a great deal to restore the balance. First, with the German conquest, and later dissolution, of the Czechoslovak state, Hitler granted, under the so-called "First Vienna Award," part of Slovakia and Ruthenia to Hungary. The remaining part of Ruthenia was turned over to Hungarian jurisdiction in March 1939. The "Second Vienna Award" of 30 August 1940 ordained by Hitler required Romania to hand over northeastern Transylvania to Hungary (this area had been in Romanian hands since 1919 and reverted to her at the end of the Second World War). The defeat of Yugoslavia in 1941 brought Hungary further gains - this time in the shape of the Bačka and Baranja regions** (the northern "tip" of Yugoslavia contiguous with Hungary). All these acquisitions carried within them substantial German minorities. More than half a million ethnic Germans found themselves under Hungarian tutelage. They were to prove something of a thorn in the flesh for the enlarged Magyar state.

There was little natural affection between Teuton and Magyar, but patently Hungary owed a not inconsiderable debt of gratitude to the German Leader, and it also shared his animosity towards Communism - something which Hungarians had experienced to their sorrow at first-hand during the brief but bloody regime of Bela Kun (1918-1920). This had been ousted by a right-wing coup in 1920, and from then on Hungary had been under the quasi-fascist rule of Admiral Nicholas Horthy (appointed "Regent" in 1920 and accorded virtually dictatorial powers as head of state in 1926). It was, therefore, natural

*1. Czechoslovakia received 65,000 sq. km. and 3.5 million people.
 2. Yugoslavia received 65,000 sq. km. and 4 million people.
 **This is the Serbo-Croat spelling. The Hungarian spelling is Bácska; the German spelling, Batscha.

enough that the Hungarians, albeit without great popular enthusiasm, should have joined Hitler's "crusade" against communism. They entered the war on 27 June 1941 having up to that time remained, at least in theory, neutral, notwithstanding their armed assault on Yugoslavia two months previously.

Hitler rated the Hungarians as little better than the Italians as soldiers. During the massive Soviet counter-attack from Stalingrad in February 1943, when the full force of the Russian Army struck and broke through the weakest sector of the front between the Romanian and Italian forces, it descended upon a poorly equipped and supplied Hungarian 2nd Army. It was the Hungarian's inability to withstand this onslaught that largely resulted in the German 6th Army being encircled and finally destroyed at Stalingrad in the winter of 1942/43.

THE HUNGARIAN NAZIS

Before the war there had been a bewilderingly large number of Hungarian "Nazi" parties. This was due less to the widespread popularity of fascism than to the national sense of grievance, endemic anti-Semitism, and the failure of any one leader sufficiently strong to draw together the various rival factions (there were never less than ten of these at any given time!). Worthy of mention is the Hungarian National Socialist Workers' Party *(Nemzeti Szocialista M.M.P.)* founded in 1932 by Zoltán Böszörmény, which adopted the brown shirt of German Nazism with the "scythe cross" as its emblem. A break-away United Hungarian National-Socialist Party was formed the following year by Count Fidel Pálffy which openly used the swastika. In 1934, Count Alexander Festetics formed yet another Hungarian National-Socialist Party, also with the swastika as its principal emblem. But by this time, Hitler had come to power in Germany, and the Hungarian government was inclined to regard the swastika as a "foreign" importation. Its use in politics was, consequently, banned. Count Festetics' party substituted for the swastika a traditional Hungarian symbol - the so-called "Arrow Cross." This device was later to be purloined

Emblem of Count Festetics' National Socialist Party (1934). 1st design (swastika upon which is a map of Hungary).

Second design of emblem of Count Festetics' National Socialist Party (Arrow Cross and map of Hungary).

by another emergent fascist party which was to prove vastly more successful and win more popular support than all the others combined.

This movement was formed in March 1935 as the Party of National Will by Ferenc Szálasi (born in 1897 of Armenian ancestry in Transylvania) and managed to win to its side many of the small "Nazi" parties then extant. In 1939 it adopted the "arrow cross" emblem of Count Festetics and took this as its new title. The Arrow Cross Movement rapidly won nation-wide support due mainly to the personal charisma of Szálasi. It gained 30 seats in the Hungarian parliament. But its very success (and violence) caused Horthy to see it as a threat to the stability of the state, and in February 1939 it was declared illegal.* It was not "legalized" again until after the German invasion of Russia in June 1941. In the meantime, an "official" Hungarian National-Socialist Workers' Party *(Nemzeti-Szocialista Magyar Munkás Párt)* had been created. Formed in July 1940, it was permitted to sport the swastika but only in patriotic colors (a green swastika on a white background within a red circle - green/white/red being the national colors of Hungary). But this

Lapel badge of the "official" Hungarian Nazi Party.

government-authorized Nazi party was never a serious rival to Szálasi's Arrow Cross which came more and more to dominate Hungarian politics as Hitler tried to prop up the defeatist Hungarian government. Indeed, the more the Hungarians sought to disengage from the war, the more formidable did Arrow Cross influence become, until, in March 1944, the party was (under German pressure) declared the *only* permitted political movement in the state.** When, in October 1944, Horthy tried unsuccessfully to make a separate peace, he was kidnapped by an S.S. commando group. Szálasi was then made Prime Minister. On 4 November 1944 he was promoted to the rank of National Leader - a post which was, however by this time, largely nominal since the country was in a state of near total chaos with the approach of the Red Army which encircled Budapest, the Hungarian capital, on December 24.

Szálasi was jailed in 1938 and released on 16 October 1940. After being made Prime Minister, his government lasted from 5 October 1944 to 4 April 1945.

**It was now called the "Hungaria" Movement, and it added an "H" to the center of its emblem. The name Arrow Cross was, however, still commonly used.*

Arrow Cross Leader, Ferenc Szálasi (in civilian clothes) with an officer of the Movement (note Arrow Cross brassard).

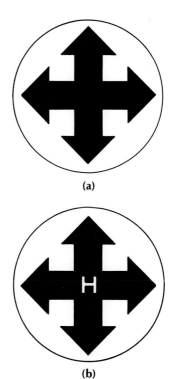

(a)

(b)

Arrow Cross emblem (a) is the original type, (b) is the type used when the Arrow Cross became the "Hungaria" Movement in 1944.

Two members of the "Hungaria" Movement with Arrow Cross brassards.

Trenka

"Hungaria" or Arrow Cross brassard. The red and white stripes derive from the Hungarian coat of arms.

Egy szív·egy akarat

Elöre a gyözelemre!

Propaganda poster showing the Arrow Cross flag between the flags of Germany and Hungary. Wording means (roughly) "One heart, one desire, forward to victory."

Arrow Cross men at Party headquarters in Budapest.

Black brassard with white death's head and crossed daggers worn by the so-called "Death Squads" of the Arrow Cross. These squads were responsible for the rounding up and deportation to death camps of Hungarian Jews.

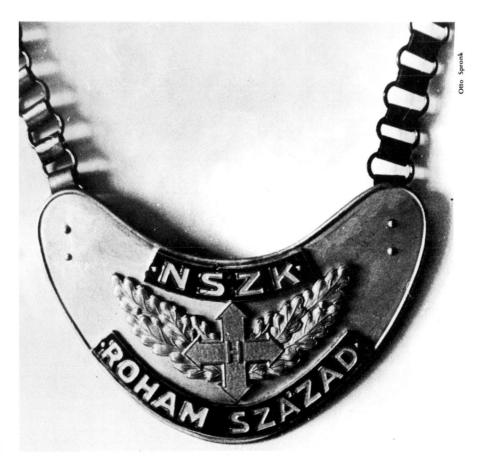

Gorget of the Storm Troop (or "Assault Company") of the Arrow Cross (or "Hungaria" Movement). This example (from the Military Museum in Budapest) is obviously German made.

While still on the subject of Hungarian fascism, reference may here be made to the Levente Movement. Although not strictly a political party, this movement, founded in 1920 and taking its name from Prince Levente of Hungarian historical renown provided physical and para-military training on a compulsory basis for all young males between the ages of 12 and 18 years. A female Levente was formed in 1941, also compulsory. In 1942, the Levente was officially made part of the Hungarian armed forces. At this time it had around 1,300,000 members (of both sexes).

Levente Youth cap badge. The motto means: "God, Fatherland, King." Worn on front of forage cap.

NOTE:
The above motto was changed in 1932 to "For a Better Tomorrow."

Levente Youth Breast Badge (green, white, and red).

Levente Youth on parade in Budapest.

Levente Youth Parachutist's "wings."

Levente Youth Marksmanship Badge.

Trenka

**Levente Youth
Leader's Badge**

**Levente Youth civil lapel
badge (metal)**

THE VOLKSDEUTSCHE

As has already been mentioned, there was a substantial minority of Hungarian citizens who were of German, or Austro-German, origin - the so-called *Volksdeutsche*. Not all were, of course, pro-German, much less pro-Nazi. Some wished for complete Magyarization, others wanted to be good Hungarian citizens while at the same time preserving their German way of life and German language, still others saw themselves as Germans who happened to reside outside the Reich in a physical sense while belonging to it spiritually. Predictably the Foreign Departments of the Nazi Party and of the S.S. encouraged this last category and sought to exploit their pan-German sentiment.

In November 1938, an Ethnic Union of Germans in Hungary *(Volksbund der Deutschen in Ungarn,* or V.D.U.) was formed under the pro-Nazi Franz Anton Basch, who in 1939 was granted the title of *Volksgruppenführer* (Racial Group Leader). Under a Hungarian-German protocol of 30 August 1940, the German *Volksgruppe* was accorded a privileged position within the state and recognized as a separate, largely self-regulating, ethnic community. The V.D.U. consciously modeled itself on the German N.S.D.A.P. In place of the "square" Nazi swastika, it adopted the "sun wheel" *(Sonnenrad)* often referred to as a mobile swastika. The V.D.U. had its equivalent of the German S.A., known as the *Deutsche Mannschaft* (literally German Manhood) and its counterpart of the Hitler Youth, the *Deutsche Jugend* (as will be seen from other chapters in this series, this term was common to all *Volksdeutsche* youth formations outside the Reich). The *Deutsche Mannschaft* (D.M.) wore white shirts and black ties, black trousers or black breeches (with top boots) and a black ski cap. Officers were allowed to wear a black tunic. On the left arm a red brassard with a yellow sun wheel on a white circle was worn. Initially the D.M. was a voluntary organization, but later membership was made obligatory for all physically fit male Party members on attaining the age of 18. In the D.M., physical and para-military training was carried out on the basis of tests leading up to an award of the German National Badge for Physical Training. In the spring of 1942, however, the V.D.U. was allowed to institute its own version of this badge. In general appearance it is similar to its German original, but is slightly smaller and has the letters F.D.S. *(Volksdeutsche Sportabzeichen)* in place of D.R.L. *(Deutsches Reichsabzeichen für Leibesübungen)*, and the "square"swastika at the base of the badge is replaced by the V.D.U. "sun wheel."

Civil lapel badge of the German Racial Group in Hungary. Gold mobile swastika on white with red surround and gilt lettering.

A D.M. officer addressing a meeting.

Brassard of D.M. and V.D.U. Political Leaders. Yellow "sun wheel" on white circle on a red brassard.

Emblem of the Deutsche Volkswohlfahrt (German Peoples Welfare Organization). This was the Hungarian racial German groups' equivalent of the "Winter Help" in Germany.

Sports Badge of the German Racial Group (the monogram V.D.S. stands for Volksdeutsche Sportsabzeichen).

"Victory" ("Victoria") device adopted by German racial community in Hungary during the war (around 1943).

110

The D.M. was not normally armed (officers were allowed to carry revolvers) until the autumn of 1944 when it was renamed the *Heimschutz* (Home Guard) to become the local equivalent of the *Volkssturm* in Germany (set up at the same time, and equally useless!) To bolster up morale in the *Heimschutz,* the Waffen S.S. secunded to it eight officers and fifteen senior NCOs as cadre personnel.

Flag of the German Racial Group in Hungary. Yellow "sun wheel" on a white background, enclosed by a red circle.

The V.D.U. flag was white with, in the center, a yellow "sun wheel" within a red circle. It may be noted that this version of the "sun wheel" is virtually closed, i.e. the circular arms actually touch the transverse arms of the cross, thus completing the "wheel" effect. But most other versions of this device employed by the uniformed organizations of the V.D.U. have a space between the curved arms and the straight arms thus giving a "mobile swastika" appearance rather than a wheel.

The *Deutsche Jugend* dressed at first in a junior version of D.M. uniform (white shirt, black shorts, and a black forage cap), but later adopted Hitler Youth garb - the only difference being in the brassard on which the German swastika was replaced by a black "sun wheel." The *Deutsche Jugend* (D.J.) was subdivided, like its Reich counterpart, by age and sex as follows:

D.J. - boys 14 to 18 years

D.Jv *(Jungvolk)* - boys 10 to 14 years

D.M.B. *(Deutsche Mädelbund)* - girls 14 to 18 years

J.M. *(Jungmädelbund)* - girls 10 to 14 years old

The organizational structure was identical to that of the Hitler Youth rising through *Kameradschaft, Schar, Gefolgschaft* and *Stamm* to *Bann* (the largest   **111** formation). There were seven *Banne* in enlarged Hungary (i.e. including the newly-acquired territories).

Up to 1943, the D.J. based its training on tests designed to lead to an award of the Hitler Youth Achievement Badge (about 300 had been won by this time), but thereafter the D.J. was allowed its own *Leistungsabzeichen*. This is virtually identical to the previous badge except for the substitution of the "sun wheel" for the German swastika and the alteration of the sham runic legend to read *Für Leistungen in der D.J.* (in place of *in der H.J.*).

Achievement badge of the Deutsche Jugend.

Boys of the Deutsche Jugend on the march with their flag (colors same as for the brassard).

Emblem of the Deutsche Jugend.

Brassard of the Deutsche Jugend.

Although the D.J. may have shared a common fascist outlook with the Hungarian Levente, there was no love lost between the two. Indeed, clashes between youths from the two organizations were by no means uncommon!

Other replications of Nazi German originals were the *Frauenschaft* (for female Party members), the *National-Socialistische Erziehungsheime* (national-socialistic training homes), counterpart of the "Napolas" of Germany, and the *Deutsche Volkswohlfahrt* (German peoples welfare) corresponding to the "Winter Help" organization of the Reich.

MILITARY VOLUNTEERS

Hungary, as an independent sovereign state, had, of course, its own army, air force, and river forces. Its *Volksdeutsche* minority were not exempt from conscription into any of these, but the S.S. worked doggedly (and ultimately successfully) to circumvent this and procure the young racial Germans for itself. Until 1941, direct German recruiting in Hungary was illegal. This did not, however, prevent the S.S. from spiriting away two or three score of lads from their Hungarian homeland to the Reich where they enlisted in the Waffen S.S. Most of these ended up in the 6th S.S. Mountain Divison "Nord" in Finland.

The acquisition of the former Yugoslav Bačka region by Hungary in 1941 brought with it a further large addition of *Volksdeutsche* who, as outsiders never previously under Hungarian rule, were of very dubious loyalty. The S.S. was not slow in attempting to exploit their uncertain allegiance. In this they appear to have been fairly successful, since by December 1941 they had managed to recruit some 2,000 young men from this region (most went into the "Das Reich" Division), while the German army and the Todt Organization gained a further 1,000 men apiece. This interference in its domestic affairs resulted in an official Hungarian protest to Berlin. As a consequence, Germany's Foreign Minister von Ribbentrop met Prime Minister Bárdossy of Hungary in January 1942 in an attempt to regularize the recruitment of young *Volksdeutsche* into the German forces. Bárdossy was opposed to any sort of encroachment on Hungarian rights, but under heavy German pressure, was prepared to condone recruitment provided three prior conditions were met. These were:

(a) Enlistment must be strictly *voluntary*

(b) Minors must have the written permission of their parents or guardians.

(c) All those who enlisted in the German armed forces would automatically forfeit their Hungarian citizenship.

Despite these restrictions, the S.S. managed, in the course of an intensive recruiting drive carried out within Hungary between 22 March and 3 May **113**

1942, to raise 16,527 volunteers, although of these only 12,067 were accepted as physically fit for service. A second drive in mid-summer produced a further 9,041 (of whom 5,793 were passed as fit). Most of the recruits raised by these two drives went to either the "Prinz Eugen" Division in Yugoslavia or to the 8th S.S. Cavalry Division "Florian Geyer" (known at that time simply as the S.S. Cavalry Division) on the eastern front.

The loss of their Hungarian citizenship was a grievous blow to the *Volksdeutsche* volunteers, many of whom spoke only broken German and often preferred, among themselves, to converse in Magyar. Thus they found themselves in the unhappy and ambiguous position of being looked on as "dirty Krauts" by their fellow Hungarians and as "Hungarian pigs" by their *Reichsdeutsche* comrades-in-arms! This was made the more bitter by the knowledge that loss of citizenship did not apply to *Volksdeutsche* volunteers from other countries such as Romania, Slovakia, or Croatia.

As a token encouragement to their ethnic brothers to "do their bit," 25 senior leaders of the V.D.U. (including *Gruppenführer* Basch himself) signed on with the Waffen S.S. and went through a (nominal) period of active duty at the front. The S.S. mounted a fresh recruiting campaign in the autumn of 1943; the upper age limit was now raised to 35, and, as a result, a further thirty to forty thousand volunteers were enlisted. The majority went either to the 11th SS Volunteer Panzer-Grenadier Division "Nordland" on the eastern front or to the 16th S.S. Panzer-Grenadier Division "Reichsführer S.S." in Italy.

V. Duchac

Silver and black cloth badge issued to those who volunteered for the Waffen S.S. Wording is: S.S. volunteer of the German racial group in Hungary.

S.S. volunteers before being kitted out with uniforms. Note the S.S. runes badge pinned to the jacket.

◀ Deutsche Mannschaft (D.M.) after volunteering for the Waffen S.S.).

By the early months of 1944, Hungary had come to resemble more a German occupied satellite than an independent state. On 14 April Himmler succeeded in forcing the Hungarian government to revoke its law under which S.S. volunteers were obliged to forfeit their citizenship. Henceforth, such volunteers would enjoy joint German-Hungarian nationality - at least until the end of the war. At the same time the previous option of performing military service either in the Hungarian or German armed forces was abrogated. In the future, young *Volksdeutsche* males would have no choice - they could serve *only* in the Waffen S.S. Conscription was now frank and undisguised.

The first "Hungarians" upon whom the harsh asperity of S.S. conscription was to fall were the young men of the Bačka, and this the result of an ironic mischance. It happened in the following manner. Now that the bestowing of names as well as numbers on its divisions had become the custom in the Waffen S.S., Hitler wanted to know why no S.S. division bore the name of Nazi Germany's most celebrated martyr, Horst Wessel. He suggested to Himmler that a new division be created and this name bestowed upon it. Since Horst Wessel had been an S.A. leader, the Führer delivered himself of the opinion that it would be appropriate for the new S.S. formation to consist mainly of S.A. personnel. Himmler must have been more than a little taken aback by this latter proposal. Not only were relations between the S.A. and the S.S. notoriously (and traditionally) bad, but at this stage of the war, the once-vast reserve of active manpower represented by the S.A. had been virtually drained away. There were, in any case, already in existence units of the Army and Luftwaffe which were earmarked to receive S.A. personnel and these were, for the most part, undersubscribed.

Himmler, however, determined at least to carry out his leader's wish that the name "Horst Wessel" be appended to a freshly-raised S.S. division. But where was he to find the necessary recruits? Only one as yet not fully tapped resevoir of manpower remained. This was the young manhood of the *Volksdeutsche.* Thus, the lads of the Bačka, once technically Yugoslavs, now technically Hungarians, but in the eyes of the S.S. expatriate Teutons, found themselves subject to the inexorable logic of Heinrich Himmler that all men of Germanic ancestry, however remote (and settlement in the Bačka dated back to the days of the Empress Maria Theresa!) must, in Germany's hour of need, bear arms on her behalf.

The result was that the *18 S.S. Freiwilligen Panzer-Grenadier Division* which bore the name of Nazidom's sacrificial hero, Horst Wessel, was made up, for the most part, of non-Germans! Although its cadre was drawn from a supposedly *Reichsdeutsche* formation - the 1st Motorized S.S. Infantry Brigade, this too was, to a large extent, of *Volksdeutsche* composition - for example, most of the volunteers from Danish North Schleswig had been assigned to this brigade. A further irony was its designation as a "Volunteer" (Freiwilligen) Division. This attribution was customarily attached to Volksdeutsche divisions of the Waffen S.S., and at one time had been reasonably accurate, but it had long since lost all meaning. Applied to the entirely conscripted "Hungarians" of the "Horst Wessel," it can be seen only in a rather sardonic light!

Training began in the winter of 1943, and by the following spring, some units were "blooded" in active engagements with Tito's partisans in Yugoslavia. But German losses in the east were now so crippling that any trained or half-trained S.S. unit was liable to find itself rushed to the front to plug a gap in the line. This was true of the, as yet, unfully trained "Horst Wessel" recruits. In July 1944, a "battle group" from the division was hastily transported to the Ukraine where, under the name of S.S. Kampfgruppe Schäfer (alternatively S.S. Kampfgruppe "Horst Wessel" - both terms were applied to it), it was employed to bolster up a collapsing front. It remained on active duty as a semi-independent unit until December 1944 when the remainder of the division came out from their training depot in the Bačka to join it at the front. The division, commanded by S.S. Oberführer August-Wilhelm Trabandt, later by S.S. Oberführer Georg Bochmann (and, for a very brief period in the closing stages of the war, by S.S. Standartenführer Heinrich Petersen, secunded to it from the "Prinz Eugen"), served actively against the Red Army and also the partisans of the "National Uprising" in Slovakia. All three of its commanders were holders of the Knight's Cross.

Recruitment of female Volksdeutsche was introduced in May 1944. Girls between 17 and 30 were required to belong to the S.S. Helferinkorps (S.S. Women's Auxiliary Corps).

Himmler's demands on the Volksdeutsche of Hungary were stepped up. In June 1944, he announced his intention of raising two further S.S. divisions from among their number. He did not fail to point out that the percentage of volunteers which had come out of Hungary was considerably lower than that from Romania, Croatia, or even tiny Slovakia. One division, he said, would be cavalry. For this purpose, the S.S. requisitioned some 20,000 horses from cavalry barracks, remount depots, and private riding schools throughout Hungary. Press-gang methods were now resorted to in order to find sufficient "volunteers." Whole villages were cleared of their young men by S.S. organized razzias. Only about 200 V.D.U. officials were left at their posts; the rest found themselves in field grey.

By October 1944, Hungary no longer *looked* like a German occupied country, it now *was* one. Thereafter, the ruthless conscription methods of the Waffen S.S. were applied to the Hungarians as well as to the Volksdeutsche.

In addition to the two projected *Volksdeutsche* divisions, Himmler envisaged the creation of four all-Hungarian divisions within the Waffen S.S. In these Hungarian divisions, Magyar would be used as the word of command; in the *Volksdeutsche* formations it would be German. The *Reichsführer S.S.* appears to have been unaware that many of the *Volksdeutsche* hardly spoke German or that the supposedly all-*Volksdeutsche* divisions often contained many "pure" Hungarians. Indeed, in a racially mixed country like Hungary, precise ethnic definitions were impossible. Frequently a German-sounding surname and an ability to comprehend elementary military instruction in the German language were sufficient to catagorize a young man as being *Volksdeutsche* (whether or not he thought of himself as German).

Using as its ground unit *(Stamm)* the 17th Regiment of the 8th S.S. Cavalry Division, a fresh division was raised in Hungary during the summer of 1944. It was given the designation: 22nd S.S. Volunteer Cavalry Division "Maria Theresa" (Hungarian No. 1). This final appendage, "Hungarian No. 1 *(ungarische Nr. 1)*, seems to have been an error on the part of the S.S. authorities and has been a source of confusion for students of the S.S. ever since as the same designation was borne by no fewer than three different S.S. divisions (simultaneously!).

Known initially simply as the S.S. Division "Hungary"*(S.S. Division Ungarn)* - it did not receive the number 22 or the name "Maria Theresa" until September 1944. It consisted of *Volksdeutsche* and "pure" Hungarians indiscriminately intermixed (with the former being in the large majority). As this resulted in intractable language problems, the "pure" Hungarians were pulled out and transferred to a smaller unit, *S.S. Kampfgruppe Ney* (Battle Group Ney - the name deriving from its Hungarian commander, *S.S. Obersturmbannf.* Károly Ney). It remained attached to, although not an integral part of, the 22nd Division. Its members wore the same "cornflower" collar patch as the rest of the 22nd Division. The only half-trained and largely untested 22nd Division was virtually anihilated in the battle of Budapest. *S.S. Kampfgruppe Ney* (variously known as *S.S. Brigade Ney* and *S.S. Regiment Ney*) survived to carry on fighting until May 1945 when it surrendered to the U.S. Army at Salzburg in Austria. Its strength at this time was around four or five thousand men.

The activation of Himmler's projected second *Volksdeutsche* division took place amid conditions of such chaos and disorganization in the autumn of 1944 that there was barely time to kit out its members with proper uniforms. Many had only civilian headgear. This won it the sarcastic nickname "Slouch hat division" *(Schlapphut-Division)*. It was allocated the number 33, but such was the confusion at S.S. headquarters as to the racial composition of its own divisions that it too was styled *ungarische Nr. 1!* The 33rd S.S. Volunteer Grenadier Division was, in reality, never fully activated. Ill equipped and ill

A soldier of "Maria Theresa" and a "Hungaria" Movement member standing guard on a bridge in Budapest.

prepared, it was thrown into the line at Pécs in southern Hungary where it was crushed out of existence by the steam-roller advance of the Red Army. The number 33 was then reassigned to the French "Charlemagne" Division (see Volume 1 of the current series).

Of the four projected "pure" Hungarian divisions, only two ever got beyond the planning stage. These were the 25 Waffen-Grenadier-Division der S.S. "Hunyadi" which was given (at last correctly!) the designation ungarische Nr. 1, and the 26 Waffen-Grenadier-Division der S.S. "Hungaria" (ungarische Nr. 2). The two other planned, but unformed, divisions were to be known as the "Gömbös" and "Görgey" Divisions (taking their names from heroes of the 1848 uprising in Hungary). As it transpired it was quite out of the question to find arms, equipment, and transport for four divisions, with the result that personnel ear-marked as cadre for "Gömbös" and "Görgey" were reallocated to the "Hunyadi" and "Hungaria" Divisions.

Two other hastily assembled S.S. divisions drawing their personnel, at least in part, from the Hungarian Volksdeutsche were the 31st S.S. Volunteer Grenadier Division and the 37th S.S. Volunteer Cavalry Division "Lützow." A reference to the 31st Division will also be found in the chapter on Croatia. Its basis was the Germans and Volksdeutsche remnants of the disbanded 23rd Mountain Division "Kama" whose Moslem recruits had been sent back to their native Bosnia. Their place was taken in the autumn of 1944 by further drafts of *Volksdeutsche* from the Bačka and Baranja regions supplemented by some two or three thousand "Arrow Cross" fanatics. The division consisted of three "Grenadier" (i.e., infantry) regiments plus a "Fusilier Battalion" formed from the ex-Arrow Cross men. The division played an active part in the defense of Hungary against the Soviet advance but was decimated in the process. The divisional commander was a German, S.S. *Brigadeführer* Gustav Lombard.

The 37th Volunteer Cavalry Division "Lützow" was an even more hurriedly convoked unit. The Hungarian Plains are famous for their herds of wild horses and, for this reason, horse-power in the most literal sense of the word was more readily available than mechanical power in these last days of the war. In February 1945, Himmler decided that it would be possible to augment the two existing cavalry divisions of the Waffen S.S. (the 8th and the 22nd) by a third freshly raised division which would draw its men and mounts from Hungarian sources (although not from Hungary itself which by this time had been occupied by the Russians). In theory the division comprised two cavalry regiments, but it is extremely doubtful if either of these ever reached anything like full strength. Given the short life of this division (19 February to 8 May 1945) it is hard to imagine that it could have achieved any sort of effective cohesion. It was granted the name Lützow (Freiherr Lützow was a hero of the War of Liberation of 1813) in April 1945.

Use was also made of Hungarian cavalry by the German army. In the summer of 1944, the cavalry regiments of Prinz Karl zu Salm-Hordomar and Prinz zu Sayn-Wittgenstein (both German) were amalgamated with the 1st Hungarian Cavalry Division to form the Hartenek Cavalry Corps (under German Army command).

UNIFORMS AND INSIGNIA

Without doubt the 18th Division had a cuff title Horst Wessel, but the S.A. monogram collar patch so often attributed to this division in post-war histories of the Waffen S.S. was almost certainly *not* worn. A photograph which purports to show an S.S. sentry wearing this special collar device is not authentic. The original photo from which this was "adapted" is, in fact, of an R.A.D. sentry - not even a genuine S.S. man! Members of the division wore the normal S.S. runes. It is true that the S.A. monogram collar patch was put into production and *bona fide* examples are to be found (as well, of course, as numerous fakes) but these in all probability never left the main S.S. clothing store at Dachau and were "pilot" types only. Doubtless hostility to wearing any S.A. insignia would account for its non-adoption by the S.S. Prejudice against their "brothers" in the Storm Troop on the part of members of the S.S. (who regarded themselves as more than just a cut above the "brown scum" of the S.A.) must have made the idea of wearing such a device abhorrent. Similarly, it is doubtful if the S.A. monogram was used as the vehicle sign of the 18th Division - although again this is often shown as such in post-war sources. It is conceivable that the vehicle sign was simply a sword pointing upward at a 45-degree angle.

Cuff title for the 18th Division. This was certainly both manufactured and worn.

S.A. monogram said to be for 18th Division but almost certainly never worn.

S.A. monogram said to be the vehicle sign of the 18th Division but unconfirmed by any photographic evidence.

The 8th Cavalry Division being, despite its complement of *Volksdeutsche* recuits, classed as a *Reichsdeutsche* Division, did not have a special collar patch. It wore standard S.S. runes. Prior to March 1944 when it was granted the title "Florian Geyer" (in honor of a 16th century leader of the Peasants' Revolt in Germany) and authorized to wear a cuff band with this name, it had no *official* cuff title. It is true that a Czech-made "S.S. Kavallerie Division" cuff title does exist and may have been worn by some members of this unit, but if so, it was certainly without official sanction.

The 22nd Division wore as its collar patch a cornflower. As the cornflower has traditionally been a symbol for Germans outside the Fatherland, it was not inappropriate. The vehicle sign of the 22nd Division was also a cornflower. The illustrated history of the Waffen S.S. (original German title: "Wenn alle Brüder schweigen") shows as the arm shield of the 22nd Division a black cornflower upon a background of the red/white/green national colors of Hungary. There is, however, no evidence to suggest that such an arm shield was anything other than theoretical. The same German source illustrates as the arm shield of the *25 Waffen Grenadier Division der S.S. "Hunyadi"* a

Collar patch of the 22nd S.S. Volunteer Cavalry Division "Maria Theresa" (certainly issued and worn).

Vehicle sign of 22nd S.S. Volunteer Cavalry Division.

A projected arm shield for the 22nd S.S. Division, but very doubtful if ever issued or worn.

black raven holding in its beak a ring on a background of the Hungarian national colors. (The raven and ring was the emblem of the Hunyadi family.) Again, this is extremely doubtful. If the 25th Division *did*, in fact, wear an arm shield (and there is no photographic evidence to substantiate this), it was much more likely to have been that illustrated on the S.S. map (see page 96). That is to say, the crown of St. Stephen of Hungary above the "Arrow Cross" emblem on a background of red/white/green. Confirmation of this comes from (a) the book *"Die Werbeaktionen der Waffen S.S. in Ungarn"* which describes (although it does not illustrate) this device, and (b) the fact that the vehicle sign of the 25th Division is an Arrow Cross and two stylized crowns. The collar patch with a large H was intended for the Hunyadi Division. This was certainly both made and worn (by at least *some* members of the division). Due to the chaotic conditions at this time, it is doubtful if the H collar patch was ever issued on a wide scale or if the St. Stephen's Crown and Arrow Cross arm shield was ever issued at all. In fact, a variety of dress was worn in these cursorily assembled divisions. Hungarian army khaki mingled with German field grey, S.S. rank insignia with Honvéd grades!

Collar patch of 25th Waffen-Gren. Division "Hunyadi." (Certainly issued and worn.)

Officers of the 25th ("Hunyadi") Division of the Waffen S.S. In the center is the divisional commander, Lt. General Grassy. Note that the officer on left wears the "H" collar patch. The officer on the right still wears the uniform of the Hungarian army.

Projected arm shield of 25th Waffen-Grenadier Division der S.S. "Hunyadi." This is as shown on the S.S. map. Colors are unknown but are most probably oblique red/white/green upon which a gold or white Hungarian crown and "arrow Cross" emblem is placed. Not known if this was ever issued.

123

An alternative projected arm shield for 25th Division. Very unlikely to have ever been made or issued. The raven with a ring in its beak was the emblem of the Hunyadi family. Janos Hunyadi was a 15th century Hungarian military hero who was largely responsible for driving out the Turks (he died in 1456).

Vehicle sign of the 25th Division. Note the use of the "Arrow Cross" emblem.

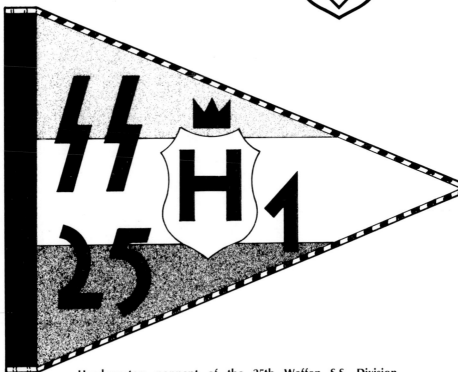

Headquarters pennant of the 25th Waffen S.S. Division "Hunyadi." Black against a background of the Hungarian national colors: red (uppermost), white, and green. (The above sketch is based on a drawing supplied by an ex-member of the Division.)

The 26th Division also had an Arrow Cross, this time with three stylized crowns, as its vehicle sign. It has been suggested that the H collar patch may have been intended for *both* the "pure" Hungarian divisions, since it could equally well stand for "Hungaria" as for "Hunyadi." It may be noted in favor of this theory that in the book *"Wenn alle Brüder schweigen,"* the putative arm shield of the 26th Division is shown as being a large black H on a background of the Hungarian national colors (again there is no evidence of the actual existence of such an arm shield). Very probably, the collar patch for the 26th Division was either the standard issue S.S. runes, or simply a plain black patch.

Projected arm shield for the 26th Waffen-Grenadier Division der S.S. "Hungaria." Very doubtful if this was ever made or issued.

Vehicle sign of 26th Waffen-Grenadier Division der S.S. "Hungaria." Note the use of the "Arrow Cross" emblem.

The 33rd Division (i.e. the Hungarian, not the French one) may have had a "sun wheel" collar patch and "sun wheel" vehicle sign, but this is unconfirmed. Once again, the collar patch was, in all likelihood, either plain black or normal S.S. runes.

Collar patch which may have been intended for the 33rd Division and not, as suggested in Vol. 1 of the present series, for Danes in the Nordland Division.

The scratch 31st and 37th Divisions do not appear to have had any special collar patches or arm shields; although it is possible that since some members of the latter came from the shattered 22nd Cavalry Division, the cornflower collar patch may have been carried over (by these) into this division.

Two versions of vehicle sign for the 31st S.S. Volunteer-Grenadier-Division.

Vehicle sign of 37th S.S. Volunteer Cavalry Division "Lützow."

Vehicle sign of 33rd Division. Although unconfirmed, this would seem to fit in with the "sun wheel" emblem used by the Hungarian Volksdeutsche who made up most of this Division (as would the "sun wheel" collar patch).

HUNGARY AT WAR

Hungary's contribution to the Axis war effort was considerably less than that of her neighbor, Romania. But, as one of the defeated of the First World War, Hungary had been subjected to severe restrictions on the size of her armed forces, while Romania, which had been on the side of the victors, suffered no such limitations.

When Hitler invaded Russia, the Hungarian army (or Honvéd) was poorly armed and inadequately motorized. Its armor consisted of only 65 Italian-made Ansaldo light tanks and 95 Swedish Toldi machines. Transport was available for hardly one third of the existing forces. The first Hungarian units to be sent to Russia comprised one armored and two motorized brigades, along with ten battalions of alpine troops. This combined force was styled "The Hungarian Mobile Army Corps" and came under the command of the German 17th Army operating in the southern sector of the Russian front. Due to very heavy casualties (more than half its men and three-quarters of its armor lost), the Corps had to be withdrawn from active service in December 1941. The following year Hitler informed the Hungarian High Command that he wished them to send "twenty-five divisions to Russia." Since, at this date, the entire Hungarian army amounted to only 21 divisions, it was a requirement that was not likely to be met! Horthy agreed to send three army corps, each of three divisions, plus "a strong mobile unit." This force, known as the Hungarian 2nd Army, consisted of the 3rd, 4th, and 7th Army Corps plus an independent armored division - in all some 250,000 men. It took up its battle station along the banks of the Don on the northwest flank of the German 6th Army.

Shortly after it had assumed responsibility for this sector of the front, it had to face the full fury of the Red Army's counter-offensive from Stalingrad - an action launched on 12 February 1943. Poorly armed, inadequately clothed against the bitter weather, and even insufficiently fed, the Hungarian forces were unable to withstand the weight of the enemy's assault and began to disintegrate. The 9th Division, under General Oszlányi, did, however, hold its ground and was, in fact, the last Axis unit to pull back - for which it was commended in the official Wehrmacht communique. Similarly, the Hungarian 13th Division had to take heavy losses while covering the withdrawal of the German 168th Alpine Division from Ostogozhak. In the course of the whole operation, Hungarian losses amounted to 147,971 men.

After this debacle, the Hungarian army more or less opted out of the war. What troops that were left in Russia (about nine divisions) were used only on garrison, or security, duty in the rear. It was not until March 1944, when the Russians reached the Carpathians, that Hungarian land forces found themselves

Hitler greets General Vörös, chief of the Hungarian General Staff. Between them is Döme Sztojay, the Hungarian Prime Minister. German with back to camera is probably Field Marshal Keitel. (June 1944)

once more in the front line. By September 1944 the Red Army was pouring into Hungary. There were large scale Honvéd defections. In an attempt to stiffen resistance, the Wehrmacht often integrated German and Hungarian military units (naturally under *German* command). On 15 October 1944, Admiral Horthy attempted to negotiate peace with the Russians. It proved abortive. Thereafter, the Germans assumed direct control over the country. It was the end of any pretense of an independent Hungary.

HUNGARIAN ARMY (Commissioned Ranks)

XI

Korossy

Officer cadet: silver star, gold horizontal bar.

Trenka

NOTE:
Hungarian army color-of-service (Waffenfarbe) was Infantry: green; Artillery: red; Cavalry: light blue; Armored Troops: black; Technical and Supply units: brown; Generals: red (with gold braid center).

Infantry Warrant Officer's dress tunic.

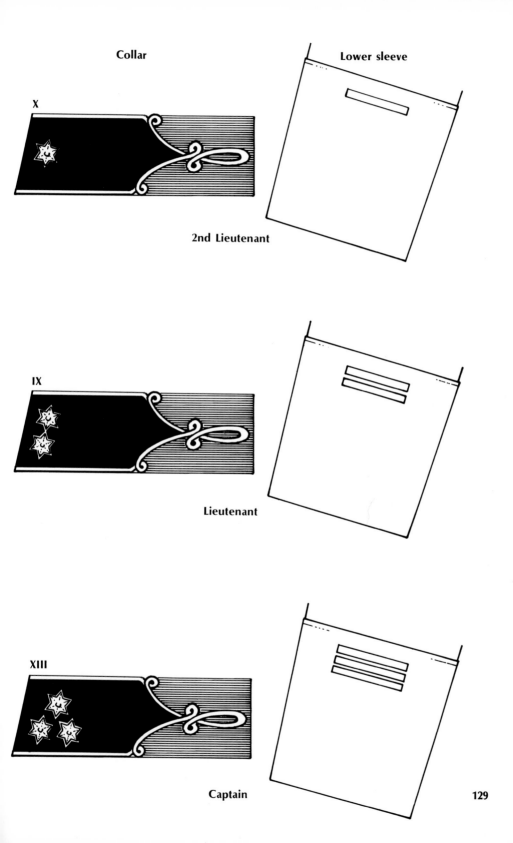

Collar

Lower sleeve

X

2nd Lieutenant

IX

Lieutenant

XIII

Captain

129

VII

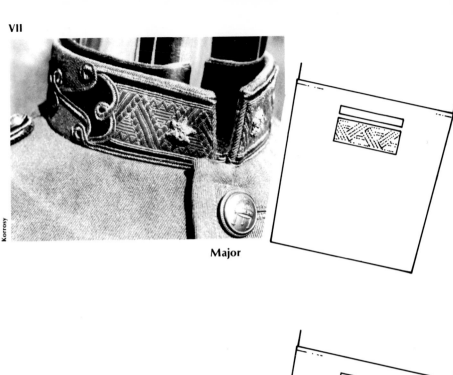

Major

VI

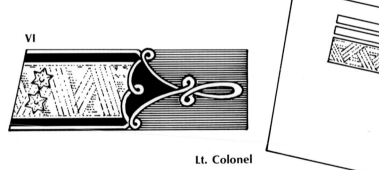

Lt. Colonel

V

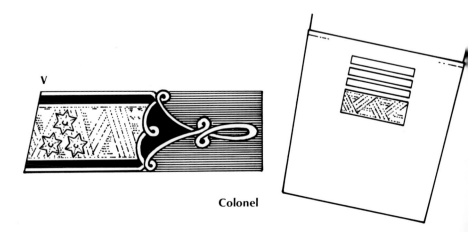

Colonel

IV

Major General

III

Lt. General

II

General

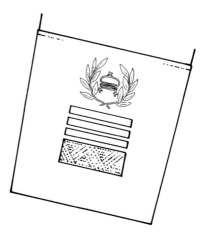

General Gusztáv Jány, the commander of the Hungarian 2nd Army in Russia. In addition to the Knight's Cross of the Iron Cross, he wears Hungarian Order of Merit Knight's Cross (both with and without swords), upon the ribbon of the first of these he wears a miniature of the Grand Cross (indicating that he holds this grade although it is not being worn in full on this, his active service uniform). Above the Iron Cross 1st Class he wears "Knight of Valor" badge. The other two medals are probably the Large Gold Medal with Crown of the "Signum Laudis" decoration and the Officer's 25 years service cross.

I

Korossy

Field Marshal

COMMISSIONED RANKS

(X) 2nd Lieutenant: color-of-service patch, gold star, gold piping
(IX) 1st Lieutenant: as above but two gold stars
(VIII) Captain: as above but three gold stars
(VII) Major: color-of-service patch, gold braid, one silver star
(VI) Lt. Colonel: as above but two silver stars
(V) Colonel: as above but with three silver stars
(IV) Major General: red patch, gold braid, gold piping, one silver star
(III) Lt. General: as above but with two silver stars
(II) General: as above but with three silver stars
(I) Field Marshal: a gold leaf ornamentation replaces the stars

The French army style rank "bars" worn on the cuff are gold; generals have the addition of the Hungarian crown in a laurel wreath above this.

Korossy

General's greatcoat collar insignia

HUNGARIAN ARMY (Non-Commissioned Ranks)

COLLAR

LOWER SLEEVE

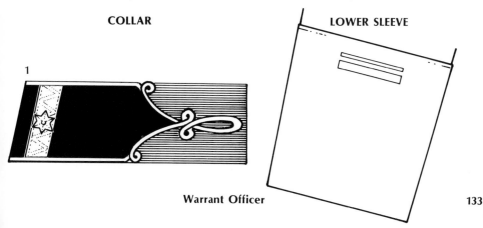

1

Warrant Officer

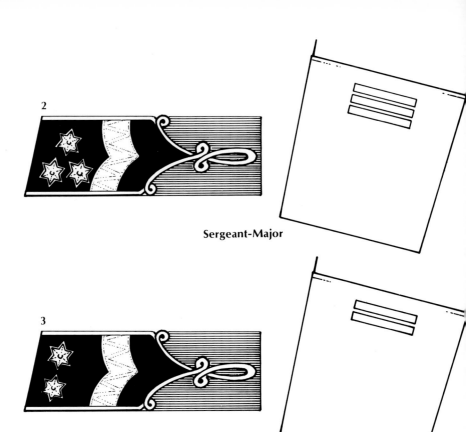

2

Sergeant-Major

3

Staff Sergeant

Trenka

All regular NCOs of the Hungarian army and air force wore on the upper left arm a silver triangle outlined in black, then in appropriate Waffenfarbe (e.g., red for Artillery).

Infantry Staff Sergeant tunic. The stripes on each sleeve indicate graduation from high school, allowing the individual to advance in rank at a faster pace.

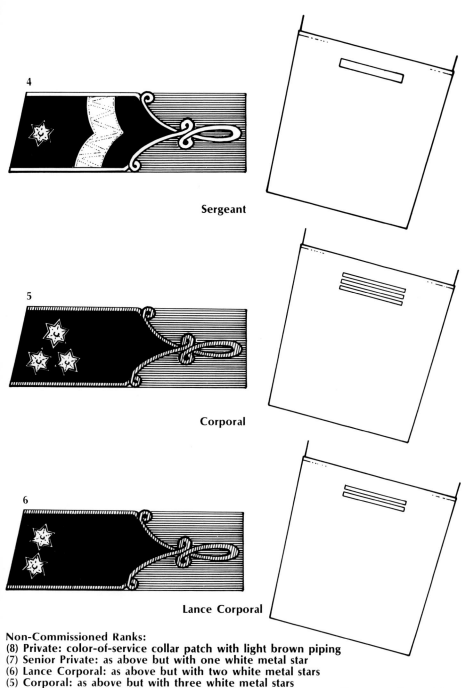

4

Sergeant

5

Corporal

6

Lance Corporal

Non-Commissioned Ranks:
(8) Private: color-of-service collar patch with light brown piping
(7) Senior Private: as above but with one white metal star
(6) Lance Corporal: as above but with two white metal stars
(5) Corporal: as above but with three white metal stars
(4) Sergeant: color-of-service collar patch, silver braid chevron, silver star, silver piping
(3) Staff Sergeant: as above but with two silver stars
(2) Sergeant-Major: as above but with three silver stars
(1) Warrant Officer: color-of-service collar patch with vertical gold braid bar on which is a silver star, gold piping

The rank "bars" on the cuff are light brown for junior non-commissioned ranks, silver for senior NCOs, and, for Warrant Officer, one silver, one gold.

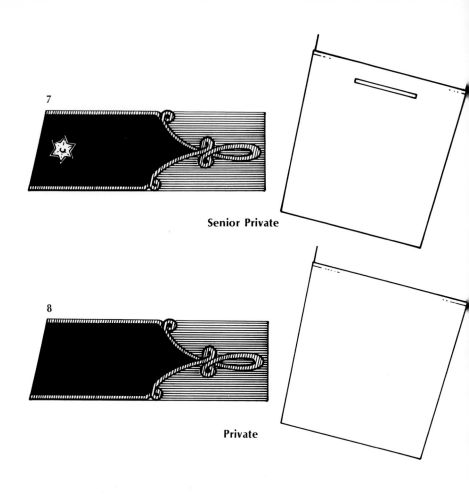

7

Senior Private

8

Private

Badge worn on left side of
forage cap by lower ranking officers (the color of the triangle
is in the appropriate "Waffenfarbe").

Badge worn on left side of
forage cap by senior officers, in
gold wire.

Badge worn on left side of forage cap by light infantry (here 24th Regiment).

Badge worn on left side of forage cap by alpine troops.

Badge worn above right breast pocket by members (and former members) of the Frontier Guard. It is silver wire on a grass green background for officers only. Other ranks were in green embroidery on a brown background.

Korossy

Badge for front of forage cap of Hungarian army and air force. The center piece is in the Hungarian national colors (red/white/green) and is the same for all ranks, but the surround is gold for officers, silver for senior NCOs, and brown for others. Also the number of chevrons varies with rank (increasing number or width with increasing seniority), and these are, as before, gold for officers, silver for senior NCOs, brown for junior NCOs (the lowest rank, private, is without a chevron of any sort). Illustrated example is for Lt. Colonel.

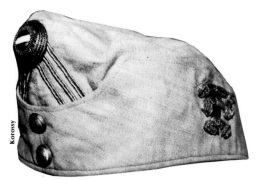

Summer forage cap for rank of Captain.

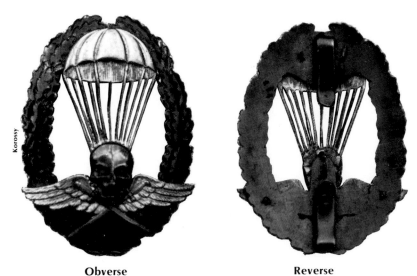

Obverse   Reverse

Master Parachute badge (metal: green
and bronze).

Officer's Paratrooper Badge

il lapel miniature of the
itrooper's badge (the actual size is
•y 15mm).

Korossy

Hungarian paratroopers.

Korossy

Enlisted ranks paratrooper badge

139

Tank Destroying badge of the Hungarian army.

Gorget of the Military Police (or, literally, "Field Security") of the Hungarian army (an example in Andrew Mollo Collection).
There is a similar gorget with the word CSENDÖR (Gendarme) in place of Tábori Biztonsag.

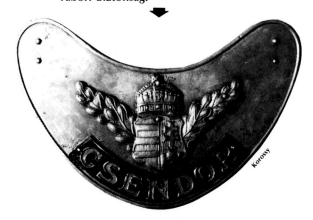

Hungarian airmen had, perhaps, a slightly more successful record than their compatriots on the ground. The Hungarian Air Force, although small (just over 300 aircraft of all types at the start of the Russian campaign), sent two fighter squadrons to the front immediately. These were equipped with Italian-made aircraft - the obsolescent Fiat CR 42 biplane and the more modern Reggiane RE 2000 monoplane (known to the Hungarians as the Héja II). The Hungarian squadrons formed part of Luftflotte 4, which at this time was operating from bases in the Ukraine. Losses were heavy and both squadrons were brought home in December 1941 for re-fitting. In June 1942, a new Hungarian "Air Brigade" joined Luftflotte 4 at the front. This comprised one fighter, one bomber, and two reconnaissance groups (each of two squadrons) - at a total of around one hundred aircraft. The fighter component was now entirely RE 2000s, the bombers were Italian Caproni Ca 135s (by now outdated), while the reconnaissance squadrons were equipped with German Heinkel He 111s (for long-range work) and Heinkel He 46 and Weiss Manfred 21 high wing monoplanes for short-range operations (these latter types proved so vulnerable that they were almost at once downgraded to antipartisan work in the rear where there was no air opposition!)

By the autumn of '42, the Germans had begun to replace the RE 2000s with Messerschmitt 109 Es - a process speeded up after the Hungarians lost the bulk of their fighter strength in the air battles above Stalingrad. In November 1943, one of the two front line fighter squadrons was recalled to the homeland to defend Hungarian air space against an ever mounting Allied Saxon bombing offensive. The Hungarian Air Force also formed six new home defense fighter squadrons which the Luftwaffe equipped with the latest makes of its own fighters - Me 109 Gs, Me 210s, and Focke-Wulf 190s.

This seeming generosity on the part of the Germans was not engendered so much by confidence in their Hungarian allies as by the ironic fact that the

HUNGARIAN AIR FORCE RANK INSIGNIA

| Airman | Junior Lance Corporal | Lance Corporal | Senior Lance Corporal | Sergeant |

German aircraft industry was now turning out planes faster than it was possible to train pilots to fly them! After the occupation of Hungary by the Red Army, the Hungarian Air Force fought on. Two of its fighter squadrons operated from airfields in Austria right up to the end.

The Luftwaffe carried off some 16,000 young Hungarians (about one third of them girls) to act as Flak helpers in the defense of the Reich.

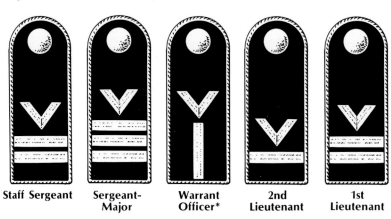

| Staff Sergeant | Sergeant-Major | Warrant Officer* | 2nd Lieutenant | 1st Lieutenant |

*The same type of shoulder strap but with gold piping instead of silver denotes an Officer Candidate.

2nd Lieutenant's shoulder strap, technical engineer (gold on wine red).

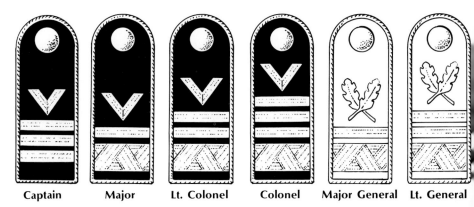

| Captain | Major | Lt. Colonel | Colonel | Major General | Lt. General |

Bomber pilot, Captain Emery von Myiradi-Szabo.

NOTE:
Air Force dagger without eagle on cross guard used in Peoples' Republic (1945-1948).

Trenka

Air Force officer's belt buckle

Hungarian air force officer's dagger

Trenka

A Hungarian airman shows a German comrade-in-arms the beauty of his city, Budapest.

Badge of rank (here for staff sergeant) worn on both cuffs of flying suit. This follows exactly the same scheme of insignia as for the shoulder straps.

Officer in service dress.

Staff sergeant in flying overalls.

Cap badge for senior NCOs (in silver)
and officer (in gold wire).

Cap badge for junior NCOs and men
(in bronze).

Major Paul Szabados is shown wearing the officer's cap badge
and pilot badge.

Collar badge for NCO ranks

G. Petersen

Pilot's badge. In gold for officers, in silver for others.

German pilot Günther Ludigkeit wears a metal version of the above pilot's badge.

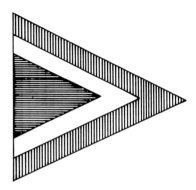

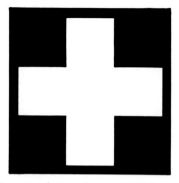

1st type of wing and rudder marking of hungarian air force aircraft.

Wing and fuselage marking of Hungarian air force aircraft, 2nd type. Rudder and aileron striped in red/white/green.

Korossy

Unit emblem of the famous "Puma" squadron.

(a)   (b)

Examples of Hungarian arm shields which exist but may have been only tentative designs, never, in fact, issued. (b) is an extremely well made item (by Bevo-Wuppertal) from an example in the Forman Collection. It is, of course, the Hungarian national coat of arms (in full color) but seems too elaborate to have ever been intended for wear on combat uniform. (a) is also a Bevo item and may belong to a tentative series, all of which have, as here, the name of the country *in German*.

River Forces cap badge

SAINT LASZLO DIVISION

After the occupation of Hungary by the Red Army, scattered units of the Hungarian army and air force were regrouped under over-all German command in Croatia and Austria. One such formation was the Saint Laszlo Division, commanded first by Major

General Szugyi, later by Lt. General Kudriczy. It saw action against the Russians in the Drava valley (of Croatia) and later in Carinthia (Austria) where it surrendered to the British.

The division had its own emblem - an oval stamped aluminum badge measuring 65 by 42mm with the crown and battleaxe of Saint Laszlo and, on a scroll at the base, the words *Szent Laszlo Hadosztaly* (Saint Laszlo Division).

Saint Laszlo, or Ladislaus, was king of Hungary from 1077-1095. As the patron saint of both military men and exiles, his was an appropriate choice of name for a division which was formed (and destroyed) in exile.

**Badge of the
Saint Laszlo Division**

ROYAL HUNGARIAN GENDARMERIE

The Royal Hungarian Gendarmerie was a para-military police force first raised in 1881. During the Second World War, in addition it its normal constabulary duties in the homeland, it also took an active part in operations against the resistance in the rear of the Hungarian front and in security duties in those territories which, as a result of the Vienna Awards, Hungary had acquired from her unwilling and sometimes hostile neighbors (Slovakia, Romania, Yugoslavia). By late 1944 the Gendarmerie was acting as part of the armed forces of the country. Five Gendarmerie divisions, some 3,-000 men and 160 officers, played an important role in the 52-day defense of the capital, Budapest, which ended with the capitulation of that city to the Red Army on 15 February 1945.

The Gendarmerie wore a uniform virtually the same as that of the Hungarian army, but with one very distinctive feature - a large bluish-green rooster feather worn on the left side of the cap.

149

Officer's field cap (here for Captain) with the distinctive rooster feathers on the side.

Badge worn by senior NCOs of the Gendarmerie when "on watch."

Gendarmerie cap badge as it existed in World War II.

One last joint German-Hungarian enterprise remains to be mentioned. This was the *Erntschutz* (Harvest Guard) which consisted of three-man patrols (two Germans and one Hungarian) whose task it was to protect crops or other agricultural produce against sabotage. The Germans would appear to have had a rather make-shift uniform - possibly the "left overs" from S.A., or other stores. Their belt buckle was, for example, a discontinued *Jungvolk* type (replaced in 1936 by a standard Hitler Youth design), and their cap badge would seem to have originated by the Technical Emergency Service (Teno)! The *Erntschutz* was permitted to carry small arms.

Volksdeutsche "Erntschutze" (Harvest Guard) receive instruction in fire arms from an NCO of the L.A.H. (July 1944). Note "Sigrune" belt buckle (similar to "Jungvolk" belt buckle) and what appears to be a "Teno" cap badge.

HUNGARIAN ORDERS, DECORATIONS, AND MEDALS

ORDER OF ST. STEPHEN

This Austro-Hungarian Order was revived by this Hungarian government in August 1938. It is in three grades: Knight (as illustrated), Commander (worn at the throat), and Grand Cross (breast star and sash). The ribbon is red with green edges. The cross is dark green enamel outlined in gilt. In the center is the Hungarian arms (white cross, green "hills," red "sky"). On the white surround is the Latin motto "Publicum meritorium praemium" (Reward for public merit). The commander grade has the same cross on a white ribbon. The grand cross sash has the same cross as the sash "badge." The breast star of the Grand Cross is eight pointed with the same cross, but in this case the white surround and Latin motto is replaced by a circular wreath of green oak leaves.

Order of St. Stephen, Knight.

Order of St. Stephen breast star. Breast star for officers only.

ORDER OF ST. STEPHEN
COLLAR OF THE GRAND CROSS

It is in gold and consists of 13 double S's (St. Stephen) and 12 MT monograms (the initials of its founder in 1764, the Empress Maria Theresa) plus 24 crowns of the St. Stephen variety (different from the so-called "Holy Crown of Hungary" which features on all other Hungarian orders and devices).

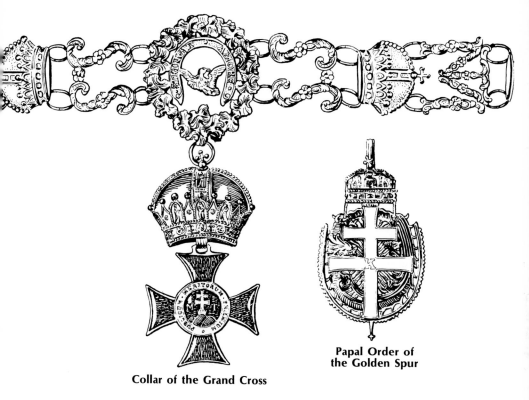

Collar of the Grand Cross

**Papal Order of
the Golden Spur**

A unique badge was worn on the ribbon of the Order of St. Stephen (although it is not connected with that Order). It is illustrated above. Basically it is the Papal Order of the Golden Spur, but it is combined with not only the Holy Crown of Hungary and the double-barred Patriarchal cross (both common Hungarian symbols) but also with the ancient emblem of the 15th century Hungarian Order of the Dragon (which creature appears within the spur and behind the white enamel cross which has a K (Karl) in the center. This unique device was awarded on the occasion of the coronation in 1916 of the last Austro-Hungarian monarch (the Emperor Karl I of Austro-Hungary, or, to the Hungarians, King Karl IV of Hungary).

**Military Order of Maria
Theresa, Knight.**

THE MILITARY ORDER OF MARIA THERESA

Another traditional Austro-Hungarian Order revived by the Hungarian government (in November 1938). It is in three grades: Knight (as illustrated), Commander (neck decoration), and Grand Cross with sash. In fact, the first award of this rare and prestigious Order was not made until 28 January 1944 when it was conferred on Major General K. Oslanyi, commander of the 9th Light Infantry Division of the Hungarian army.

The cross is white enamel outlined in gilt. The center piece is red/white/red with the motto "Fortitudini" (For bravery). The ribbon is red/white/red in equal proportions.

Star to the Grand Cross of the Military Order of Maria Theresa.

Military Order of Maria Theresa, Commander.

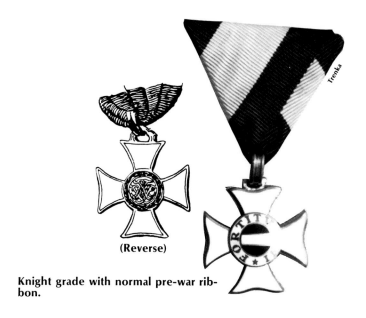

(Reverse)

Knight grade with normal pre-war ribbon.

ORDER OF MERIT

Instituted in June 1922 as the Hungarian Cross of Merit, and originally in only three grades: a bronze, a silver, and a gilt cross; but later expanded into an Order in six grades as follows:

Knight

Officer

Commander

Grand Commander

Grand Cross

Grand Cross with Holy Crown of Hungary.

The ribbon (or sash) for all grades was plain green except for the Grand Cross with Holy Crown of Hungary whose sash was edged with white and red (red being the outer color). In 1939 the "war decoration" ribbon (red with narrow white/green edges) was introduced for all grades including the sashes of the Grand Crosses. However, it may be noted that on the sash of the Grand Cross with Holy Crown of Hungary the green edge stripe is about three times wider than the white stripe (and not the same width as is the case for all the other grades).

The Knight is a white enamel cross with gilt edges. In the center is the double cross and "hills" on a red background, whole being enclosed in a circular wreath of gilt-outlined green laurel leaves. It was worn from a triangular ribbon on the left breast.

The Officer is the same cross (but slightly larger), worn without a ribbon as a pin-back decoration on the left breast pocket.

The Commander is the same type of cross worn from a ribbon around the neck.

The Grand Commander is as above but with an eight-pointed breast star (on which the same type of white enamel cross). There is no sash.

The Grand Cross is a rather larger version of the same but with a sash and sash "badge" (i.e., the same white enamel cross at the juncture of the sash).

The Grand Cross with Holy Crown of Hungary is an eight-pointed breast star upon which is the white enamel cross between the arms of which are gilt rays and upon whose upper arm is a gilt crown. At the juncture of the sash is the sash "badge" - the white enamel cross but, in this case, surmounted by a gold crown.

Knight grade with swords and "war decoration" ribbon.

Officer grade without swords.

Officer grade with swords and "war decoration" green laurel leaves.

Any grade of the Order could have the addition of crossed swords and/or the "war decoration" green laurel leaves (between the lower arms of the cross). When this was the case, the ribbon was, of course, the "war decoration" type. When only the ribbon was worn, a fascimile of the cross (or breast star) was worn on it. Generally speaking, the grade awarded depended on the rank of the recipient.

Commander grade neck decoration with swords.

Grand Commander grade.

Hungarian Order of Merit, Grand Commander (worn interchangeably with the Grand Commander breast star).

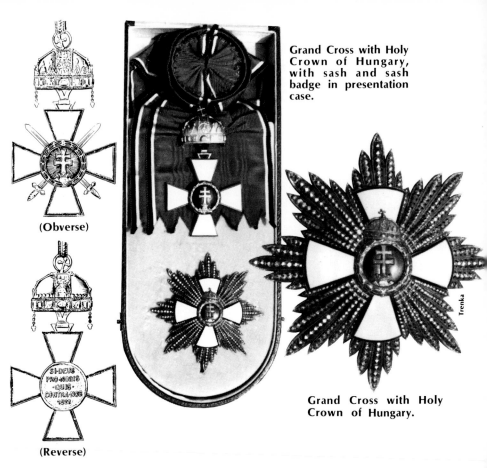

(Obverse)

(Reverse)

Grand Cross with Holy Crown of Hungary, with sash and sash badge in presentation case.

Trenka

Grand Cross with Holy Crown of Hungary.

Korossy

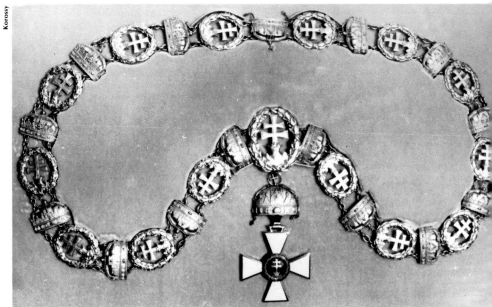

Grand Cross and neck chain given to Hungarian government officials.

As mentioned above, the original Order of Merit consisted only of a bronze, silver, and gold cross, but after the creation of the Order, the three crosses continued to exist and a Medal of Merit (in two grades: bronze and silver) was added. This counted as a fairly low award since even the Cross of Merit in gold ranked below the "Signum Laudis" in bronze. The two grades of the medal are on the same ribbon - plain green; the three grades of the cross are on the same ribbon - green with two red stripes at the edges. The bronze cross is all bronze; the silver, all silver; but the gold class has a red background to the center-piece gold double cross and "hills," and the wreath is gilt outlined green laurel leaves. When only the ribbon was worn, a small metal facsimile of the medal or cross was worn on it.

The inscription "A Hazáért" means "For the nation."

Obverse   Reverse

Cross of Merit in bronze

Medal of Merit in bronze
(green/white/red/white/green ribbon
of the "War Decoration")

Medal of Merit in silver
(green ribbon)

ORDER OF THE HOLY CROWN OF HUNGARY

Instituted in 1942, this Order was intended only for non-Hungarian subjects who "in peace or war have rendered meritorious service to the Kingdom of Hungary." The official (published) date of institution was 3 March 1943.

The order was subdivided, in the manner of other Hungarian Orders, into five grades:

Grand Cross

Grand Officer

Commander

Officer

Knight

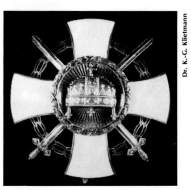

Officer grade with "war decoration" wreath and crossed swords

There was, in addition, three medals (or crosses) - bronze, silver, and gilt.

The basic "badge" of the Order is as illustrated above (for the pin-back officer grade). Any grade could have the addition of the "war decoration"wreath and, presumably for bravery in action, crossed swords. The ribbon of the Order is described as being of the "war decoration" type.

Presumably Germans would have been the most frequent recipients of this "for foreigners only" Order. It is, in fact, extremely rare, possibly due to the late date of its institution.

THE "SIGNUM LAUDIS"MEDAL

The "Signum Laudis" medal was instituted in June 1922 and was then in two classes: a bronze and a silver medal. The ribbon for both was green with narrow white/red edges (red being the outer color). In April 1939 the "war decoration" ribbon (red with narrow white/green edges) was authorized for this medal. At the same time a new, and much higher grade, was introduced: the Large Gold Medal with Crown. This latter is a gold oval medal with an outer edge of gilt outlined green laurel leaves. The suspension is a gilt V surmounted by a gilt crown. For bravery in action, gilt swords can be added at the base of the V and the ribbon is the "war decoration" type. For other merit the swords are omitted and the ribbon has narrow white and *red* edges (instead of the white and *green* of the "war decoration"). A second award of the medal with swords was indicated by the gilt swords being on a silver "bar" attached to the ribbon. When only the ribbon was worn, a facsimile of the medal was worn on it.

"Signum Laudis" medal in bronze with "war decoration" ribbon and crossed swords.

"Signum Laudis" medal in silver with normal civilian ribbon.

(Below) Large Gold Medal reverse with swords.

Large Gold Medal with Crown of the "Signum Laudis."

"Signum Laudis" medal "For Bravery." The Hungarian text which accompanies the original illustration of this medal with the unusual red/white ribbon describes it merely as "Bravery Medal" (*Bátorsági Érem*). Since there would appear to have been a more than adequate number of medals for bravery in the field, it is possible that this medal was awarded for civilian, or peace-time, bravery (as at fires, life-saving, or other emergencies). It is a silver medal with a ribbon which has four red and three white stripes of equal width.

DEFENSE OF THE NATION CROSS

Instituted on 1 March 1944 for merit in the military defense of Hungary in the face of the advancing Red Army. The ribbon is green with a white/red/white central stripe.

Dr. K.-B. Klietmann

THE FIRE CROSS

"Fire Cross" instituted on 24 November 1941 for merit in the war or the defense of the nation which could include being wounded, etc. It is in three types: (a) for combatants; (b) for non-combatants; (c) for those mobilized for home defense.

(a)

(b)

(c)

The ribbon is the same for all three grades: alternate white/green horizontal stripes between red and white vertical edges. For the wounded, a metal "bar" was worn on the ribbon.

Officer's Combat Leadership badge. A green wreath and "hills," the rest gilt. It was awarded to officers for examples of sound leadership in battle.

NOTE:
Could be awarded to army or air force personnel.

"Order of Heroes (Vitézi Rend). Hungarian arms in full color, blue background. On left, green oak leaves; on right, gold ears of corn. A very high award for military or civil distinction instituted in August 1920. Worn on left breast pocket. Recipient had the title *Vitéz* (Knight) which could be passed on to his eldest son. By 1943, over 14,000 had been awarded. No Jew could be a member of the Order.

BRAVERY MEDAL

Originally instituted in 1922 in one class (silver), but in April 1939 expanded to the following:

Bronze Medal   Large Silver Medal
Small Silver Medal   Large Gold Medal.

It was intended to be a fairly low-ranking award given only to non-commissioned ranks, but in September 1942 an Officer's Large Gold Medal was added to the above grading.

The ribbon is the same for all grades: the "war decoration" type; red with narrow green/white borders. The Officer's Large Gold Medal has the addition of the Hungarian crown, open laurel wreath, and crossed swords in gilt metal upon it.

The obverse is a bust of Admiral Horthy. The reverse has the coat of arms of Hungary, crossed swords, and the word Vitézségért.

Small silver Bravery Medal

The order of precedence of this award seems to follow a slightly illogical pattern. Whereas the bronze medal ranks *below* the bronze Medal of Merit (and only one "step" above the "Fire Cross"), the Silver Medal ranks *above* the silver Medal of Merit, but below the silver Cross of Merit. The Large Gold Medal ranks above the gold Cross of Merit, but below the bronze "Signum Laudis." The Officer's Gold Medal, however, ranks above even the gold grade of the "Signum Laudis"!

Crown, crossed swords, and wreath device worn on the ribbon of the Officer's Gold Medal.

When the ribbon alone was worn, a facsimile of the medal (in the appropriate color) was worn on it, except in the case of the Officer's Gold Medal, which had, instead, a facsimile of the crown, crossed swords, and wreath device in gilt metal.

NATIONAL DEFENSE CROSS

Instituted on 11 December 1940 and given for countering communist influences on the home front. The ribbon is red and green (red uppermost) with a narrow white central stripe. In one class only.

Commemorative Medal of the War of 1914-18, non-combatant

COMMEMORATIVE MEDAL OF THE WAR OF 1914-1918 FOR NON-COMBATANTS

The medal for combatants is the same except that swords appear behind the shield on the obverse. Both were instituted in May 1929. The ribbon for non-combatants is white with broad red and green stripes, slightly inset from the edges (red being the outer color). The ribbon for combatants is alternate white and green horizontal stripes in a "ladder" between red and white vertical stripes (white being the outer color). This is, in fact, the same ribbon as that of the "Fire Cross" of the Second World War. The Commemorative medal was also awarded to Hungary's allies of the 1st World War and is often found on German medal groups.

Medal for combatants

AWARDS FOR MILITARY LONG SERVICE

Awards of military long service consisted of the following: for non-commissioned service; 6, 10, 20, and 35 year crosses. For officers: 15, 25, and 35 year crosses.

The non-commissioned cross has the Roman numeral VI, X, and XX (on silver for the latter two), to indicate the years of service, but the 35 years' cross has the arms of Hungary enclosed in a wreath of oak leaves (all in silver) in the center. The ribbon is the same for all four: red with white and green broad edges (green being the outer color). More than one could be worn at a time.

The officer's 15 years' cross is gilt with the crown of King Stephen in the center. The ribbon is white with a red (right) and a green (left) side stripe and red/white/green in the center. For 25 years, the cross has green inset edges and the arms of Hungary in silver in the center.

Cross for 6 years' service (non-commissioned ranks)

The ribbon is green with red and white edges (red the outer color) and a very narrow central red stripe. For 35 years, the arms of Hungary are in gilt and there are gold angels as "supporters" on either side. There is also a gold oak leaf added to the suspension. The ribbon is the same as for non-commissioned ranks.

| Cross for 20 year's service (Non-commissioned ranks) | 25 years' service (Officers) | 35 Year's Service (Officers) |

HUNGARIAN RED CROSS DECORATIONS

In March 1930 the Hungarian Red Cross instituted a number of awards. There were: a 1st and 2nd Class decoration, a bronze, silver, and gold medal.

The medal is oval and has the double armed white cross on which a small red cross and a gold crown is placed. The bronze class has a bronze background, the silver a silver background, but the gold class has a black background with only the outer edge being gold. The ribbon is the same for all three: white with slightly inset red/white/green edge stripes (red being the outer color). The 2nd Class decoration is a pin-back green enamel cross with gold rays between its arms; in the center is a white shield with a red cross, this is surmounted by a gold crown. The 1st Class Decoration is

1st Class Decoration

the same upon an eight-pointed silver breast star. For merit in war, the so-called "war decoration" consisting of an open wreath of green oak leaves could be added to any grade. There was, however, no "war decoration" ribbon for the medals. When only the ribbon was worn, a small metal facsimile of the medal (or decoration) was worn on it.

2nd Class Decoration of the Hungarian Red Cross.

Medal in bronze of the Hungarian Red Cross.

NOTE:
The "War Decoration" oakleaves are placed on the medal or cross just below the red cross.

COMMEMORATIVE MEDALS

This trio of medals commemorates three bloodless victories in as many years. The first celebrates the so-called "1st Vienna Award" by which, on orders from Hitler, Slovakia had to cede part of its southern territory to Hungary. The obverse shows Prinze Rákóczi, a Hungarian military hero. The reverse has the date "1938." The ribbon is red and blue in equal proportions (red being on the left). Date of institution: 4 November 1938.

The second medal is for the "2nd Vienna Award" when (again on orders from Hitler) the Hungarians gained north Transylvania (or in German, the *Siebenburgen*) from Romania. The obverse shows a portrait of King Matthias Corvinus and the date "1940". The ribbon is plain blue. Date of institution: 1 October 1940.

The third medal is for the occupation of the Bačka-Baranja district of Yugoslavia after that

(1) Occupation of South Slovakia
1938

country's defeat by Germany in the spring of 1941. Obverse design is a knight on horseback (Hunyadi). The ribbon is blue and yellow in equal proportions (the blue being on the left). Date of institution: 4 September 1941.

Although the designs are well executed, the medals look rather shabby, being in dull grey zinc.

(2) Occupation of North Transylvania 1940

(3) Occupation of the Bačka-Baranja Region 1941

YUGOSLAVIA
(CROATIA, SERBIA, SLOVENIA)

Yugoslavia was created in December 1918 by the fusion of the kingdom of Serbia with the south Slav regions of the former Austro-Hungarian Empire (that is to say, Slovenia, Croatia, and Bosnia-Hercegovina). Shortly before the end of the First World War, the tiny principality of Montenegro had voluntarily united itself with Serbia. The newly created state, under the Serbian royal house, was known as the Kingdom of the Serbs, Croats, and Slovenes (S.H.S.) until 1929 when the name Yugoslavia (literally "South Slavia") was officially adopted.

It was, from the start, an unstable union. The Roman Catholic Croats resented the dominance of the Greek Orthodox Serbs with their "eastern" habits, so different from their own Vienna-oriented "European" outlook. Friction between Croat and Serb threatened the very existence of the state. Most Croats wanted at the least a federal state in which Croatia and Slovenia would be on equal terms with Serbia. A few extremists demanded nothing less than the establishment of an entirely autonomous Croatia. The most militant among these latter was the Insurgent Croat Revolutionary Organization (*Ustaška Hrvatska Revolucionera Organizacija,* usually abbreviated to, in its plural form, *Ustaše*). This movement, founded in 1929 by a Zagreb lawyer, Ante Pavelić, was destined to play a significant role in the country's subsequent history. At first Pavelić looked towards Italy for aid and support. Mussolini was willing enough to give shelter and financial assistance to *Ustaše* fanatics when they were outlawed in their own homeland. The *Duce* had dreams of incorporating a future Croatia within his Italian Empire and seems to have imagined that a grateful *Ustaše* would cooperate in the achievement of this aim. Hitler, on the other hand, showed little interest in the Balkans and even after the outbreak of war in September 1939, wanted nothing of Yugoslavia except cooperative neutrality. The whole situation was, however, dramatically altered as a result of Mussolini's unprovoked and unjustifable assault on Greece in October 1940. The Italian leader, jealous of his Axis partner, yearned for a military triumph of his own. Unfortunately for both leaders, this plan miscarried disastrously. The Italians were unable to overwhelm the Greek army, and Hitler was obliged to step in to pull the *Duce* out of his difficulties. This he did not so much out of a sense of comradeship as from a fear that should the British establish a bridgehead in Greece, it might be impossible ever to evict them. From Greece the vital Romanian oil fields were within easy bombing range. An attack on Greece could be more easily mounted through Yugoslavia, or at lease with Yugoslav compliance. Hitler, therefore, sought to bring the Yugoslavs within the Axis orbit by getting them to adhere to the so-called Tripartite Pact (an alliance originally only between the three powers: Germany, Italy, and Japan, but later joined by Hungary, Bulgaria, Romania, and Slovakia). After considerable pressure the Yugoslav Regent, Prince Paul, agreed to sign the Pact. He was almost immediately deposed by a clique of Serbian officers. Hitler regarded this as tantamount to a repudiation of the agreement, even though the new Yugoslav government grovelingly pleaded that it was merely a matter of internal politics and (in a written note to the German Ambassador) professed its continued "loyalty" to Germany and its willingness to stand by the provisions of the recent agreement. Hitler disdained such professions of friendship and determined to destroy Yugoslavia by a single massive blow. This fell, unpreceded by any declaration of war, on 6 April 1941 with an air attack on the Yugoslav capital, Belgrade, followed by a lightning campaign (it lasted only 12 days) in which Yugoslavia's armed forces were beaten into the ground by the combined might of Germany, Italy, and Hungary.

After her defeat, Yugoslavia was carved up among the victors in the following manner: Croatia (including Bosnia-Hercegovina and Dalmatia) was declared to be an independent state, although permanent German and Italian garrisons remained behind in two separate "zones of influence" (the Italians in the western, or Adriatic coast, half of the country, the Germans in the eastern landlocked region). It was Mussolini's intention that an Italian prince should become king of the new Croatia and thus forge a permanent bond between the two states. Aimone, Duke of Spoleto, was selected for this role and even accorded a title - King Tomislav II. In fact, the whole transaction was a pure charade. The "king" never set foot in his "kingdom," and it was German, rather than Italian, influence that predominated from the very start.

Serbia was reduced to roughly the size it had been prior to the Balkan wars of 1912-13. It was placed under a German military governor but allowed to have its own civilian administration and raise self-defense forces on a limited scale.

Slovenia was partitioned between the two Axis partners, Germany taking the lion's share. Italy's segment was named the Province of Ljubliana.

Montenegro was enlarged by having its frontiers extended to embrace part of the Dalmatian coast and granted theoretical "independence" under Italian patronage. As with Croatia, it was Mussolini's dream that an Italian prince would occupy the "royal" Montenegrin throne (vacant since its last occupant fled in 1918), but no one could be found willing to accept this unrewarding function!

Other alterations to the former frontiers were that Macedonia (or South Serbia) was given to the Bulgarians (although they had contributed virtually nothing to the recent campaign). The historic Kossovo Region of Serbia was accorded by Hitler to Albania (which latter country had been annexed by Italy in April 1939). The Vojvodina, that region which forms the northern "corner" of Yugoslavia between Hungary and

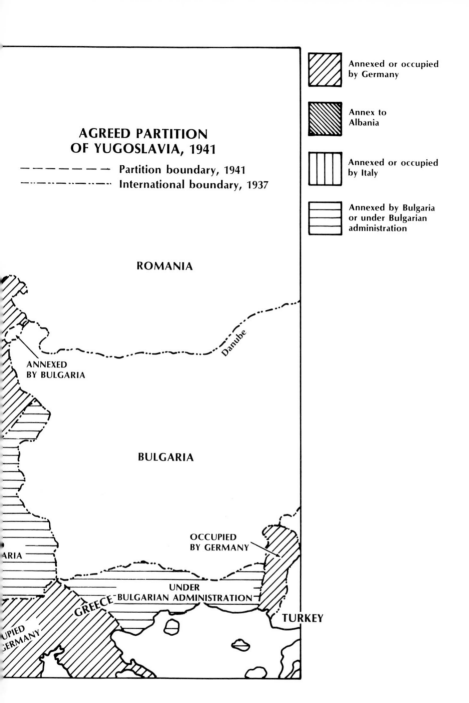

AGREED PARTITION
OF YUGOSLAVIA, 1941

– – – – – – – Partition boundary, 1941
–·–·–·–·–·–·–·· International boundary, 1937

Annexed or occupied
by Germany

Annex to
Albania

Annexed or occupied
by Italy

Annexed by Bulgaria
or under Bulgarian
administration

ROMANIA

Danube

ANNEXED
BY BULGARIA

BULGARIA

OCCUPIED
BY GERMANY

...ARIA

UNDER
BULGARIAN ADMINISTRATION

GREECE

TURKEY

...UPIED
...ERMANY

Romania and comprises the three districts of Bačka, Baranja, and the Banat, was divided between Germany, Hungary, and Romania.

Conditions in the above new territories were as follows:

CROATIA

The "battle of Yugoslavia" was not yet over when the Croats, with German and Italian backing, declared their independence. To Pavelić and some 300 *Ustaše* émigrés under Mussolini's protection in Italy, news of the German attack on their homeland came as a complete surprise. It was not Pavelić but one of his principal henchmen in Croatia, Colonel Slavko Kvaternik, who, on 10 April 1941, announced the setting up of "a free and independent State of Croatia" and appealed to the people to take an oath of loyalty to Ante Pavelić as its leader. Pavelić reached Zagreb on 14 April and at once declared himself *Poglavnik* (leader) of the new Croatia. Slavko Kvaternik was rewarded with the post of Commander-in-Chief of Croatia's armed forces (at that moment in time, non-existent!). On 17 April Pavelić declared war on Great Britain, thereby making Croatia an ally of the Axis.

Hitler spoke of the presence of German troops in the supposedly independent state as "purely temporary." In reality, foreign troops never quit Croatia's soil for the entire war, and Croatia became increasingly a vassal of Nazi Germany.

Dr. Ante Pavelić, Croatia's "Leader."

Pavelić and Kvaternik wasted no time in putting the country on a war footing and instituting a fascist-military dictatorship. Croatia established its own army, known as the *Domobrana* (roughly, Home Defense or Home Army), in which service was obligatory for all physically fit males (in three categories) from 18 to 55 years. Most of the commissioned ranks were officers of the former Royal Yugoslav army who retained at least their previous status and, in many cases, received a greatly advanced grading. Colonel Kvaternik was a prime example of this accelerated promotion since he became first a general, later a field marshal! The Home Army consisted mainly of infantry units, but there were some armored formations (equipped with obsolete German Pz.Kpfw. IV G and IV N tanks, and Hungarian CV 33 and CV 35 tankettes).

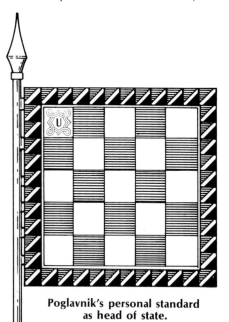

Poglavnik's personal standard as head of state.

There seems to have been something resembling nostalgia for the old Austro-Hungarian army (in which many of the senior *Domobrana* officers, including Kvaternik, had once held commissions), reflected by the "Austrian" style of rank insignia worn on the collar.

All ranks wore a gilt oval cap badge with NDH (*Nesavina Država Hrvatska* - Independent State of Croatia), but, presumably for artistic convenience, the letters appear as NHD. Officers wore this on the peak of their German-style cap above a wreath of linden leaves (the national flower of Croatia as it is of Czechoslovakia) which enclosed a cockade in the Croat national colors: red/white/blue. Generals had the wreath and chin strap in gilt, lower grade officers had a silver wreath and a silver braid chin strap. Non-commissioned ranks wore a mountain cap whose style was again a throw-back to the Austro-Hungarian army. On the front of this they wore the oval gilt cap badge as described above.

At first ex-Yugoslav army khaki was worn, but later this was replaced by field grey (Bosnian Moslem units, however, retained the brown uniform with which they were allowed to wear the red fez prescribed by their religion).

German style peaked cap worn by officers. Black band. Red piping for senior officers.

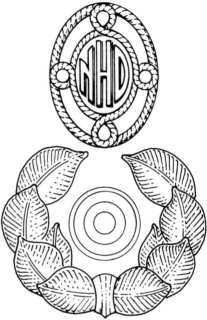

Cap badge for officers. Generals have a gold wreath; other officers have a silver wreath, but for all officers the upper part of the badge (the oval metal part) is gilt.

Visor cord for generals (gold). Senior officers have the same but in silver.

Visor cord for lower ranking officers (silver). The same differences in the style of the visor cord also applied in the Croat Air Force.

Bundesarchiv

The Croat Oberleutnant at left wears an M-43 style visored cap with a gilt oval metal badge, as for the peaked cap above. NCOs also wore the same cap and badge.

Red fez with black tassel for Moslem units. Same oval metal badge as for others.

Officers wore top boots and breeches. General staff officers had, like their German counterparts, a red stripe down the outer seams. Non-commissioned ranks wore puttees. Belts, ammunition pouches, etc., were brown leather. German steel helmets were worn on parade or active service duty. Buttons were gilt for generals, silver for other officers, and black for non-commissioned personnel. Collar patches were in the color of the branch of the service:

Generals: red

General Staff: red and black

Infantry: carmine

Artillery: light red

Cavalry: yellow

Technical troops: black

Medical: dark blue

Veterinary: brown

Engineers: dark green

Catering Corps: light blue

Commissariat: dark brown

DOMOBRANSTVO RANKS (Worn on Collar)

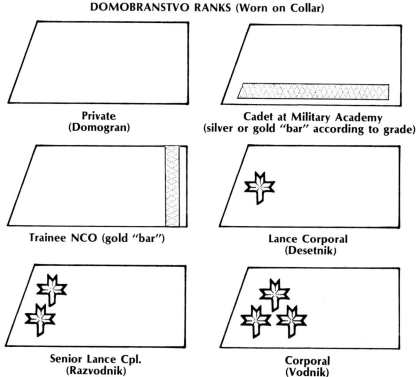

Private
(Domogran)

Cadet at Military Academy
(silver or gold "bar" according to grade)

Trainee NCO (gold "bar")

Lance Corporal
(Desetnik)

Senior Lance Cpl.
(Razvodnik)

Corporal
(Vodnik)

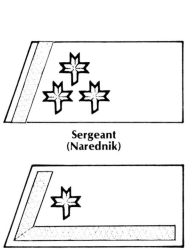

Sergeant
(Narednik)

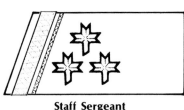

Staff Sergeant
(Častnički Namjestnik)

Sgt. Major
(Stožerni Narednik)

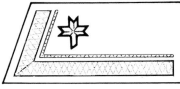

Officer Cadet, or
Ensign (Zastavnik)

2nd Lieutenant
(Poručnik)

1st Lieutenant
(Nadproučnik)

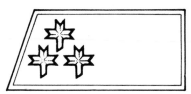

Capt.
(Satnik)

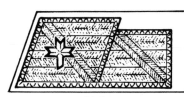

Major
(Bojnik)

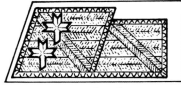

Lt. Colonel
(Podpukovnik)

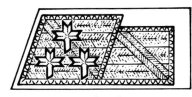

Colonel
(Pukovnik)

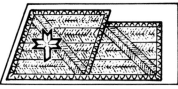

Major General
(General Bojnik)

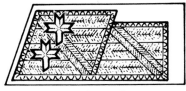

Lt. General
(General Poručnik)

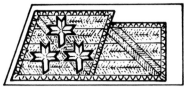

General
(Pukovnik)

Marshal of Croatia
(Hrvatski Vojskovodja)
A unique rank held by
Slavko Kvaternik

Croat Marshal Kvaternik and Foreign Minister von Ribbentrop at the Führerhaupt-
quartier on 21 July 1941.

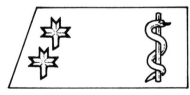

Senior Lance Corporal in Medical Branch

Lance Corporal in Signals Branch   181

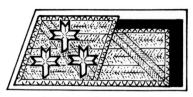

Colonel on the General Staff

Lance Cpl. to Captain   **Major to Colonel**   **Major General to General**
(white metal)   **(gilt metal)**   **(silver metal)**

The above detail of the trefoil rank badges of the Croat Home Army are from a German publication *"Uniformen der Kroatischen Wehrmacht"* (May 1942).

In place of the old Austro-Hungarian stars of rank, the *Domobrana* wore silver or gold trefoils. The *Domobrana* expanded from an original six divisions in November 1941 to fifteen before the end of the war. There was, in addition to the regular divisions, a special Leader's Bodyguard Division and a Replacement Division. There was also an Officer Cadet School, a Cavalry School, and a Battle School. Although large in numbers, the Home Army was unimpressive in combat. It was poorly equipped and politically unreliable. Its unwilling conscripts frequently deserted to the resistance, often taking their weapons with them. The Home Army was dubbed "the supply unit of the Partisans"! When a major operation was mounted against the resistance, the Home Army was seldom accorded more than a supporting role. Threatened with invasion by the Red Army in the last months of the war, the *Domobrana*, by pooling all its available resources, could muster only *one* battle-worthy formation: the 1st Croat Storm Division. This was raised in the winter of 1944/45 and was kitted out with surplus Finnish army uniforms (supplied by the Germans from stocks in the Reich undelivered to Finland at the time of that country's unilateral defection from the war). A special emblem was worn above the right breast pocket. It takes the form of the Croat shield surmounted by the *Ustaše* emblem and the letters H.U.D. *(Hrvatska Udarne Divizje -* Croat Storm Division) flanked, on either side, by tapering "wings" in red/white/blue. (Philatelists may be interested to note that this emblem is featured on a stamp issued

Badge of the Croat Storm Division.
Worn above the right breast pocket.

by the Croat Post Office in 1944). The Storm Division, equipped with second-hand French tanks, went into action on Christmas Day, 1944, against the Red Army in the Drava River sector. It can be said to have met with some success.

Marshal Kvaternik on a state visit to Germany carries his Marshal of Croatia baton* (also a Croat army dagger). His Iron Cross 1st Class derived from the First World War.

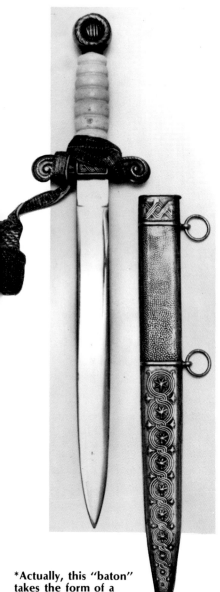

Croat Army dagger

*Actually, this "baton" takes the form of a ceremonial axe.

Officer cadet of Croat Home Army (gold tress bar on collar patch). His steel helmet appears to be of the 1914-18 German variety.

Ante Pavelić with soldiers of the Croat Home Army. They wear, unusually, Czech steel helmets (with the Croat checkerboard shield on the side).

The *Volksdeutsche* of Croatia had their own German-speaking unit within the *Domobrana*. This will be dealt with later in this chapter.

Under the "Pact of Rome" which Pavelić had signed with Mussolini at the time of the defeat of Yugoslavia, Croatia was not permitted to have a navy of its own. This did not, however, prevent the Croats (who have a long naval tradition) from serving as individual volunteers in the German *Kriegsmarine,* or from forming a "Naval Legion" (see later). After Italy quit the war, the Croats were free to form a navy. This they based on the former Naval Legion. The first uniform was similar to that of the Italian or French navy with, on both shoulders, gold bars (known as *passants),* but this was soon replaced by German navy style shoulder straps and officers epaulettes - worn in addition to the more-or-less international scheme of gold "rings" round the cuff.

On their cap, ratings wore a band with *Rata Mornarica* (literally "War Navy"). Above this they had the same gilt oval badge with NHD as worn by the land forces. Petty officers wore peaked caps with an oval badge with a "fouled anchor" (an anchor with its cable twisted round it). Officers had peaked caps which had, within a wreath of linden leaves, an anchor. Superimposed on the anchor was a horizontally oval badge (possibly bearing the letters NHD, although this detail cannot be vouched for with certainty). On the first type of officer's uniform, this badge was surmounted by a red/white/blue cockade. Later this cockade was replaced by a winged Croat checkerboard with the *Ustaše* emblem above. On the visor of the peaked cap, officers of the rank of captain and above wore a single row of gold intertwined braid (known as "troplit") in the same way as German naval officers wore oak leaves. Those with the rank of rear admiral and above had a double row of "troplit."

On the left side of their trench coats, officers wore a rectangular dark blue cloth patch on which was a trefoil above a short gold bar, or bars, corresponding in number and width to the "rings" worn on the cuff.

The Italians raised no objection to the Croats forming their own air force and even contributed towards its creation by donating some aircraft. This was, perhaps, a rather less generous gesture that it might at first appear since the aircraft they handed over (Fiat G 50 fighters) were, in all respects, inferior to the ex-Royal Yugoslav Air Force Hawker "Hurricane" fighters which they expropriated for themselves! The bomber wing of the new Croat Air Force consisted of those Royal Yugoslav Air Force Dornier Do.17 Ks which had survived the brief "war" (about half the original 70 Dorniers were still serviceable). The Luftwaffe supplemented these with some of its own Dornier Do 17s which were being replaced on squadron service by the more up-to-date Junkers Ju 88 bombers.

The Croat Air Force at first wore the uniform of the former Yugoslav Air Force, dropping the royal insignia and adding Croat emblems. In May 1942 a new uniform was introduced virtually identical to that of the Luftwaffe. The scheme of ranks was also almost exactly the same. There were, in fact, only the following minor differences: the "birds" worn on the collar are rather less V-shaped than their German counterparts, and the oakleaves (of Luftwaffe officers) are replaced by linden leaves. The Croat Air Force officer's cap badge bears a rather odd resemblance to that of the present-day West German Air Force! Officers were permitted ceremonial daggers. Aircrew qualification badges, modeled on the German pattern, were introduced in 1942 to replace the rather modest eagle (somewhat like the R.A.F. Pathfinder badge) which had, previously, acted as the aircrew device (it was, in fact, the only surviving part of the former Royal Yugoslav Air Force pilot's badge - the rest having been jettisoned since it incorporated the arms of Yugoslavia).

The branch of service color (or *Waffenfarbe*) of the Croat Air Force, which was worn as the underlay of the officer's epaulette or piping of the non-commissioned ranks' shoulder strap as well as being the basic color of the collar patch, was:

Generals: scarlet
Flying personnel: sky blue
Flak gunners: red
Technical branch: carmine
Medical personnel: dark blue
Supply services: black
Auxiliaries: grey

The home-based Croat Air Force was, from time to time, called upon to assist the Luftwaffe in air operations against the Partisans. Only in the later stages of the war did it have to defend its own skies against enemy aircraft.

CROAT VOLUNTEERS IN THE GERMAN FORCES

The Croat Legion Within days of Hitler's invasion of Russia, Pavelić had issued an appeal for Croats to rally to Germany's side in the "crusade against bolshevism." The response was immediate. An infantry regiment was raised in a matter of weeks. Two battalions were formed at Varaždin, while a third, composed entirely of Bosnians, was established at Sarajevo. All three were then moved to Döllersheim in Austria and amalgamated into a single unit under the designation of 369th Re-inforced (Croat) Infantry Regiment *(369 Verstaerktes Infanterie Regiment (Kroatisches))* - the term "reinforced" indicating that it had its own complement of artillery. It consisted of three infantry battalions, one machine gun company, one anti-tank company with 37mm guns, three batteries of 105mm calibre field guns, in addition to the usual headquarters staff and supply company.

The regiment, or legion, as it was more popularly called, had an effective strength of about 5,000 officers and men. There were around 700 base personnel at its depot at Stockerau in Austria. The majority of the regiment were Croats, but there were also some German officers and NCOs. The 369th was a regiment of the German army, *not*

(a)   (b)

Two variants on the arm shield, (b) has the word for Croatia in its German form.

(b) was almost certainly not issued or worn (one of a series of un-issued BeVo arm shields with place name in German).

The type of arm shield worn by Croat volunteers in the Italian sponsored Croat Legion. Since these were volunteers in the Italian, not the German, forces, this does not properly belong to this study, but is included for purposes of comparison.

of the Croat *Domobrana*. Its uniform and ranks were entirely German. The only distinguishing feature was a red and white checkerboard shield worn on either the left or the right upper arm (photographs show both!) There are at least three variants of this shield: (a) with *Hrvatska*, (b) with its German equivalent, *Kroatien*, and, (c) without wording of any sort. The regiment was awarded a flag. It is the horizontal red/white/blue standard of Croatia upon which is the grandeloquent motto *"Sto Bog da i sreča junačka"* ("By the grace of God and the deeds of heroes").

On 22 August 1941, the 369th Regiment set out *on foot* to join the German 100th Light Division currently fighting on the southern sector of the Russian front. It saw its first action at Valki that September and thereafter fought with considerable courage and loss of life at Kharkov, Kalatch, and along the Don. As part of the German 6th Army, it was drawn into the Stalingrad cauldron, where its commander, Colonel Viktor Pavečić, was killed. About 1,000 Croat wounded were flown out to safety. By January 1943 in the beleaguered city, the 369th was reduced to less than one battalion (attached to the German 24th Division), but by 1 February it was listed simply as a "battlegroup" (a rather vague term). It perished with the rest of the 6th Army.

By building on the base personnel at Stockerau, the recovered wounded, and by mounting a fresh recruiting drive in Croatia, the Germans succeeded, between September and December 1942, in raising two new infantry regiments which were designated the 369th Infantry Division. It took the name *Vrazja Divizija* - Devil's Division. Actually a more literal, if less flattering, translation would be Diabolical Division! This had been the soubriquet of the 42nd (Croat) Infantry Division in the old Austro-Hungarian army. The Germans preferred to call the 369th the "Chess Board Division" *(Schachbrett Division)* - a reference to its red and white arm shield. The divisional

Croatian volunteers in the Italian forces (above) are shown wearing the white-based shield as illustrated at left.

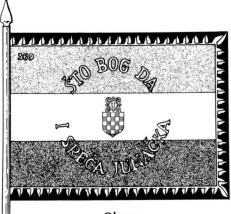

| Obverse | Reverse |

Flag of the 369 Division. Obverse is red (upper) white (center) and blue (lower) with, in the white center, the red and white checkerboard arms of Croatia with a blue "U" in a gold ornamental "frame." In the left upper quarter is 369 in gold. Around the center piece is the motto (in gold) STO BOG DA I SREĆA JUNAČKA ("By the grace of God and the deeds of Heroes"). The fringe on three sides of the flag is red/white/blue. The reverse is white and has in the center the A.P. (Ante Pavelić) monogram in gold surrounded by, also in gold, ZA POGLAVNIKA I ZA DOM ("For the Leader and the Fatherland").

Pole top for the flag of the 369th Division.

Presentation of flag to the 369th Division on 16 May 1944.

commander was a German, Lt. General Fritz Neidholt. Veterans of the 369th "Legion" were awarded a commemorative badge which was worn at first on the left side of the cap, later on the left breast pocket. It takes the form of a linden leaf on which is the Croat checkerboard and the words *Hrvatska Legija* (Croat Legion) and the date, 1941.

Croat Legion Commemorative badge (white metal)

Due to the rising tide of resistance within Croatia, it was decided that the 369th Division would be employed only on counter-insurgency operations in its homeland. The same applied to the two later Croat divisions raised by the Germans. These were:

373 Infanterie-Division (Kroat.) formed at Döllersheim in January 1943 and comprising two infantry regiments (I.R. 383 and I.R. 384), one artillery regiment, one pioneer battalion, a medical, and a signals company. It took the nickname "Tiger" *(Tigar)* Division. Its commander was Lt. General Emil Zellner, a German.

392 Infanterie-Division (Kroat.) formed, also at Döllersheim, in September 1943. It had, like its sister, two infantry regiments (I.R. 846 and I.R. 847) and an artillery regiment. It also had an antitank company and a reconnaissance battalion. It took the name "Blue Division" *(Plava Divizija)*, a rather presumptious title since this was already borne by a much more distinguished (Spanish) division. The divisional commander was Lt. General Hans Mickl, a German.

All three above mentioned divisions were part of German army and wore its uniform and rank insignia. They were distinguished only by the red and white checkerboard arm shield of Croatia. In operations against the Partisans, only the 369th Division played any significant role.

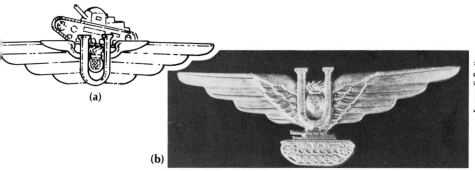

(a)

(b)

Forman Collection

Two versions of Home Army tank crewman's badge.

The Croat tank crewmen above are wearing protective helmets with the checkerboard shield on the side. Note the man at right is wearing a version of the tank crewman's badge on his upper right breast.

Croat officer candidates in June 1944 (note checkerboard shield on side of helmets.

Croat Legion arm shield as shown in photo above. HRVATSKA is the Serbo-Croat word for Croatia.

Parachutist's Badge of the Croat Home Army. Very obviously modeled on that of the German Luftwaffe, it is silver-colored with, at the base, the red and white shield of Croatia in colored paint. At the top of the badge is the N.D.H. monogram. (Adrian Forman Collection)

Forman Collection

191

CROAT NAVAL LEGION

As mentioned above, the Italians, while they were still in the war, ruled out the creation of a Croat navy, but this had not stood in the way of the Croats when they formed a "Naval Legion" within the *Kriegsmarine*. This expeditionary force was under the command of a Croat officer, Andre Vrkljana, who held a commission as a *Fregatten-Kapitän* in the German Navy. Formed in July 1941, the Naval Legion consisted of around 900 officers and ratings who manned an improvised "fleet" of 47 converted fishing boats engaged mainly on mine-sweeping in the Black Sea and the Sea of Azov. In the summer of 1943 the Naval Legion was augmented by a Croat coastal artillery battery, and the make-shift vessels were replaced by authentic mine-sweepers on loan from the German navy.

The Croats succeeded in recruiting to their ranks some former Red Navy personnel of Ukrainian origin who changed sides and, in some instances, brought their ships with them! The Croats wore standard *Kriegsmarine* uniform with only the red and white checkerboard shield of Croatia to distinguish them. This shield could be with or without the word HRVATSKA at the top. The Ukrainian volunteers wore a mixture of German and Red Navy garb. The Croat coastal artillery battery adopted the normal coastal artillery field-grey with, again, only the checkerboard arm shield to indicate their origin. The Naval Legion was superceded by, and absorbed into, the Croat Navy when this was established following the collapse of Italy (see below). Veterans of the Naval Legion, like those of the land and air legions, were awarded a commemorative badge. This is an oval wreath of linden leaves with the words *Hrvatska Pomorska Legija* (Croat Naval Legion). Inside the wreath is an anchor upon which is the Croat checkerboard shield and the date, 1941.

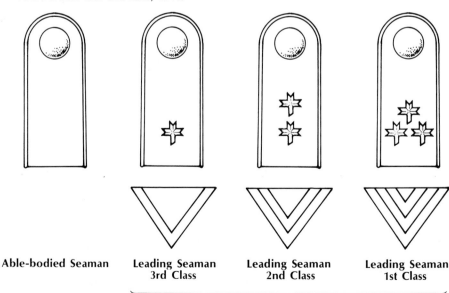

| Able-bodied Seaman | Leading Seaman 3rd Class | Leading Seaman 2nd Class | Leading Seaman 1st Class |

(Red chevrons on left arm. Gilt trefoils on shoulder strap).

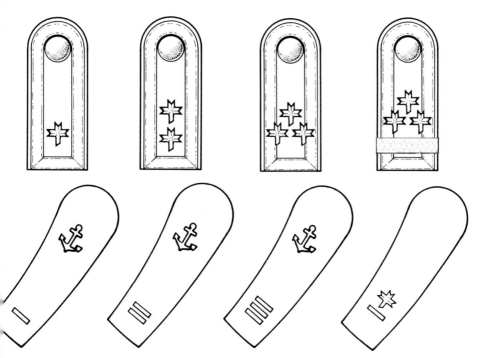

Petty Officer   Chief Petty Officer   Warrant Officer   Midshipman
(Gold bars on cuff, golden tress round shoulder strap, gilt metal trefoils)

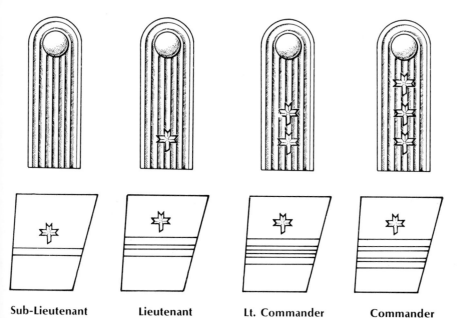

Sub-Lieutenant   Lieutenant   Lt. Commander   Commander
(All the epaulettes are silver with gilt trefoils, except Admiral which is gold and silver interwoven.)

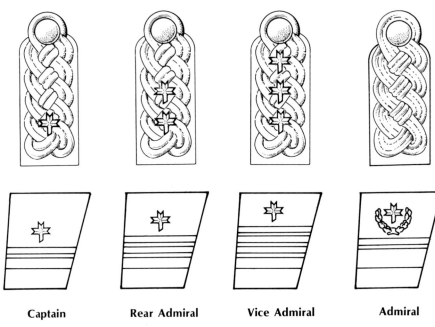

| Captain | Rear Admiral | Vice Admiral | Admiral |

Croat Navy seaman in what would appear to be a German Navy tunic. His cap band has RATNA MORNARICA in yellow.

Naval ratings short coat and sea-going blouse.

Petty Officers' sea-going and dress jackets.

Sailor's collar. In each corner at back is a yellow trefoil.

Petty Officers' and Officers' trench coats showing rank on left arm for petty officer and on left breast for officer.

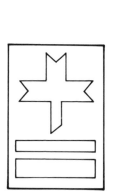

Rank insignia as worn left side of officer's trench coats (here for rank of captain). Gold on dark blue.

First design of officer's peaked cap.

Badge as worn on second design officer's cap.

Second design of officer's peaked cap.

"Troplit" ornamentation worn on visor of cap - a single row for captains, a double row for admirals.

Sailor's cap badge (gilt metal)

Marshal Kraternik (center) with an officer of the Luftwaffe and (right) a senior officer of the Croat Navy. Note that neither Kraternik nor the naval officer wear eapulettes. The naval uniform is the first design with a rosette above the wreath on the cap and "passants" on the shoulders instead of, as from 1944, German style epaulettes.

Naval Legion badge. This is found in various versions, some have a colored shield, others have not. Usually silvered white metal, but some have a brown wreath and a white enamel anchor.

Croat rating in the German Navy. He wears the Croat shield with the word "HRVATSKA" (Croatia) similar to the type worn by the army volunteers.

Unidentified gilt metal badge worn on right breast . Possibly only for officers. (From a photograph)

Frailey

German and Croatian sailors laying mines in the Black Sea in mid-1942. Note the national arm shield without "HRVATSKA."

CROAT AIR FORCE

The Croats contributed two squadrons, one fighter, one bomber, to the German air war in the east. The bomber squadron, consisting of Dornier Do 17 Z medium bombers, arrived at Vitebsk in October 1941 where it was designated at 10 (Kroat.) K.G. 3 (the 10th Croat Squadron of Bomber Group No. 3). It commenced operations the following month, but after losing six of its aircraft in the first few weeks, it was withdrawn to Croatia for further training. It returned to the front in July '42 as 15 (Kroat.) K.G. 53 but was brought back to Croatia that November to be incorporated into the Croat Air Force. It did not return to Russia but remained at home taking part from time to time in anti-partisan operations.

The Croat fighter squadron had, on the other hand, a long and successful tour of front-line duty. It served at 15 (Kroat.) J.G. 52 (the 15th Croat squadron of Fighter Group 52) under the command of Major Franjo Dzal (who later became commander-in-chief of the Croat air force). The squadron was equipped with Messerschmitt Bf 109 G fighters and served on the southern sector of the eastern front. The Croat pilots acquitted themselves well. The first Croat to be awarded the Iron Cross 1st Class was an airman. No less than 14 Croat fighter pilots achieved the status of "ace" (that is to say, shot down ten or more enemy aircraft). The most successful was Cvitan Galić who scored 36 victories before himself being shot down over his homeland by U.S. Air Force "Mustangs" (in the spring of 1944). In all, the Croat fighter squadron chalked up an impressive total of 283 aerial victories.

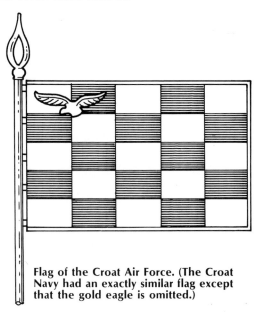

Flag of the Croat Air Force. (The Croat Navy had an exactly similar flag except that the gold eagle is omitted.)

The Croat volunteers wore standard Luftwaffe uniform with only an "Air Legion" badge to distinguish them (they did not wear an arm shield). The Air Legion badge, a winged Croat checkerboard surmounted by the Ustaše emblem, was normally worn

Above and below: two versions of the Air Legion badge.

on the right breast pocket (German personnel sometimes wore this above the left breast pocket), but it could also be worn in a cloth version on the right or left arm (photographs show either). At first the Croats wore only an eagle (as we have noted) as their qualified aircrew member's badge, but later a whole range of flying insignia (for different types of aircrew function) was introduced.

First version of Croat Aircrew badge. Gold metal eagle worn above right breast pocket.

Pilot's badge, 1st design.

Note: both designs also existed in silver wire on black cloth.

Pilot's badge, 2nd design.

Wireless-operator's badge, 1st design.

Wireless-operator's badge, 2nd design.

CROAT AIR FORCE RANKS

Private   Acting Lance Corporal   Lance Corporal

(white metal trefoils)

CROAT AIR FORCE WAFFENFARBE

Generals: scarlet   Medical personnel: dark blue
Flying personnel: sky blue   Supply services: black
Flak gunners: red   Auxiliaries: grey
Technical branch: carmine

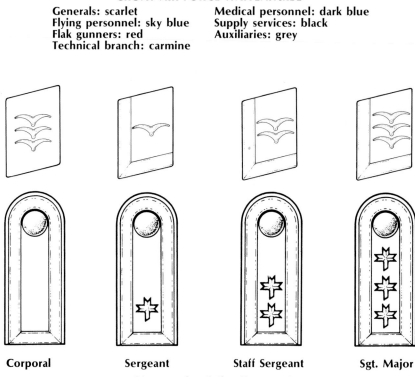

Corporal   Sergeant   Staff Sergeant   Sgt. Major

(white metal trefoils, silver tress)

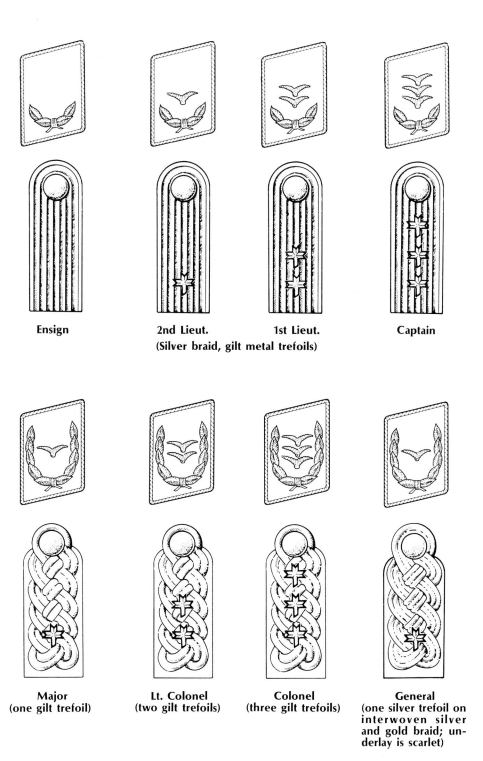

Ensign

2nd Lieut.
(Silver braid, gilt metal trefoils)

1st Lieut.

Captain

Major
(one gilt trefoil)

Lt. Colonel
(two gilt trefoils)

Colonel
(three gilt trefoils)

General
(one silver trefoil on interwoven silver and gold braid; underlay is scarlet)

Collar patch and underlay of epaulette in "Waffenfarbe"

Marshal of the Air Force (crossed silver metal batons on interwoven silver and gold braid). Underlay is scarlet.

Colonel Kren (center) of the Croat Air Force being welcomed on his arrival in Germany. Note his dagger and the absence of shoulder straps (these must have been a later addition). Just behind the saluting officer one can make out an admiral of the Croat Navy (his rank insignia of one broad, one narrow "ring" with, above these, the Croat trefoil in an open wreath of oak leaves is just discernible).

Cap badge for air force officers. Lower part is silver wire, upper part is silver metal. Non-commissioned ranks wore only the upper part (in white metal) on a forage cap. Generals had both parts in gold.

Croat naval officer, air force officers, and a Luftwaffe Major.

This Croatian NCO wears the Croatian Legion Badge (metal and embroidered) and the first version of the Aircrew Badge.

Major Rathmann of the Luftwaffe welcomes Croat Air Legion officers on their arrival in Russia. The Croat volunteers wear normal Luftwaffe uniform. Note Air Legion badge, also the small eagle above the Luftwaffe emblem on the right breast.

Newly graduated officers of the Croat Air Force take the oath of loyalty. They wear the uniform of the Croat Air Force, obviously closely modeled on that of the Luftwaffe.

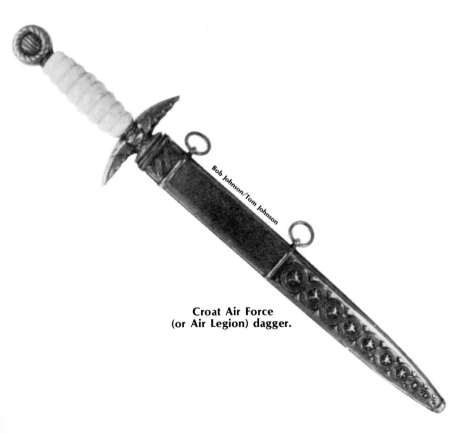

Bob Johnson/Tom Johnson

Croat Air Force
(or Air Legion) dagger.

The Croat bomber squadron flew under Luftwaffe markings with a Croat shield surmounted by the *Ustaše* symbol on the nose of their aircraft. The figher squadron originally also flew under Luftwaffe colors, but later the Croats developed their own wing and fuselage marking. This was the characteristic Croat trefoil in black outlined first white and then in narrow black. The original wing and fuselage marking for the Croat Air Force at home was simply the red and white checkerboard. When the black trefoil was introduced, the checkerboard insignia was relegated to the tail fin.

JU-88 of the Croat bomber squadron with the Croat shield surmounted by the Ustaše symbol on the nose of the aircraft.

Emblem for wings and sides of fuselage of Croat Air Force aircraft. The tail marking was the red and white checkerboard of Croatia.

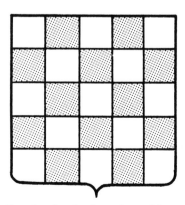

Croat checkerboard emblem worn as tail marking, but originally as the wing and fuselage emblem.

Although the peoples of Yugoslavia are ethnic Slavs, the race "experts" (or charlatans) at S.S. Headquarters were able to convince Himmler that the Croats were really the descendants of the Goths who had once overrun the region and were therefore a "nordic" people suitable for recruitment to the Waffen S.S. The Waffen S.S. raised, or attempted to raise, no fewer than three divisions from Croatia. These were:

7th Volunteer Mountain Division "Prinz Eugen"

13th Mountain Division "Handschar"

23rd Mountain Division "Kama."

The first of these, the "Prinz Eugen," was *Volskdeutsche* and, as such, will be dealt with later in this chapter. The "Handschar" and the "Kama" were Croat.

The raising of a division from among the Moslems of Bosnia-Hercegovina was first ordered by Himmler in February 1943. It may be necessary to say at this point that although the bulk of the population of Bosnia-Hercegovina are of the Moslem faith, they are ethnically identical to their Christian compatriots. Their conversion to Islam was one of those strange accidents of history. Their forefathers once belonged to a much-persecuted Christian sect known as the Bogomils who, in gratitude for the more tolerant attitude extended towards them by the Turks (who overran the Balkans in the 15th century) adopted the religion of their conquerors. Thus they became that unique phenomenon - a European people who embraced the Moslem faith (along with its dress and social customs).

Croatia's dictator, Ante Pavelić, had neither been consulted nor forewarned by Himmler that the Germans intended to inveigle his Moslem subjects into their service. He was furious and reacted by placing as many obstructions in their path as he could devise. (He dared not, of course, countermand Himmler's orders.) He was convinced that the Germans were trying to undermine his authority by deliberately playing Catholic off against Moslem. He raised innumerable objections. When all these had been overruled by Himmler, the *Poglavnik* requested that recruitment be restricted to members of the *Ustaše* (thereby doubtless hoping that it would be confined to those whose loyalty to himself was beyond question) and asked that the new division be named the S.S. *Ustaše* Division. Both requests were ignored. Himmler instructed S.S. *Gruppenführer* Konstantin Kammerhofer, the Higher S.S. and Police Leader in Croatia, to use the full weight of his authority to ensure that by 1 August a division of not less than 26,000 men had been activated. To strengthen Kammerhofer's hand, the *Reichsführer S.S.* promoted him and credited him with two million Reichsmarks to be spent on an intensive propaganda campaign. Kammerhofer rode roughshod over all opposition. The required 26,000 volunteers were conjured up even though many were, as the French say, "volunteers in spite of themselves." To Pavelić's fury, Moslems were frequently combed out of his own forces and transferred, voluntarily or otherwise, to the Waffen S.S.

Originally known as the Croat S.S. Volunteer Division (and a little later as the Croat S.S. Volunteer Mountain Division), it was given the number 13 in October 1943 to become the *13 S.S. Frei. Gebirgs Division (kroatien)*. In May 1944 it was renamed the *13 Waffen-Gebirgs-Division der S.S. "Handschar" (kroatische Nr. 1)*. The word "handschar" is Turkish for a scimitar, which symbol it displayed on its collar patch above a swastika (the scimitar is the emblem of Bosnia). A scimitar was also used as the divisional vehicle sign.

Collar patch with "Handschar" (scimitar) and swastika.

A clear photo of the collar patch being worn. Since the personnel of this division were Moslems, they were allowed to wear a fez with the S.S. emblems.

Standard field-grey was worn but, as Moslems, the fez was permitted as headgear. This was red for parade and "walking out" dress, field-grey for normal service usage (in both cases with a black tassel). On the front of the fez was a death's head surmounted by the S.S. eagle and swastika. The special "handschar" collar patch seems to have been introduced about October/November 1943. Prior to that, either the S.S. runes or a plain black right hand collar patch was worn. Not all the personnel of the division were, of course, Moslem. Many of the officers and senior NCOs were either Germans or *Volksdeutsche*. They were permitted the option of wearing the normal S.S. mountain cap. All members of the division, as supposedly "mountain troops," were entitled to wear an oval edelweiss badge on the right upper arm. On the left upper arm, below the S.S. eagle (or, in the case of the *Feldgendarmerie,* below the Police emblem), all members of the division wore a red and white checkerboard on a black background. This can be found either in the straight-sided version usually associated with the S.S. or in the more shield-shaped type favored by the army. As far as can be ascertained, neither of these was surmounted by the word HRVATSKA (as used on the legion version). After the introduction of the special "handschar" collar patch, those members of the division who were also full S.S. members were entitled to wear the S.S. runes on or below the left breast pocket.

Edelweiss arm badge (white on black)

Arm shield

Full S.S. members wore the S.S. runes on the lower left breast.

Two versions of vehicle sign of 13th Division.

Two non-commissioned officers of the Gendarmerie of the Handschar Division question a Moslem girl. Note the cuff title "Feldgendarmerie" and the Gendarmerie arm badge worn in place of the S.S. eagle above the Croat checkerboard. This man is probably German since he wears the D.R.L. sports badge, the German Horseman's badge, and (below this) the S.S. runes.

The straight sided arm shield (as worn in the above photo). This was worn as an alternative to the curved sided "army" type.

Himmler did not get much joy from his Moslem soldiers. In September 1943 the division was moved to Le Puy in the south of France for further training. There it made history as the only S.S. division ever to mutiny. Almost all the cadre personnel were, at this stage, either German or *Volksdeutsche* (seconded from other divisions, notably the "Prinz Eugen"). To have placed Moslem recruits in the hands of Christian (or perhaps more correctly, non-Moslem) officers and NCOs would, at the best of times, have been an insensitive action; but to turn them over to the tender care of the S.S., a body not noted for its piety or tolerance, was to invite trouble. The Germans scarcely concealed their contempt for the *Mujos* or *Muselgermanen* (a sarcastic term for these honorary Germanics!) In fairness it must be said that Himmler did decree that his Moslem S.S. men were to be afforded "the undeniable right to their religious demands," and that their dietary regulations were to be respected. With typical Teutonic earnestness, the *Reichsführer S.S.* attempted at the same time to outlaw "those jokes and facetious remarks about Moslem volunteers which some of our comrades find so amusing.'" It would seem that despite this injunction, the disparaging "jokes and facetious remarks" continued, since on 16 September some of the Moslem trainees (obviously deficient in an S.S. sense of humor) killed a number of their officers and sparked off a major mutiny. This was quelled only after some further loss of life - this time on the part of the mutineers. Order was eventually restored, the ring-leaders shot, and discipline reimposed. By the end of the year (1943), the division was deemed fit for active service but only in an internal security capacity. The division comprised 21,065 men (360 officers, 1,931 NCOs, and 18,774 other ranks) - well above normal German divisional strength. During 1944, the "Handschar" took part in several operations mounted by the Germans against Tito's Partisans. It distinguished itself mainly by the number of atrocities it committed in what was, on both sides, a singularly brutal campaign. By the end of the year, a major withdrawal of German forces from southeastern Europe was well underway, and the "Handschar" was, for all practical purposes, disbanded as a division. The local Bosnians were officially allowed to revert to civilian status - possibly in order to prevent them from doing so *unofficially* (taking their weapons with them!) The German and *Volksdeutsche* component, about 6,000 men, were remustered as a *Kampfgruppe* (Battle Group) called variously *Kampfgruppe Hanke* or Regimental Group "Handschar." It fought in Hungary and Austria until the end of the war.

The other Moslem Croat formation, the 23rd Mountain Division "Kama," was even less distinguished. In view of the 13th Division's poor record for indiscipline in camp and unruly behaviour in the field, Himmler's continued faith in Moslems as appropriate S.S. material is hard to understand. Possibly he reckoned that the Moslems' traditional hatred of the Serbs would make them good anti-resistance fighters (most of the Yugoslav resistance was Serbian; the Croats and Slovenes began to flow into Tito's armies only late in the war). The official date of the activation of the new division was 17 June 1944. It was given the designation *23 Waffen-Gebirgs-Division der S.S.*   213

A recruiting poster urging Croats from Bosnia and Hercegovina to join the Croat S.S.

"Kama" in September of the same year. Like the "Handschar," it consisted mainly of Bosnian Moslems (about eight or nine thousand) with a cadre of German and *Volksdeutsche* personnel along with some Croat Moslem officers and senior NCOs secunded from the "Handschar." Basic training was performed in Hungary, but with the Red Army steadily closing in, it became impossible to carry on. After having been in existence for less than four months, the division was disbanded in October '44. Its German and *Volksdeutsche* personnel were used to form the cadre of a new division, the *31 S.S. Freiwilligen-Grenadier-Division* (31st S.S. Volunteer Infantry Division) - a scratch formation consisting mainly of *Volksdeutsche* from southern Hungary and native Hungarian collaborators (see chapter on Hungary). The Moslem recruits were sent back to Croatia. The number 23 was reallocated to a Dutch division (see chapter on Holland in Volume 2 of this present series).

A collar patch with a sun flower was designed for the "Kama" Division, but there is no evidence that this was ever either manufactured or worn. Due to the short time the division was in being, it is most likely that either a plain black collar patch or the standard S.S. runes were worn. As with its sister Moslem division, the headgear of its Islamic personnel was a field-grey, or red, fez. All members of the 23rd Division wore the checkerboard shield of Croatia as used by the 13th "Handschar" Division.

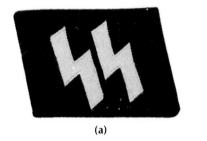
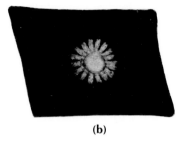

(a)   (b)

Collar patches of the 23rd Waffen Gebirgs Division der S.S. "Kama" (Kroatisches. Nr. 2).
(a) normal S.S. runes; (b) special sunflower patch which does not appear ever to have got off the drawing board.

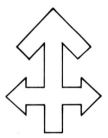

Vehicle sign of "Kama" Division

CROAT INTERNAL SECURITY AND UNIFORMED POLITICAL FORMATIONS

The Ustaše   The Ustaše, the political movement founded by Ante Pavelić, although certainly commanding only a minority of active support in Croatia, came eventually to dominate the entire life of that country. Pavelić's original followers from his days of exile in Italy could be numbered only in hundreds, but soon these few were expanded into a vast uniformed militia (Ustaška Vojnica) which eventually reached a strength of some 20 battalions. Most of these acted as static garrison troops, but some became "active service," or, "emergency battalions" (Pripremne Bojne), taking on a semi-independent character. Often instead of a battalion number, they took the name of their commander. Two of the most celebrated, or notorious, were Boban's Battalion (Bobanova Bojna), and Colonel Francetić's Francetićeva Bojna. This latter, on account of its unique black uniform, was nicknamed the Black Legion (Crna Legija). It was the best equipped, most fully mechanized, and certainly the most brutal of all the Ustaše militia battalions.

At first the Ustaše bully-boys directed their fury against the Serbian minority in Croatia, only later did they turn their attention to the forces of the resistance.   **215**

Ustaše units wore either ex-Royal Yugoslav, or ex-Italian army, uniforms. Later they acquired their own (home produced) uniforms, but these were worn only by officers. This locally devised garb consisted of a British army style tunic, breeches, and riding boots with a white shirt and black tie. Headgear was a peaked cap (again more British looking that German) with a small *Ustaše* U and grenade badge on the cap band.

Collat patches were red with a large U and exploding grenade emblem (the badge of the *Ustaše* movement). Veterans, that is to say, those who had shared Pavelić's exile in Italy, wore blue/white/red collar patches (the national colors of Croatia). These veterans formed the basis of Pavelić's personal bodyguard known as the P.T.B. (*Poglavnikova Tjelesna Bojna* - Leader's Bodyguard Battalion). Later this title was changed to P.T.S. (*Poglavnikova Tjelesna Sdrug**), or, Leader's Bodyguard Regiment.

Three versions of the Ustaše Militia collar patch. The first two are red cotton with white metal emblems. The last one is metal with a gilt colored metal emblem. This type of collar patch was worn by Ustaše Militiamen who joined the P.T.S. but were not original P.T.S. members entitled to the types shown below.

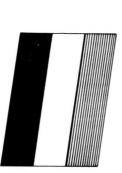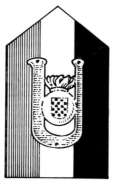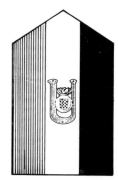

Collar patches of the P.T.S. (The Leader's Personal Bodyguard). The first is the pre-war and early war type. The second was introduced in 1942 and was for non-commissioned ranks, the third type was for officers, but these could be worn only by original (i.e. pre-war) members of the P.T.S.   The collar patch colors are "mirror image," that is to say on one side red/white/blue, on the other blue/white/red - the blue part being the color facing inwards (towards the wearer's tie).

**Serbo-Croat language specialists may query the spelling of this last word. Certainly Zdrug is more usual, but the substitution of S for Z was one of the linguistic "purifications" introduced by the Pavelic regime!*

Ustaše militiamen guarding Pavelić during a speech.

This "Regiment" may, at its peak, have had a strength of over 10,000 men, but of these only about one hundred were employed as actual bodyguards. The P.T.S. was allowed the "honor" of wearing the blue/white/red collar patch - but in this case the order of the colors was reversed and the *Ustaše* U and grenade emblem added.

Ustaše officer's belt buckle (blue U on red background).

Forage cap with U badge in front and rank "stars" on side.

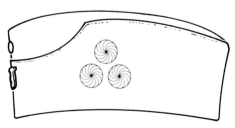

Cap badge set. The upper part is an A.P. monogram standing for Ante Pavelić

Ustaše officer, Marijan Nosić, wears the second style (non-Italian) type of Ustaše uniform with peaked cap and cap badge set as shown on right.

Emblem of the Black Legion of the Ustaše.

Forman Collection

Belt buckle of the Pripremne Bojne (the active service battalions of the Ustaše).

Emergency Bns

Ustaše volunteers (on left of photo) sign on in the Waffen S.S.

Marshal Kvaternik (standing) with Pavelić.   On his collars Pavelić wears red/white/blue collar patches.

Non-commissioned ranks (worn on both upper arms)

Cadet N.C.O. Lance Corporal Corporal Sergeant Staff Sergeant

Sergeant Major

Commissioned ranks (worn on both lower arms)

Officer Cadet 2nd Lieutenant Lieutenant Captain Major

Lt. Colonel Colonel Brigadier-General

Three variants of rank circle. Last shows Major (Bojnik) rank with ornamental "bar."
The rank insignia could also be worn on the left side of the forage cap.

This is possibly the P.T.S. type.

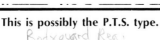
Bodyguard Reg.

Flag party of Croat Ustasë in the Italian type uniforms. The standard-bearer is a sergeant (note on his left upper arm he has two circles and a bar to denote his rank).

The U and grenade device was used as a cap badge and as a belt buckle motif. Rank was indicated by red circles and red bars worn on the upper arm or, by officers, on the cuff. Rank also was shown on the left side of the forage cap. On active duty, a steel helmet could be worn. This was either an obsolete German type (the 1916-1935 version) or the French variety (as used previously by the Royal Yugoslav army). In either case, a U badge was worn on the front. Other *Ustaše* formations were:

(a) The Railway Guard Battalions of the *Ustaše (Ustaška Zeljeznička Bojna)*. These were first formed in October 1941 and had the duty of protecting the railways against Partisan attack. There may have been as many as 20 battalions before the end of the war.

(b) The *Ustaše* Security Service, or U.N.S. *(Ustaška Nadzorna Služba)*. This was a sort of Croatian Gestapo which worked in close cooperation with the S.D.

(c) *Ustaše* Reserve Service *(Ustaška Pripremna Služba)*

Two versions of non-commissioned Ustaše belt buckle.

Ustaše Railway Guard's belt buckle (actual size).

Collar patch of the Ustaše Railway Guards

(d) *Ustaše* Youth *(Ustaška Mladež).* This was divided into three age groups:

7-14 year olds

12-15 year olds

16-21 year olds.

It was open to both sexes and was voluntary. Uniform was grey-green with, on the forage cap, the same U and grenade emblem as for adults.

Hitler Youth boy (left) talks to a young member of the Ustaše Youth at a rally of European youth in Vienna.

Lads of the upper age group of the Ustaše Youth on the march.

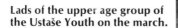

Boys of the 12 to 15 years age group of the Ustaše Youth on parade with their officers. On the right are members of the Home Army (Domobrana).

Badge of the Ustaše Youth (Ustaška Mladež). Worn on left breast - probably an award for merit or sport achievement.

Cap badge set of the Ustaše-Gendarmerie.

(e) *Gendarmerie (Oružničtvo)*. This was, until 1942, under the command of the Home Army, but after that time it was made part of the *Ustaše* Security Service and became the *Ustaše* Police *(Ustaško Redarstvo)*. It was not part of the State Police *(Redarstvena Straža* - literally, the Police Guard).

The *Ustaše* militia battalions sometimes acted as auxiliary guards at German installations in Croatia. They also furnished a volunteer division for the Croat Home Army. In the summer of 1944, the *Ustaše* Militia and the Home Army were fused as a single military force.

223

STATE LABOR SERVICE

On 20 August 1941, Croatia introduced a State Labor Service - the *Državna Castna Radna Služba* (literally the State *Honor* Labor Service, although this second word appears to have been dropped since it was always referred to simply as the D.R.S.) It was quite patently modeled on the German R.A.D. Service in the D.R.S. was obligatory for all physically fit males between the ages of 19 and 25 who were required to serve 12 months in its ranks prior to call-up for military service in the Home Army. There were, of course, regular serving cadre personnel (specially trained for the task at R.A.D. centers in Germany). By the summer of 1942, the D.R.S. had a membership of 90,000.

The D.R.S. emblem was a wreath of barley heads enclosing a spade upon which is the checkerboard shield of Croatia surmounted by the *Ustaše* emblem. Uniform consisted of an open-necked tunic (color unknown, but probably brown) with which officers wore a collar and tie and other ranks a sweat-shirt. Officers could wear breeches and top boots, other ranks had trousers and black shoes. Normal headgear was a forage cap, but officers could wear a peaked cap. Belt buckles followed the German style - round for officers, "square" for other ranks - in both cases featuring a spade within a wreath of barley.

Emblem of the Croat Labor Service.

The scheme of ranks is not known but would appear to have been one, two, and three bars (possibly silver for lower, gold for higher, ranks) worn on the shoulder straps. Collar patches (possibly black) were worn on both sides; senior officers wore on these a head of barley (probably in silver thread). The commander of the D.R.S. was General Palcić. Although originally conceived as a work service, the D.R.S. could, and in emergencies *did*, act as combat engineers in cooperation with the armed forces (for example, during major offensives against the Partisans).

Member of the German racial section of the Croat Labor Service. His sweat-shirt badge is that of the German National Sports Association (D.R.L.).

Labor Service Sports badge (in three classes: bronze, silver, and gilt).

The leader of the Croat Labor Service, General Palcić, inspects Croat officer trainees at an R.A.D. camp in Germany.

Two "blow ups" of Croat postage stamps issued to honor the Croat Labor Service.

Tentative illustration of cap badge set.

GERMAN RACIAL MINORITY IN CROATIA

The State of Croatia had a population of some 6.3 million, and of these more than 150,000 were registered as being of German origin - the so-called *Volksdeutsche*. Not unnaturally, the German minority demanded, and received, preferential treatment. They became, in effect, a state within the state. A German Cultural Union *(Kulturbund)* had existed within Yugoslavia since 1920, but it was not until 1938 that the leadership of the *Bund* passed into the hands of dedicated Nazis. Thereafter, its "cultural" activities tended to give place to more military pursuits. A parallel formation to the S.A., known as the *Deutsche Mannschaft* (D.M.), was formed for men between the ages of 18 and 45 years, with a Hitler Youth-type junior offshoot called the *Erneuerer* (the Renewers, or Rebuilders). Hitler had shown no great interest in Yugoslav affairs in the inter-war years. His main concern even after the outbreak of hostilities had been to preserve peace in the Balkans (from which area raw materials essential to the German war effort flowed). Some enthusiastic young D.M. lads had, it is true, crossed over into Austria to sign on with the S.S., but it was not until January 1941 that the S.S. began to recruit actively within Yugoslavia. It set up "clandestine S.S. regiments" *(getarnte S.S. Standarte)* among the German racial communities and exhorted *Volksdeutsche* youngsters to evade Yugoslav military service. Among the German forces invading Yugoslavia in April 1941 were *Volksdeutsche* lads from Croatia (serving with the *Leibstandarte* Adolf Hitler).

After the setting up of the Independent State of Croatia, Pavelić signed a series of decrees (21 June, 31 July, and 30 October 1941) granting the ethnic Germans the right to establish a *Volksgruppe* (Racial Community). The leader of this community was Branimir Altgayer who was given the rank of State Secretary in the Croat cabinet. In July 1941, Himmler authorized the creation, from the ranks of the D.M., of what amounted to the Croat-*Volksdetusche* equivalent of the *Allgemeine S.S.* It was known as the *Einsatzstaffel,* or ES (roughly, "Action Squad") and was open, on a voluntary basis, to all physically fit men between the ages of 17 and 22 who could sign on for periods of service varying from four years to as little as six months. In November of the same year, a regular active service unit, the *Verfügungsbataillon* (approximately, "Everready Battalion") was activated within the framework of the E.S. It consisted of six companies and was granted the name "Prinz Eugen" in memory of Prince Eugene of Savoy, the Austrian military hero who, in the 18th century, had been responsible for clearing the Turks from Croatia. A second regular E.S. battalion was raised shortly thereafter, in addition to four *Bereitschaftskompanien* ("Readiness Companies") and a *Stabswache* (Headquarters Guard Unit) with companies in Zagreb, the Croat capital, and Essegg, the main town of "German" Croatia.

The uniform of the E.S. was field-grey with a dark green collar on which was (on the right) two stylized "wolf hook" emblems (bearing a strong resemblance to the letters S.S.) Sometimes the two "wolf hooks" are close together, sometimes more widely spaced (doubtless due to differences in local manufacture). On the left hand side was a black collar patch with the rank of the wearer indicated by a system which is virtually identical to that of the Waffen S.S. (although the names of the rank follow army, rather than S.S., usage). Rank was also indicated on the shoulder - again the scheme is virtually the same as that of the army/Waffen S.S. The S.S. eagle was worn by all ranks on the left upper arm. Due to shortages of equipment, many items of accoutrement were ex-Royal Yugoslav Army while the steel helmets were old 1914-18 war, German stock! The tunic could be worn either open or closed at the neck. If open, a khaki shirt and black tie was worn with it. A forage cap with the S.S. eagle on the front was worn by non-commissioned ranks; officers wore a peaked cap with the S.S. eagle above, not the customary death's head, but a wreath (probably of linden leaves) enclosing a cockade (conceivably in the red/white/blue of Croatia).

Right hand collar patch.

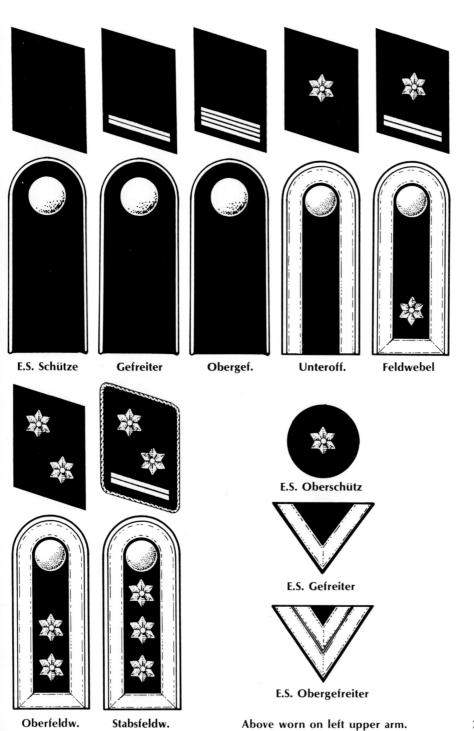

E.S. Schütze **Gefreiter** **Obergef.** **Unteroff.** **Feldwebel**

E.S. Oberschütz

E.S. Gefreiter

E.S. Obergefreiter

Oberfeldw. **Stabsfeldw.**

Above worn on left upper arm.

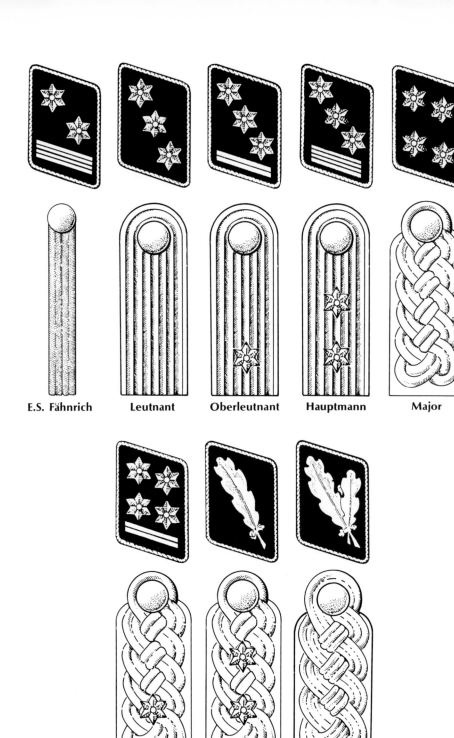

E.S. Fähnrich	Leutnant	Oberleutnant	Hauptmann	Major

Oberstleutnant	Oberst	E.S. General (silver and gold interwoven thread)

Bronze badge which, although not positively identified, is almost certainly related to the Einsatzstaffel (E.S.) of the German Volksgruppe in Croatia. The curious type of double runes (or wolf hooks) are the same as those worn on the E.S. collar patch. It is, therefore, possible that this may be a Sports, or Military Sports Badge of the E.S. (Photo approximate actual size, from an example in the collection of VerKuilen Ager of New York.)

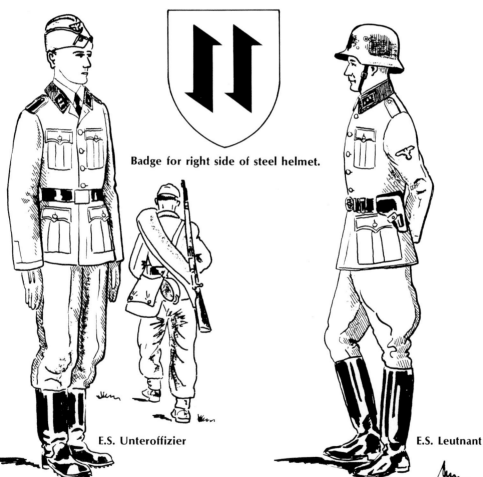

Badge for right side of steel helmet.

E.S. Unteroffizier

E.S. Leutnant

Uniform is field-grey with dark green collar. Black collar patch with two white "Wolfsangeln." Rank on a black patch on other side. Khaki shirt, black tie. Black belt, black boots. Steel helmet is 1914-18 type. Field equipment partly ex-former Yugoslav Army.

The *Volksdeutsche* were not exempt from service in either the Croat Home Army or the Croat Labor Service, but in both they were allowed to have their own all-German units. Within the Home Army a German-speaking *Jäger* (Light Infantry), battalion was set up in December 1941; its uniform and rank insignia were the same as the normal *Domobran* except that on the left upper arm a white swastika in a circular wreath of white oak leaves was worn. There was also a *Volksdeutsche* Railway Security Battalion to protect the rail lines running through the *Volskgruppe* region. In the early months of 1943, the *Jäger* Battalion and the Railway Security Battalion were taken over by the S.S. The younger and fitter members of these two formations were remustered into active service divisions of the Waffen S.S., the older or less fit were posted to police, or other internal security, units.

The uniform was that of the former Royal Yugoslav Army, a brownish-green color. Steel helmets were often of First World War type. Collar patch color may have been Jäger green. All insignia was standard Croat Home Army (including the dagger); the only exception was the swastika on the left upper arm.

Private in working uniform showing wreathed swastika arm badge.

Commemorative badge of the Police (Obrana) of the Independent State of Croatia. (From an example in Marburg Museum in Yugoslavia.)

Cap badge for the State Police (Redarstvena).

Badge (possibly of merit) of the National Relief (Pomoć means aid or relief) founded in 1941 as the Croat equivalent of the "Winter Help" of Germany.

Medal (or Honor Badge) to commemorate the foundation of the Croat State, mentioned on page 161 of the author's "Orders, Decorations, Medals and Badges of the Third Reich" Volume 2, but (at the time of publication) no illustration was available. Instituted in March 1942 and awarded in silver to Ustaše men who had joined before 1934 and in bronze to those who had joined after 1934 but before April 1941.

THE PRINZ EUGEN DIVISION

Beyond doubt, the most celebrated Waffen S.S. Division raised from among *Volksdeutsche* communities outside the Reich was the 7 S.S. Volunteer-Mountain-Division "Prinz Eugen." Its story is as follows:

The Waffen S.S. had, from the very start of the occupation, tried to recruit men for its combat divisions from among the *Volksdeutsche* of Yugoslavia. In this it had not been markedly successful. Less than one thousand volunteers had come forward, and these had simply been distributed piece-meal among whatever S.S. units were in most need of replacements (many of the volunteers ended up in the "Das Reich" Division). Word reached Himmler's ear that more volunteers might be forthcoming if they were permitted an ethnic formation of their own and not required to serve in predominately German divisions. It was decided, therefore, to raise a division which could consist mainly of *Volksdeutsche* from Croatia and the Banat. In March 1942, a Volunteer Mountain Division *(Freiwilligen-Gebirgs-Division)* was activated. The following month it was granted the name "Prinz Eugen." In October 1943, it joined the list of numbered Waffen S.S. divisions (the practice of numbering did not occur before this time) as the 7th Division. Despite its prefix of "Volunteer," by no means did all of its members come into this category. Moral pressure, and in the ultimate analysis, outright conscription had to be applied. In April 1943, all the active service units of the E.S. were incorporated into the "Prinz Eugen." Recruitment was carried out not only in Croatia and the Banat but also in Serbia, Romania, and Hungary (among the *Volksdeutsche* communities in these places).

Finding equipment for the new division was frought with difficulty. The war on the eastern front was a constant drain on German resources. Front line units had priority, anti-partisan formations had to take second best. The "Prinz Eugen" was obliged to commandeer 9,000 rifles from the *Postschutz* (Postal Defense Service) and scavange weapons from the arsenals of defeated foes. The result was a strange mixture of weaponry: Belgian antitank guns, French howitzers, Yugoslav army field guns, Czech machine pistols, and Italian mortars!

The commander of this largely *Volksdeutsche* division was Artur Phleps, himself a *Volksdeutsche* (from Transylvania) and one-time general in the Romanian army.

The "Prinz Eugen" took part in its first major offensive against the Partisans in January 1943. This action, code-named *"Weiss"* is perhaps better known as the Battle of Neretva. Although the whole operation (the largest mounted to date against Tito's forces) certainly inflicted heavy losses on the Partisans, it could by no means be claimed as a victory. The insurgent forces escaped encirclement to fight again - which they did with ever increasing effectiveness until the end of the war. The "Prinz Eugen" was called on to participate in most of the subsequent actions mounted against them. It never, except in the very closing days of the war, actually served in the front line. Artur Phleps was replaced as divisional commander by *S.S. Brigadeführer* Carl von Oberkamp in July 1943. Later commanders were Otto Kumm (August 1944 to January 1945) and August Schmidhuber (January to May 1945). Both of these held the rank *S.S. Brigadeführer.*

Initially the "Prinz Eugen" consisted of two mountain light infantry regiments:
S.S. Gebirgs-Jäger-Rgt. 1
S.S. Gebirgs-Jäger-Rgt. 2
Also one artillery regiment, two squadrons of cavalry and pioneer, signals, reconnaissance, etc., support units. In October 1943 the composition of the division was:
S.S. Volunteer Mountain Rgt. 13
S.S. Volunteer Mountain Rgt. 14

Two squadrons of cavalry (Cavalry *Abteilung* 7)

Volunteer Mountain Artillery Regiment 7

The supporting pioneer, signals, Flak, dispatch-rider, antitank, and reconnaissance, etc., *Abteilungen* also all bore the number 7.

The uniform of the "Prinz Eugen" was standard Waffen S.S. field-grey (the Panzer company wore normal Panzer black). The right collar patch had an Odal rune (the symbol of kinship or family). One photograph shows *S.S. Standartenführer* Heinrich Peterson, commander of the artillery regiment, wearing the Odal rune on *both* collars, but this seems to have been exceptional (although possibly not unique). German officers and NCOs secunded from other divisions could continue to wear their normal S.S. runes collar patch. If they opted for the Odal rune patch, they were entitled to wear their S.S. runes on the left breast pocket - this practice was, however, expressly forbidden by Himmler in 1943. As a mountain division, members of the "Prinz Eugen" were allowed to wear the edelweiss on the upper right arm and on the left side of the mountain cap. A cuff title PRINZ EUGEN (silver on black) could be worn by all ranks. After the death of the division's first commander, Artur Phleps (on active service in September 1943), the Volunteer Mountain Regiment 13 was granted the right to wear a cuff title in his honor with ARTUR PHLEPS (again standard silver on black type) - this award was made in November of the same year.

Two versions of the special Odal rune collar patch of the Prinz Eugen Division. (Examples in Dodkins Collection)

S.S. runes as worn on the left breast pocket of Germans in the division.

S.S. Standartenführer Petersen (note Odal rune on both collars)

Being a mountain division, its members could wear the S.S. type edelweiss arm and cap badge.

Prinz Eugen

Prinz Eugen cuff title in silver-grey thread for enlisted ranks and aluminum wire for officers.

Artur Phleps

Cuff title "Artur Phleps" (silver on black) worn by members of the 13th Regiment of the "Prinz Eugen" Division, after November 1944, in honor of the former commander of the division.

White Odal rune on black worn on left upper arm by the divisional commander (Artur Phleps) but not, apparently, by any other member of the division.

Artur
Phleps

During his time as divisional commander, Phleps wore on his left arm what would appear to have been a unique arm badge - a white Odal rune on a black circle outlined in white.

An Odal rune was also used as the divisional vehicle sign.

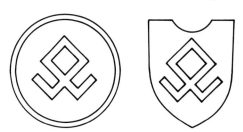

Two versions of the 7th Division vehicle sign.

POLITICAL LEADERSHIP AND YOUTH MOVEMENTS OF THE *VOLKSGRUPPE* IN CROATIA

The *Volksgruppe* in Croatia had its own facsimile of the Nazi party of the Reich. Membership of the National-Socialist German Community in Croatia *(National-Sozialistische Deutsche Gefolgschaft in Kroatien, N.S.D.G.K.)* was obligatory for all persons from the age of 18 upwards. Women had to belong to the *Allgemeinen Frauenschaft* (A.F.G.), workers to the *Deutsche Arbeitsgemeinschaft* (D.A.G.) The

Corps of Political Leaders wore a uniform which appears to have been modeled on that of the N.S.D.A.P. The red brassard had an elongated black swastika on a white lozenge. The *Volksgruppe* leader, Altgayer, wore on both collars an Odal rune within a wreath of oak leaves. Other rank insignia for political leaders is not known, but designs may have incorporated the Odal rune. A black Odal rune on a white circular background on a red field was the flag of the *Volksgruppe*.

Branimir Altgayer (born 8 November 1897), Leader of the German Racial Community (Volksgruppe) in Croatia. (Photo taken from "Jahrebuch der Volksgruppe in Kroatien" for 1943.) The Odal rune collar patch may have been unique to Altgayer.

The *Volksdeutsche* youth was organized along lines very similar to those of the German Hitler Youth as follows:

Deutsche Jungvolk (D.J.V.)   -   boys of 10 to 14 years

Deutsche Jugend (D.J.)   -   boys of 14 to 18 years

Jungmädelbund (J.M.B.)   -   girls of 10 to 14 years

Deutschen Mädelbund (D.M.B.)   -   girls of 14 to 21 years

There were four Youth *Banne* and two Independent *Stämme - Stamm Agram* (Zagreb Company and *Stamm Mittelbosnien* (Central Bosnia Company). The D.J. had a membership (according to the *"Jahrbuch"* of 1943) of 15,000. It had, like the Hitler Youth, its own cavalry, motor sport, and glider units. The *"Jahrbuch"* makes reference to a

Arm band of Political Leaders of the German Volksgruppe in Croatia.

Flag of the German Volksgruppe in Croatia.

Political leader of German Volksgruppe.

J.M.B. *Leistungsabzeichen"* (Achievement Badge of the J.M.B.) and also a D.M.B. *Leistungsabzeichen,* but does not illustrate these.

It would appear (from photographs) that the uniforms of the Croat youth movement were virtually identical to those of their Reich counterparts. The emblem of the D.J., for example, is simply the Hitler Youth badge with D.J. added. It may be noted that the term *Deutsche Jugend* as a substitute for *Hitler Jugend* was common to several *Volksdeutsche* youth movements (e.g. those of Hungary, Romania, and Slovakia as well as Croatia).

Emblem of the Deutsche Jugend in Croatia (the local equivalent of the Hitler Youth).

Pennant of a Hitler Youth company in Zagreb. It is rather unusual that the name of the Croat capital is given in the original form and not in the more usual German form of Agram.

There was, as we have seen, a German-speaking unit within the Croat State Labor Service. The German-speaking Railway Guard Battalion and the German *Jäger* Battalion in the Croat Home Army were (as mentioned above) taken over by the S.S. in the spring of 1943 as part of a general stiffening of internal security against an ever increasing Partisan threat. Police Volunteer Units *(Polizei-Freiwilligen-Verbände)* were raised by an order from Himmler dated 15 July 1943. In Croatia seven battalions (each of four companies) were activated. The volunteers were both *Volksdeutsche* and Croat, with a cadre of German Police officers and senior NCOs. Each company consisted of two German officers, ten German NCOs, while the rest (three officers and 135 other ranks) could be either *Volksdeutsche* or Croat. They wore normal German uniform. For the more elderly *Volksdeutsche* males, an *Ortsschutz* (or Local Home Guard) was formed around this time to act as a static self-defense force. That the struggle against the Partisans was taking its toll is testified by the figures quoted in the 1944 *"Jahrbuch"* which lists as "fallen in the battle against the Bolshevik Balkan Partisans," 441 names as against only 312 who had "died for *Führer* and Fatherland in the East" (this is to say up to mid-1943).

It has been estimated that the *Volksdeutsche* of Croatia contributed the following to Germany's armed forces:

To the Wehrmacht 1,386
To the Waffen S.S. 17,538
To Police formations 3,488
To the Org. Todt 2,200

More than 14,000 volunteer workers from "German" Croatia went to work in the Reich; 2,636 *Volksdeutsche* served in the armed forces of Croatia.

Dr. Budak of the Croat Foreign Department.

CROAT ORDERS, DECORATIONS, AND MEDALS

ORDER OF THE IRON TREFOIL

The Order of the Iron Trefoil was instituted in November 1941 and intended to rank as the highest award for members of Croatia's armed forces (although, like other Croat awards, it could also be conferred on members of the armed forces of her allies). It is in four classes:

4th Class: a silver outlined, black trefoil cross worn from a triangular ribbon on the left breast.

3rd Class: a similar cross but worn on a normal ribbon from the second buttonhole of the tunic.

2nd Class: the same cross but worn as a pin-back decoration (without a ribbon) on the left breast pocket.

1st Class: the same cross, but slightly larger, worn on a ribbon at the throat.

4th Class decoration, reverse

4th Class decoration, obverse

3rd Class decoration

2nd Class decoration

1st Class decoration

1st Class with "war decoration" green oak leaf wreath.

To any class the so-called "war decoration" of green oak leaves could be added for "especially outstanding acts of bravery." On the reverse is *Za Dom Spremni* (Ready to defend the Fatherland), and the date of the foundation of the state, 10.IV.1941. The ribbon is the same for all grades - the war decoration red-with-white-edges type. The choice of the second buttonhole as the place to wear the 3rd Class (like the Iron Cross 2nd Class) and the fact that the highest grade is a neck cross (like the Knight's Cross) and not, as would be normal with an Order, a Grand Cross with breast star, would seem to indicate that Pavelić hoped that the Iron Trefoil would become the "Iron Cross" of Croatia!

ORDER OF THE CROWN OF KING ZVONIMIR

The Order of the Crown of King Zvonimir was instituted in May 1941 and was in five classes: (a) 3rd Class: a white enamel, gilt outlined cross worn from a ribbon; (b) 2nd Class: a similar cross but worn as a pin-back decoration without a ribbon; (c) 1st Class: a similar cross but worn on a ribbon round the neck; (d) 1st Class with Star: as above but with a breast star, no sash; (e) Grand Cross: an eight-pointed silver breast star with sash and sash "badge."

Any class could have crossed swords (for military action). For bravery in the field the "war decoration" wreath of green enamel oak leaves could be added around the center piece. For civilian merit the ribbon (and sash) is white with red edges; for war merit the so-called "war decoration" ribbon was employed - red with white edges. It will be clear that much of this derived from the old Austro-Hungarian practice. The motto "Bog i Hrvati" which appeared on the reverse means "God and the Croats." The date 1076 (which also appears on the reverse) was the date of the coronation of King Zvonimir.

Reverse of the 3rd Class with swords

3rd Class with swords.

2nd Class with swords. **2nd Class with "war decoration" green oakleaf wreath.**

1st Class decoration

Grand Cross

MEDAL OF THE ORDER OF KING ZVONIMIR

Instituted in December 1941, this medal is in three grades: silver, bronze, and "iron" (this latter being, in fact, white metal or zinc). Like the Order itself, the ribbon is white with red edges or, for war service, red with white edges. For bravery in the field, a metal wreath of gilt oak leaves could be added to the ribbon. The obverse shows the king with his name Kmitar Zvonimir and the date of his coronation, 1076. The reverse features the Ustaše emblem and *Bog i Hrvati* (God and the Croats), and the date of the foundation of the Independent State of Croatia, 10.IV.1941 and the words *Za Zasluge* (For Merit).

Obverse   Reverse

BRAVERY MEDAL

Instituted in December 1941, this comes in four types: bronze medal, small silver medal, large silver medal, and gold medal. The small silver medal was given to next-of-kin of fallen NCOs and enlisted men. The large silver and gold medals were awarded for bravery in the field. The obverse has a portrait of Pavelić; the reverse has the Ustaše emblem and the words *Za Dom Spremni* (Ready to defend the Fatherland) and *Za Hrabrost* (For Bravery). The ribbon is the "war decoration" type - red with white edges. More than one class could be worn at a time.

Bravery Medal. This is a half size miniature ribbon (actual size is 15mm) with facsimile of the medal attached to it.

Suspension for the Gold Bravery Medal

Bravery Medal, obverse

Reverse

WOUNDED MEDAL

The Wounded Medal was instituted on 9 April 1943 and is in two classes: gold and "iron" (in fact, grey zinc). The gold medal was awarded only for severe disablement which resulted in the man concerned being invalided out of the service, or to the next-of-kin of a man killed in action. The "iron" medal could be given on four diferenty types of ribbon to indicate the number of times wounded. For one wounding

Medal with ribbon for being wounded once.

Reverse

the ribbon is a "ladder" of alternate white/red narrow horizontal stripes with white edges and a blue vertical stripe down the center. For two wounds the ribbon is without the center blue stripe but with two blue stripes inset beside the white edges. For three times wounded there are three blue stripes (i.e. it is like a combination of the ribbon of the once and twice wounded). For multiple wounds a gilt metal wreath of oak leaves could be added. On the obverse is *Za Poglavnika i za Dom* (For Leader and Fatherland) and on the reverse *Priznanje Domovine* (The Gratitude of the Fatherland).

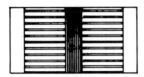

Ribbon for being wounded once.

Ribbon for being wounded twice.

Ribbon for being wounded three times.

Ribbon with gilt metal wreath for being wounded more than three times.

CROAT ORDER OF MERIT

The Croat "Order of Merit" *(Red za Zasluge)* was instituted in May 1942 and is in five classes:

3rd Class: a cross from a ribbon

2nd Class: a pin-back cross

1st Class: a neck decoration

1st Class with Star: as above but with a four-pointed star worn on the left breast. No sash.

Grand Cross: an eight-pointed breast star with sash and sash "badge."

The badge of the Order is in two types: one a red enamel cross with silver ornamentation given to Christians; the other a silver "star" with red enamel center intended for non-Christians (this meant, in practice, the Moslem citizens of Bosnia-Hercegovina who would be unwilling to wear a cross on religious grounds).

The ribbon is the same for both types and all grades (including the sash); it is white/red/white/red/white in equal proportions with very narrow red outer edges. On the reverse is the date of institution 10.V.1942 and the words *"Za Zasluge"* (For Merit). The Ustaše U and grenade emblem features on the obverse of both types.

2nd Class decoration
for Christians

1st Class decoration
for Christians

1st Class decoration
for non-Christians

Grand Cross
for Christians

1st Class with Star
for non-Christians

3rd Class on a ribbon for
ladies, non-Christian

Sash and badge of the Grand Cross (for Christians).

COMMEMORATIVE WAR MEDAL

The head of state did not wait until the end of the war before instituting a commemorative medal! On 29 December 1943 Pavelić awarded all members of Croatia's uniformed forces (including the Police, Labor Service, and Ustaše militia) a commemorative "medal." In fact, this never seems to have gone beyond the "ribbon only" stage - the medal itself does not appear to have been manufactured. This "medal" was awarded for six months active service or twelve months non-combatant duty. It could also be awarded to members of the armed forces of Croatia's allies. The ribbon is a "ladder" of alternate narrow blue and white stripes with white and red edges (red being the outer color). In the center of the "ladder" is a metal badge with the Ustaše arms above a red and white enamel shield of Croatia. It was worn, in the manner of the German Iron Cross 2nd Class, diagonally from the second buttonhole of the tunic.

Commemorative War Medal

COMMEMORATIVE MEDAL OF INDEPENDENCE 1918-1943

This medal, instituted in December 1943, commemorates not the foundation of the Independent State of Croatia, but of Croatia's independence from the Austro-Hungarian Empire at the end of the First World War. The obverse shows the badge of the Independent Croat State, the reverse has the dates "1918 5. XII 1943" (i.e., 25 years). The ribbon is red with three white stripes.

Obverse   Reverse

NOTE:
It was awarded to those who had participated in the big anti-Austrian demonstrations in Zagreb in December 1918.

SERBIA

The vassal state of Serbia was under a German military administration headed by General Heinrich Danckelmann, but was, like the "Protectorate" of Bohemia-Moravia, allowed to have its own civil government with powers to raise a prescribed number of internal security troops. Prime Minister Milan Nedić, a former chief of staff of the Royal Yugoslav Army, might be compared to Pétain in France insofar as he favored cooperation with the Germans in order to prevent his country falling prey to communist influence. The German authorities were willing to allow the arming of up to 10,000 men for self-defense purposes - obviously this would ease the burden on their own security troops.

The indigenous forces at the disposal of the Serbian government comprised:

(a) the Serbian State Guard *(Srpska Državna Straža)*, or S.D.S. An armed police force, or gendarmerie, which incorporated the Drina and Danube Regiments of the former Royal Yugoslav Gendarmerie. It had a strength of 153 officers and 1,779 other ranks.

(b) the Serbian Frontier Guard *(Srpska Granična Straža)* or S.G.S. This was a static frontier defense force.

(c) the Serbian Volunteer Corps *(Srpska Dobrovoljački Korpus)* or S.D.K. This was the most overtly collaborationist of the three. It consisted largely of members of a pre-war Yugoslav fascist party known simply as *Zbor*(Rally) or of its youthful offshoot the *Beli Orlovi* (White Eagles). Originally known as the Serbian Volunteer Command *(Komanda)*, it was formed in Belgrade in September 1941. It was popularly referred to as the *Ljotićevci (Ljotić-ites)* after its commander, the erstwhile *Zbor* chief, Dimitrije Ljotić. The S.D.K. consisted of 12 companies, each of about 120 to 150 men. In January 1943, when the name Volunteer Corps replaced Volunteer Command, the formation was reorganized into five battalions, each with three companies. Early in 1944, the five battalions were expanded into five regiments (of three battalions each, except the 5th Regiment which had only one).   At the same time an artillery "division" (it was, in fact, only about 500 men) was added. Arms for the S.D.K. were supplied both by the Serbian government and the German military authorities.

If Nedić's Serbia is to be compared to Pétain's France, the State Guard might be likened to the Vichy police or *Garde mobile,* whereas the S.D.K. could be equated with the *Milice française.* (See Volume 1 of this series.)

The uniform of the S.D.K. was basically that of the former Royal Yugoslav Army. Surprisingly even the Royal Crown and monogram (of Peter II) was retained. The regimental badge, worn on the right breast pocket, took the form of the Cross of Karadjordjević(the royal family's name)with, in the center, St. George slaying a dragon (Communism?). Around this, in Cyrillic script, is the motto: "With faith in God, for King and Fatherland. Volunteer." In the presence of the German military commander, the S.D.K. was presented with a regimental flag in the Serbian colors bearing this same device and motto. When this was reported to Himmler, he was moved to address a sarcastic letter to Field Marshal Kietel containing the words, "I consider it decidedly dubious *(sehr fragwürdig)* for us Germans to present the Serbs with a flag inscribed, 'With faith in God, for King and Fatherland.'" The offending banner was not, however, withdrawn.

Rank insignia was worn on the shoulder straps and was the same as for the Royal Yugoslav Army. Collar patches and shoulder straps were plain black until March 1943 when these were changed to dark blue. With the expansion of the S.D.K., its command had to be entrusted to someone more versed in the military arts than Ljotić. Early in 1944, General Kosta Musicki was appointed S.D.K. commander. When, in the late autumn of the same year, the Red Army liberated most of Serbia, the S.D.K., along with the State Guard, was evacuated to Slovenia. All former Serbian self-defense forces were now placed under direct S.S. command. The S.D.K. was absorbed into the Waffen S.S. on 27 November 1944. In March 1945, it was rechristened the Serbian S.S. Corps *(Serbisches S.S. Korps)*, but there is no evidence that it ever adopted S.S. uniform, and certainly there was no special collar patch even on paper.

SHOULDER INSIGNIA OF THE SERVIAN VOLUNTEER CORPS
(All shoulder straps are dark blue.)

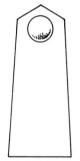    

Private*	Corporal	Sergeant	Staff Sgt.	Sgt. Major
(Dobrovoljac)	(Kaplar	(Podnarednik)	(Narednik)	(Narednik Vodnik)

Non-commissioned ranks have silver stars.

*Literally, "Volunteer."

Breast badge of the Serbian Volunteer Corps. Actual size. Bronze metal. Motto means "With faith in God, King and Fatherland. Volunteer."

(Officers have gold stars)

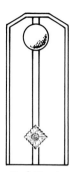  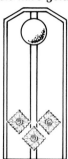  

2nd Lieut. (Potporučnik)	1st Lieut. (Poručnik)	Capt. 2nd grade (Kapetan 2 Klasse)	Capt. 1st grade (Kapetan 1 Klasse)	Major (Major)

(All shoulder straps are dark blue.)

The color of the piping around the shoulder strap and, for 2nd Lieutenant to Captain 1st Grade, the stripe down the center of the shoulder strap indicates the branch of the army. (Example: red for Infantry.)

Lt. Colonel (Potpukovnik)	Colonel (Pukovnik)	Brigadier-General (Brigadni Djeneral)

Exactly the same ranks were used in the Serbian State Guard (S.D.S.) and the Serbian Frontier Guard (S.G.S.) except that Private was called *Stražar* in the S.D.S. and *Graničar* in the S.G.S.

Two officers of the Serbian Volunteer Corps.

Cap badge with Cyrillic P (for King Peter II).

The German *Volksgruppe* in Serbia was much smaller than that in Croatia since, of course, Serbia had at no time been a part of the Austro-Hungarian Empire. There was only a single battalion of the D.M. in Serbia. As the Partisan threat increased, Himmler ordered the removal of isolated *Volksdeutsche* communities from various parts of the country to the greater security of the *Volksgruppe* region of Croatia.

In addition to the above "official" defense forces, there also existed in Serbia a privately organized defense corps which owed nothing to governmental sponsorship. This was the so-called Russian Guard Corps. Ever since the Revolution of 1917, large numbers of anti-communist Russian émigrés had found asylum in Serbia. Belgrade had come to rival Paris as a center for anti-Soviet expatriates. Hitler's invasion of the U.S.S.R. in June 1941 was greeted with jubilation by these exiles who imagined it would result in the overthrow of the Soviet system and their own triumphant return to a liberated fatherland. Thousands hastened to join the German "crusade"; even the most elderly and decayed ex-White Army officers offered to don uniform once more. All were rudely rebuffed. Hitler categorically ruled out the employment of émigrés, arguing, doubtless correctly, that they would be politically embarrassing and militarily incompetent. Denied the opportunity to fight communism at the front, some of the would-be warriors determined at least to combat its resistant manifestations at home.

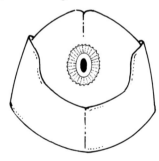

Forage cap with white/yellow/black rosette. This type of cap is more like the British army type. Certainly not Yugoslav in origin.

This private in the Russian Guard Corps wears the collar patch with a button.

RUSSIAN GUARD CORPS RANK INSIGNIA

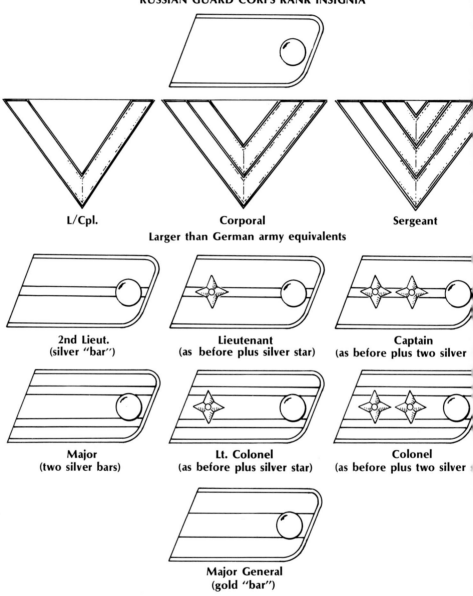

L/Cpl.

Corporal

Sergeant

Larger than German army equivalents

2nd Lieut.
(silver "bar")

Lieutenant
(as before plus silver star)

Captain
(as before plus two silver

Major
(two silver bars)

Lt. Colonel
(as before plus silver star)

Colonel
(as before plus two silver

Major General
(gold "bar")

Collar patches are in two types: (a) light blue for Cossacks and (b) crimson for infantry units.

The Russian Guard Corps was formed in September 1941, but in November 1942 it was absorbed in the German Wehrmacht and thereafter German army rank insignia was used.

An Independent Russian Corps *(Otdel'niy Russkiy Korpus)* was formed in Belgrade on 12 September 1941 by Brigadier M.F. Skorodumov. Three days later he was arrested by the Germans - presumably for acting without their authority - and removed from his self-appointed command. Major General Boris A. Shteyfon (or Steifon) took over the embryonic corps which, on 2 October, was renamed the Russian Guard (or Defense) Corps *(Russkiy Okhranniy Korpus)*. It eventually reached a strength of five regiments. The first three were activated in September-November 1941, the fourth in April 1942, the fifth in December 1943. By September 1944 it had 362 officers, 1,295 non-commissioned officers, and 9,540 other ranks. Interestingly, less than one-third were residents of Serbia, the largest single group (over 5,000) came from Romania, others from Bulgaria and other Axis satellites, some even were Soviet citizens - after the capture of Odessa by Romanian troops, a recruiting office was opened in that city.

The Guard Corps' somewhat ambiguous status of being neither part of the governmental self-defense forces nor of the occupation troops was brought to an end on 30 November 1942 when it was absorbed into the Wehrmacht as the *Russisches Schutzkorps,* known after October 1944 as the *Russisches Schutzkorps Serbien* (The Russian Guard Corps, Serbia). Shteyfon died on 30 April 1945, and command of the Corps passed to Anatoliy I. Rogozhin, commanding officer of the 1st Regiment and one-time lieutenant in the Czar's Personal Bodyguard.

Officers of the Russian Guard Corps in Serbia (Cossack section). Note the Cossack sabre carried by the officer in the picture.

Prior to its incorporation into the Wehrmacht, the Russian Guard Corps wore a Czarist-style uniform improvised from former Royal Yugoslav Army khaki with a Russian scheme of ranks worn on the collar. But rank was the subject of much vexation. Since

This officer wears a Czech steel helmet with a white St. George's Cross painted on the front.

many of the volunteers were former high ranking officers of the Czarist or White armies, there was an overabundance of colonels and generals. No one wished to accept a lower rank than his former one; a problem which was resolved by the ludicrous device of adopting a scheme of double ranks - one's current Guard Corps status indicated by one's collar, and the former grading on Imperial-style shoulder boards! Collar patches were crimson for infantry and light blue for cavalry (romantically, if inaccurately, called "cossacks"). On the front of the cap a black/yellow/white cockade was worn. On active duty ex-Czech army steel helmets were worn. On the front of these a white St. George's Cross was painted. After November 1942 and its incorporation into the German army, standard Wehrmacht uniform was worn, and the absurd double rank scheme dropped.

Armed merely with light infantry weapons and virtually without mechanical transport (there was even a company of cyclists), the Guard Corps was fit only for supporting anti-partisan operations in a modest capacity.

There was some talk of making the Russian Guard Corps part of General Vlasov's German sponsored "Russian Liberation Army" (see final volume of this series), but this came to nothing.

SLOVENIA-STYRIA

With the defeat of Yugoslavia in 1941, Slovenia was partitioned between the two Axis partners - Germany taking the lion's share. Mussolini received the "Province of Ljubliana" (that is to say, Slovenia south of the River Sava). The remainder of Slovenia was taken under German "protection" with the ultimate object of "bringing it home to the Reich" through a process of Germanization. The German-acquired area consisted of Lower Styria *(Untersteiermark)*, Carinthia *(Kärnten)*, and Upper Carniola *(Oberkrain)*. In October 1942, these three regions were incorporated into the Greater German Reich as *Reichsgau Kärnten* and *Reichsgau Steiermark*.

The Italians organized a self-defense force in their zone of Slovenia under the name Anti-Communist Volunteer Militia *(Milizia Volontaria Anti-Comunista,* or M.V.A.C.). This was a mobile strike force. There was also a static "White Guard." After Italy's defection from the Axis in September 1943, the S.S. assumed control of all the defense forces in Slovenia which they renamed the Slovene Home Army *(Slovensko Domobranstvo)*. Along the Adriatic coast this force was known as the Slovene Coastal Guard *(Primorska Slovenski Domobranci)*.

The Slovene Home Army wore a greenish-blue uniform consisting of an open-necked tunic, trousers, and forage cap. This uniform was certainly not of Yugoslav origin. It may have come from the quarter-master's stores of one of Germany's defeated foes - possibly the Royal Netherlands Navy. The scheme of ranks (worn on the shoulder) was, however, entirely Yugoslav and followed that used by the former Royal Yugoslav Army. On the front of the forage cap a cockade in the Slovene national colors, white/blue/red (white being the outer color), was worn. On the left upper arm the blue eagle of Slovenia was worn on a white shield outlined in blue. This

Cap cockade

Blue and white arms of Slovenia. Worn on left upper arm.

shield is featured on the celebrated S.S. map of February 1945, but although it was certainly worn by the Slovene Home Army, there is no evidence of its being so on Waffen S.S. uniform. The commander of the Slovene Home Army was Brigadier-General Leo Rupnik, who had the distinction of being the only non-Serb to attain the rank (before the war) of general in the Royal Yugoslav Army.

SLOVENE HOME ARMY RANK INSIGNIA

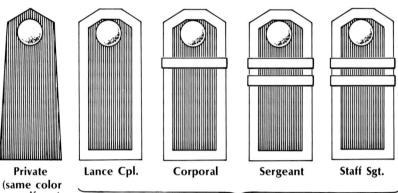

| Private (same color as uniform) | Lance Cpl. | Corporal | Sergeant | Staff Sgt. |

Dark green with silver "frame" and gold "bars"

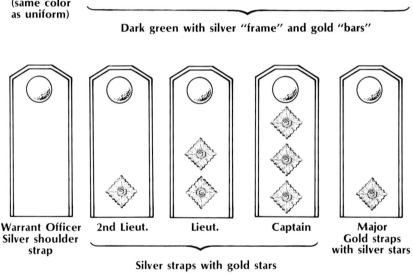

| Warrant Officer Silver shoulder strap | 2nd Lieut. | Lieut. | Captain | Major Gold straps with silver stars |

Silver straps with gold stars

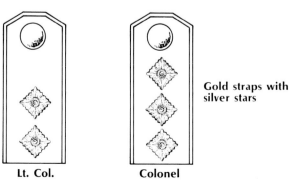

Gold straps with silver stars

| Lt. Col. | Colonel |

**Brigadier General
(gold twisted cord
with light blue
underlay)**

The Slovene Coastal Guard (or, to give it its full title, The Slovene National Security Corps of the Adriatic Littoral) was commanded by Colonel Kakalj. It consisted of 15 companies (around 1,800 men in all). The Slovene Home Army had (by 1944) six assault battalions *(Sturmbataillone)* in addition to miscellaneous static "Communications Defense Units" - a total strength of 57 companies (around 11,500 men).

Officers of the Slovene Home Army. Their uniform is described as "greenish-blue." Note the Slovene arm badge on left upper arm.

Brigadier-General Leo Rupnik, commander of the Slovene Home Army. Rupnik was the first non-Serb to attain (before the war) the rank of general in the Royal Yugoslav army.

263

In Lower Styria the local *Volksdeutsche* were formed into a *Steierscher Heimatbund* with a *Deutsche Jugend* as its youth branch and equivalent of the Hitler Youth. In Carinthia there was a *Kärtner Volksbund* with a *Volksbundjugend* as its counterpart of the Hitler Youth. After these two regions were absorbed into the Greater German Reich, the two youth movements were transformed into what were called Hitler Youth Preparatory units *(Hitler Jugend Anwärter Einheiten)*, membership of which was made obligatory for all boys between the ages of 14 and 19 years.

In the spring of 1941, physically fit males of the *Steierscher Heimatbund* were encouraged to join the *Wehrmannschaft* (roughly: Defense Militia). The same applied to young men of Upper Carniola. At first membership was voluntary, but on 17 April 1942 the chief of the Civil Administration in Lower Styria issued an order making it compulsory. The strength of the *Wehrmannschaft* in Lower Styria (in 1942) was officially quoted as being 87,400; and in Upper Carniola, 17,592 (in this latter region the *Wehrmannschaft* was known as the *Selbstschutz).*

From the best elements of the *Wehrmannschaft* in Lower Styria, a *Wehrmannschaftsbataillon Süd* (South) was formed as a mobile strike force against the Partisans. It was later expanded from one battalion to five and given the designation *Wehrmannschaftsregiment Untersteiermark* (Defense Militia Regiment Lower Styria).

The uniform of the *Wehrmannschaften* was the same as that of the *S.A. Wehrmannschaften* of the Reich; that is to say, brown tunic, trousers, shirt, and mountain cap. Collar patches are described as being "raspberry red." This color was also used as the shoulder strap piping and the lozenge background to the white metal edelweiss which was worn on the left side of the cap. A brassard was worn. This was sometimes green and white (the Styrian colors) with the black Styrian lion rampant on a white circle, but in other versions the lion is white and superimposed upon a black swastika on a square background. This Styrian lion with a sword also appeared as a decal on the left side of the brown steel helmet.

With the creation of the *Volkssturm* in Germany in October 1944, all *Wehrmannschaften* and *Selbstschutz* were incorporated into it.

Alternative type of brassard with Styrian lion without swastika on green and white (the Styrian colors).

Edelweiss for side of ski cap.

S.A. Gruppenführer Jüttner with a Wehrmannschaft man, August 1944. Note the lion on swastika brassard.

Styrian Wehrmannschaft members on a field exercise.

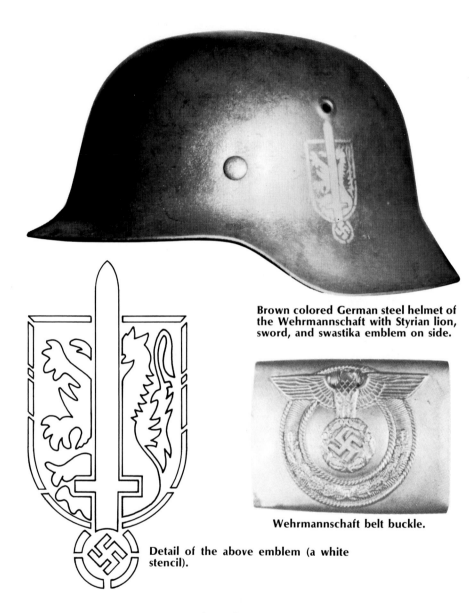

Brown colored German steel helmet of the Wehrmannschaft with Styrian lion, sword, and swastika emblem on side.

Wehrmannschaft belt buckle.

Detail of the above emblem (a white stencil).

The 24th Division

The *24 Waffen-Gebirgs-(Karstjäger) Division der S.S.* evolved from a specially trained mountain company *(S.S. Karstwehr Kompanie)* formed in the summer of 1942 to deal with Partisan resistance in the Carso (Karst) and Julian Alps. By November of the same year it was expanded to a battalion. After the fall of Mussolini in July 1943, and the resultant intensification of Partisan activity both in Yugoslavia and northern Italy, Himmler decided that it would be necessary to increase the strength of the *Kartswehr* Battalion, hopefully to divisional status by taking on locally enlisted volunteers. Recruited in the South Tirol, Istria, and Slovenia, it was, according to Paul Hausser, "a mixture of Italians, Slovenes, Croats, Serbs, and Ukrainians." A divisional headquarters was established at Udine in northern Italy, and eventually three regiments were formed: two of mountain infantry and one of mountain artillery. Its active service was confined to anti-partisan operations except for one very brief brush with the British in the closing stages of the war.

A special "Karst flower" collar patch was designed for it. This must not be confused with the flower worn by the 22nd Division which was the traditional cornflower of Germans outside the Reich. This Karst flower is illustrated on the S.S. map of February 1945, but there is no evidence that it was worn or even manufactured. In all probability the collar patch was either plain black or the standard S.S. runes (certainly for its German cadre). It has been suggested that the horizontal green/white/red arm shield with ITALIA may have been intended for the 24th which was, it is true, sometimes referred to as "the Italian Division," but again there is no confirmation of this fact. Although Istria is now part of Yugoslavia, it was, at that time, a region of Italy.

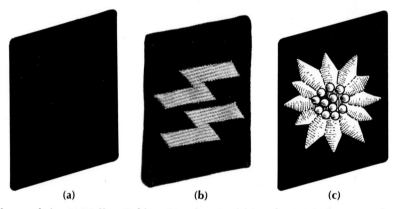

(a)　　　　　　　(b)　　　　　　　(c)

Collar patch for 24.Waffen-Gebirgs (Karstjäger) Division der S.S. is shown on the S.S. map of February 1945 as being like (c) - described as a "Karst flower,"* but there is no evidence that such a design was ever issued, and it is more likely that members of this division wore either (a) a plain black collar patch, or (b) the normal S.S. runes.

Vehicle sign of
24th Division.

*The author has to confess that despite extensive research among German botanical reference books, he has been unable to discover what is meant by a "Karst flower"!

Carso (Karst) mountains.

ADDENDUM

Corrections and Additional Information Relating to Volumes 1 and 2 of this Series.

Volume 1

NORWAY

General Secretary of N.S., Rolf Fuglesang. Note the unusual design of cap badge (compare with that shown on page 10 of Vol. 1). This resembles the arm badge and was probably the first design, later replaced.

Another first design, later replaced. This is the first pattern of the collar patch for the Førergarden (Leader's personal Bodyguard). The second pattern is illustrated on page 19. This version of the Vidkun Quisling monogram also appears on a dark blue M-35 German steel helmet in the possession of the Norwegian Army Museum in Oslo. On the other side of the same helmet is the N.S. eagle and sun cross emblem in white.

Hagelin (center) with State Secretary of the Ministry of the Interior (of Germany) Pfundtner (in civilian clothes) and State Secretary Dr. Stuckart during Hagelin's visit to Germany in April 1941.

N.S. eagle and "sun cross" of the type which would appear to be worn in the above photo. Possibly emblem of the Diplomatic Corps or State officials (high civil servants, as Beamte in Germany).

FRANCE

I am indebted to M. Jamin of Ostwald, France, for the following information on Vichy French formations and their insignia. Since part of the purpose of this series is to assist collectors, or others, in identifying items they may have, or have seen, this new information is worthy of inclusion even though it may be felt that some of these organizations *are rather obscure!*

JOFTA and SET

In September 1942 the Vichy government introduced compulsory direction of labor for males between the ages of 18 and 65 and unmarried females between 20 and 35. But liability for service outside France (i.e., in Germany) was restricted to males between 20 and 35 and even here the draft was applied in military fashion, initially only to young men in the "classes" of 1940, 1941, and 1942, that is to say to 20, 21, and 22-year-olds. The first of these left for Germany in February 1943.

To deal with the problem of sending so many young men to Germany, the French authorities set up a uniformed organization known as the JOFTA (*Jeunes ouvriers français travaillant en Allemagne* - Young French workers working in Germany). They also established special camps in Germany at which those without a trade could be taught one.

The uniform of the JOFTA was dark blue. It consisted of a "battle dress" type blouse, ski trousers worn with white gaiters or rolled down white stockings and a *beret basque*. Additional items were a blue/white/red cloth bar worn on the left upper arm and a colored rank bar above the right breast pocket. Sometimes, unofficially, an arm badge with the coat of arms of the province from which the man came was worn on the left arm (below the blue/white/red French nationality bar). Again, unofficially, an *écusson Pétain* might be worn on the left breast pocket.

In 1944 the term JOFTA was changed to SET (*Service Encadré du Travail*, roughly Paramilitary Labor Service) and some of the details of the uniform were altered. Collar patches were now introduced. These were red with a regional number or, for the headquarters staff at the Kellerman Center in Paris, a *francisque*. The rank insignia was still bars above the right breast pocket, but in slightly enlarged and altered form. On the left breast pocket a French shield with SETF was at first worn, later this was replaced by a more elaborate badge (see illustrations below).

The SET was also responsible for the care and training of French labor conscripts in the homeland as well as in Germany. A special Staff Training School (*école des Cadres*) was established at Beaufort-en-Valle (in the Department of Maine et Loire). Staff there wore the same uniform as above but had their own type of rank insignia. At first this was in the form of triangular collar patches, but after a few months this was changed to shoulder straps.

JOFTA RANKS

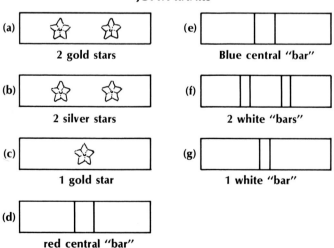

(a) 2 gold stars

(b) 2 silver stars

(c) 1 gold star

(d) red central "bar"

(e) Blue central "bar"

(f) 2 white "bars"

(g) 1 white "bar"

Headquarters Staff (on a white bar)
(a) Chef de Service 1st grade
(b) Assistant Chef de Service
(c) Chef de Service 2nd grade
(d) Clerk in Service Chief's office
(e) Clerk

General Service Units (on a red bar)
(a) Chef de Camp
(b) Assistant Chef de Camp
(c) Chef de Chantier
(f) Chef d'équipe
(g) Second d'équipe

Administrative Staff (on a dark blue bar)
(a) **Chef de Service**
(b) **Assistant Chef de Service**
(c) **Chef du Bureau**

SET RANKS AND INSIGNIA

Rank bars (dark blue with gold, except first two which have white bars):

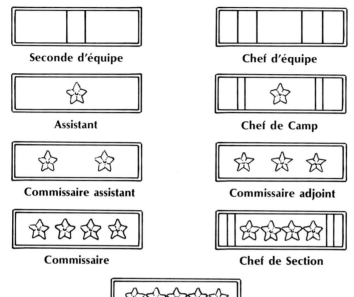

Seconde d'équipe

Chef d'équipe

Assistant

Chef de Camp

Commissaire assistant

Commissaire adjoint

Commissaire

Chef de Section

Chef de Division

Breast Badge, first design

Breast badge, second design

271

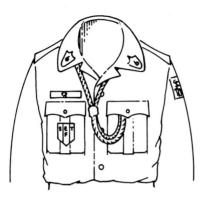

Blouse type tunic (here for an Assistant)

Shoulder strap with number

Collar patches for (a) a region (6 is Rennes) and (b) for Headquarters staff in Paris

(a)   (b)

JOFTA/SET Staff Training School (École des Cadres)

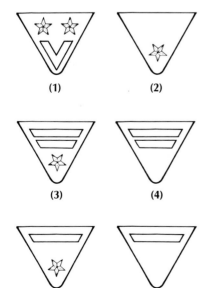

(1)   (2)

(3)   (4)

(5)   (6)

First design of rank insignia, worn on both collars.
  (1) **Directeur de l'école**
  (2) **Instructeur principal**
  (3) **Instructeur chef**
  (4) **Instructeur**
  (5) **Chef de service**
  (6) **Adjoint dans un service**

All collar patches are dark blue with green "bars" or chevron. Stars are gold.

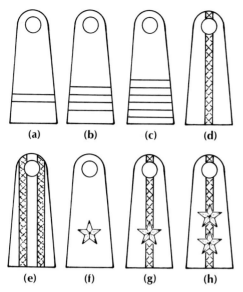

Second design ranks insignia, worn on both shoulders.
- (a) Attaché (1 red bar)
- (b) Adjoint (2 red bars)
- (c) Chef de service (3 red bars)
- (d) Instructeur (red central stripe)
- (e) Instructeur Chef (2 red stripes)
- (f) Instructeur Chef spécialisé (gold star)
- (g) Instructeur principal (red stripe, gold star)
- (h) Directeur de l'école (red stripe, two gold stars)

CORPS FRANC FRANÇAIS

An interesting but little known anti-resistance group was the so-called *Corps Franc Français* (French Free Corps) formed in Bordeaux by a French army officer with the approval of the German authorities. This small unit, perhaps no more than about 100 men, wore French army khaki (Model 1940) with, on the shoulders, German rank insignia and, on the upper arm, corresponding ranks of the French Régiments de la Garde (normally this insignia would have been worn on the cuff, not the upper arm). Above their French rank insignia they wore a "symbolic French arm shield" (the exact design is not known but it may have featured Joan of Arc or Charlemagne or some other symbol of French military history). Weapons were provided by the Germans. The unit claimed that it fought only against the Communist F.T.P. resistance and not against the Gaulliste F.F.I. resistors.

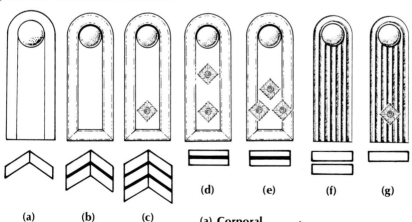

- (a) Corporal
- (b) Lance Sergeant } - gold chevrons
- (c) Sergeant
- (d) Staff Sergeant - silver bar, red center
- (e) Sergeant Major - gold bar, red center
- (f) 2nd Lieutenant - 1 gold stripe
- (g) 1st Lieutenant - 2 gold stripes

JEUNESSE ET MONTAGNE (J.M.)

The sub-section of the *Chantiers de la Jeunesse* known as *Jeunesse et Montagne* (literally "Youth and Mountain," although perhaps better rendered as Mountaineering Youth) has already been mentioned (page 138) but some further information may be of interest. This largely independent and voluntary formation wore the dark blue of the French Air Force and, on their shoulder straps, their own rank insignia, quite different from that of the rest of the *Chantiers*. This is illustrated below:

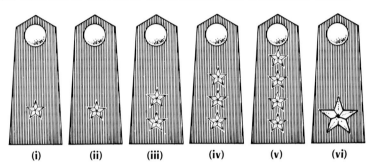

(i)   (ii)   (iii)   (iv)   (v)   (vi)

(i) **Chef d'équipe**
(ii) **Chef de Groupe**
(iii) **Chef de Centre**
(iv) **name of rank unknown**
(v) **Chef de Groupement**
(vi) **Chef de la J.M.**

All stars are gold except that of a Chef d'équipe which is silver. All shoulder straps are in color of uniform - dark blue.

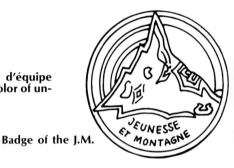

Badge of the J.M.

ÉQUIPES NATIONALES (E.N.)

The E.N. was an organization created by the Secretariat General for Youth and was open to the entire youth of France, both male and female, as a vehicle for social and civic service of all kinds. The E.M. membership consisted of two types (a) those who wished to enroll in it exclusively, and (b) those who, as members of other youth organizations, wished to participate from time to time in its activities (i.e., help out in an emergency).

The E.N. had three age groupings as follows:
Cadets: 12 to 14 year-olds
Pionniers: 15 to 17 year-olds
Volontaires: 18 to 25 year-olds
(Leaders could, of course, be over this last age as there was no age limitation in their case.)

The organization was divided into:
Main: 5 members under a Chef and Deputy Chef
Section: 3 to 6 Mains
Groupe: 2 to 4 sections
Ban: an administrative area covering various Groupes (there being normally one Groupe per town or rural region). Every Groupe had its flag and there was also a national E.N. flag.

Winter uniform consisted of a navy blue tunic and trousers, or plus-fours (girls had a navy blue skirt), navy blue beret, white shirt and black tie. In summer the tunic was left off and the white shirt worn open at the neck with the sleeves rolled up. Rank was worn on the shoulder straps in the manner shown below:

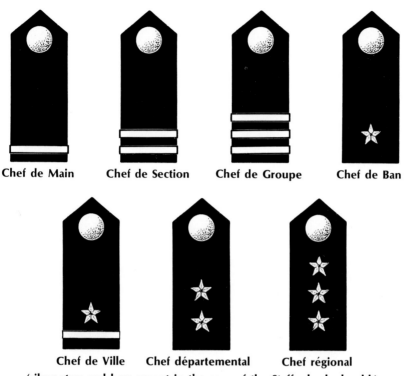

Chef de Main   Chef de Section   Chef de Groupe   Chef de Ban

Chef de Ville   Chef départemental   Chef régional

(silver stars and bars except in the case of the Staff who had gold.)

All ranks wore a white embroidered celtic cross on the left breast pocket and on the left side of the beret. Two honor badges could be awarded: one was the celtic cross in bronze, the other the celtic cross in white enamel with a red background. Both were worn above the left breast pocket. These were individual awards, but there were also "unit citations" in the form of colored lanyards:

    Blue for a Main
    White for a Section
    Tricolor for a Groupe.

In addition, custody of the national E.N. flag could be awarded to a particularly deserving region for a specified period of time dependent on the degree of merit shown. For example, on 12 November 1943 a two-month guardianship of the national E.N. flag was awarded to the Angers region in recognition of its heroic work during an (Allied) air attack on the town of Nantes.

A Civil Defense section of the E.N. was known as the *Service Interministeriel de Protection contre les Evénements de Guerre* (Interministerial Service for Protection against Acts of War) or S.I.P.E.G.

Cap badge of the E.N. This, in a miniature form, was also worn as the civil lapel badge.

page 121: the metal badge "Marcel Déat" was worn by all those who had joined the RNP before 7 March 1944, the date on which Déat became Minister of Labor and National Solidarity in the Vichy government. His followers liked to refer to this as his "coming to power."

page 139: the rank insignia of the *Compagnons de France* shown on this page is the second design. The first design took the form of slip-on tabs on which rank was shown (in much the same manner). These were worn on the left shoulder strap only.

page 167: *KRIEGSMARINE WERFTPOLIZEI*

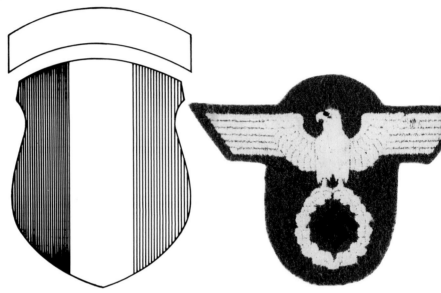

Worn on right upper arm.
French arm shield with above this a semicircle with writing (possibly the name of location of the unit in question).

Worn on left upper arm.
White police-type eagle with a black swastika on a navy blue background.

In addition to the *Kriegsmarine Wehrmänner* mentioned on pages 166-7, the German navy also employed another French volunteer guard unit. This was the *Kriegsmarine Werftpolizei* (Naval Dockyard Police) at the important U-boat base at La Pallice. This unit, formed at the beginning of 1943, was part of the German Police whereas the *Kreigsmarine Wehrmänner* were more military police. The *Werftpolizei* wore a uniform similar to that of the Danish *Marinevaegtere* (illustrated on page 111) but with a forage cap. They wore, on the right arm, a French shield of the shape illustrated with, above this, a white semi-circle with writing (the author has been unable to find out what this wording was, but it may well have been La Pallice). On the left arm they wore a version of the Police arm badge on navy blue.

page 177: The breast badge of the Groupe Spécial de Sécurite of the Milice as shown on page 177 of this series is entirely accurate (it was drawn from an actual example), but two variants of this badge have since come to light and are illustrated below. It will be noted that in (a) the arms of the gamma emblem are more turned down than normal and that the bones of the skull and cross bones badge appear below the skull and not behind it. In (b) the bones do not appear at all and the arms of the gamma are more florid. There would appear to be no wording on the upper part of the badge. It has to be said that (b) may not be entirely accurate since it is drawn from a photograph of one being worn whereas (a) is taken from an actual example in the author's possession.

(a)

(b)

page 194: the all-black uniform shown as illustration (a) was only a project which was, in fact, never worn.

page 196: the *Garde du Maréchal* did not wear the "horizon blue" uniform of the French army of World War One, but a black tunic and blue trousers (down the outer seams of which was a black stripe), white shirt, black tie, black leather gaiters, white belt, white gauntlet gloves. On guard they wore a model 1935 army crash helmet, off guard a black gendarmerie *képi*. The collar badge (as illustrated on page 197) was worn below a double inverted silver V on a black patch on both collars. This type of badge was also worn on the front of the crash helmet.

page 196: (a) first design, and (b) second design of the badge worn on right breast pocket by the Garde du Maréchal (Pétain's personal bodyguard). Type (a) was instituted in August 1942 and is a white shield with a light blue border upon which is the "francisque" in full color (the officer's version of this badge is shown on page 197). Type (b) replaced it the following year. It is a light blue shield with the seven stars of a Marshal of France and a grenade in gold surmounted by a "francisque" in full color and the motto "Toujours fidele" (Ever faithful).

(a)

(b)

Volume 2

BELGIUM

As a consequence of the generous assistance given to the author by César van Wiele of Bazel, Belgium, and the publication of Jan Vincx's five volume study of military collaboration in Flanders ("Vlaanderen in Uniform, 1940-1945") a great deal more information on Belgium is now available than was the case when volume 2 went to press. It has therefore proved possible to provide what amounts to an additional chapter rather than merely an addendum with regard to that country. For the convenience of readers this will follow the same layout as used in the original:

DINASO (pages 7 and 8)

The militia of Dinaso, the *Dinaso Militanten Orde* (D.M.O.) had three changes of uniform in the course of its history:

1st (1932-1937): green shirt, brown trousers (actually Belgian army khaki), black tie, brown ribbed velvet tunic.

2nd (1937-1940): green shirt, black tie, and black trousers or black breeches.

3rd (1940-1941): green shirt, black tie, black trousers/breeches, black tunics (Belgian army khaki dyed black), black angular peaked cap without insignia. Only the leader of the D.M.O., Jef François, appears to have worn a normal type peaked cap and badge.

The D.M.O. was organized as follows:

Cel: five men under a Celleider
Schaar: four Cellen under a Schaarleider
Vendel: three Scharen under a Vendelleider
Groep: three Vendels under a Groepsleider
Korps: two Groespen under a Korpsoverste

There were three Korps: Korps I West Flanders, Korps II East Flanders, Korps III Antwerp. Rank was indicated on the collar and shoulder as illustrated below. The belt buckle was usually the normal "civilian" two claw type, but a German army style buckle with the Dinaso emblem was less frequently employed.

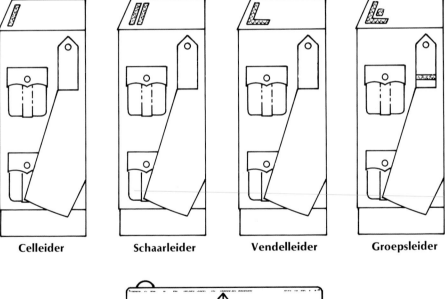

| Celleider | Schaarleider | Vendelleider | Groepsleider |

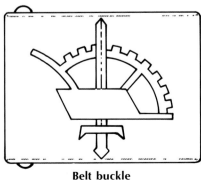

Belt buckle

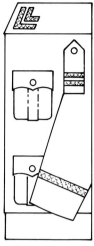

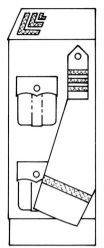

Korpsoverste   **Commandant**

Cap badge and flag emblem

Jef François, Commandant of the D.M.O. (Dinaso Militanten Orde), the "Storm Troopers" of Dinaso. He wears the Joris van Severen Commemorative Badge on left breast pocket.   279

In addition to the D.M.O. there were also the following sub-sections of the Dinaso:

(i) V.D.C. *(Verbond van Dinaso Corporaties)* which sought to establish Dinaso-run corporatives among the various trade and professional groups - food industry, transport, clothing industry, law, medicine, fine arts, etc. Its members did not wear uniform as such, only a green brassard on which was a white circle with, in black, "two hands interlocked in greeting" (i.e., shaking hands) within a cog wheel.

(ii) *Verdivro (Verbond van Dinaso Vrouwen en Meisjes)* Union of Dinaso women and girls. This was open to female persons over the age of 21. Uniform, when worn, consisted of a white blouse with the Dinaso emblem on the left side, a black skirt, and with belt with two black buttons as a fastening.

(iii) *Jongdinaso* (or *Dinaso Jeugd*) the youth organization of Dinaso was sub-divided as follows:

Klein Dinaso: 10 to 14 year old boys
Jong Dinaso: 14 to 18 year old boys.
Dinaso Meisjes Bond (D.M.B.) founded in January 1941
Jong Meisjes: 9 to 13 year old girls
Meisjes: 13 to 17 year old girls
Jonge Vrouwen: 17 to 21 year old "young women."

Boys wore a green shirt, orange tie, black trousers (or shorts) and black shoes. The girls had a white blouse and black skirt. The badge of Jongdinaso is illustrated on page 40. The age group within the D.M.B. was indicated by a runic symbol as follows:

| 9-13 years | 13-17 years | 17-21 years |

The first two were taken over unaltered by the N.S.J.V. (see later in this chapter), the third was replaced by an Odalsrune.

The Joris van Severen badge (properly: Dinasoken-teken - Dinaso Commemorative Badge) shown as a drawing on page 24 is herewith illustrated by a "from life" photograph of an example in the Forman Collection. This badge was awarded to all those who had been in the D.M.O. before May 1940 (i.e., prior to the German invasion of Belgium) and who had remained with it after its re-formation. It was given to officers in silver and to other ranks in bronze.

V.N.V (pages 9 to 32)

The leader of the Social Movement of the V.N.V. was Edgar Delvo (not Victor Leemans as wrongly stated on page 10). The party greeting was Hou Zee, not Hoo Zee (page 11). The information on the party militia of the V.N.V. (pages 11 to 29) is substantially correct but requires some minor corrections and expansions. Ranks were worn on the left (wearer's left) collar, not the right (page 12). Herewith, a more accurate illustration of the collar patch of Commandant-General (2nd design). This is taken from an example in a private collection and is silver bullion on red. Red collar patches were worn by highest ranks only.

**Commandant-General
(2nd design)**

There was, in fact, a *fourth* expansion of DM-ZB ranks increasing the overall total from 16 to 18. These are illustrated below. Since exactly the same rank insignia was used by the Vlaamsche Wacht Brigade (see later) but with different names, the DM-ZB ranks are given first, with the VW.B. equivalents beneath.

**Z.B. Weerman
V.W.B. Wachter**

**Z.B. Opperweerman
V.W.B. Opperwachter
(silver metal bar)**

**Z.B. Ploegleider
V.W.B. Brigadier
(2 silver metal bars)**

**Z.B. Opperploegleider
V.W.B. Opperbrigadier
(3 silver metal bars)**

**Onderschaarleider
Onderwachtmeester**

**Schaarleider
Wachtmeester**

**Opperschaarleider
V.B. Opperwachtmeester**

**Stafschaarleider
Stafwachtmeester**

**Stormleider
Vaandrig**

Z.B. Opperstormleider
V.W.B. Oppervaandrig

Vendelleider
Kompaan

Oppervendelleider
Opperkompaan

Z.B. Banleider
V.W.B. Hopman

Opperbanleider
Opperhopman

Heerbanleider
Heerbanleider

Z.B. Opperheerbanleider
V.W.B. Opperheerbanleider

Brigadeleider
Brigadeleider

Com. Generaal
no equivalent rank

All the above are green with, for officers, silver wire surround and, for other ranks, black piping. Stars and "bars" are silver.

The belt buckle with Het Vaderland Getrouwe (page 21) was not used by the DM-ZB, but was for Political Leaders of the V.N.V.

Chin straps (on peaked caps) for non-commissioned ranks of the DM-ZB were green, not black, and the arm badge was a black wolf-hook on orange, not yellow (both page 23). The style of cap badge illustrated on that page is correct, but in 1942 a new design of badge was introduced. The oakleaf wreath part was retained, but the V.N.V. delta in a circle emblem was replaced by a wolf-hook. On the peak of the cap was a newly created symbol: a *Blauwvoet* (Stormy petrel) holding in its claws the delta badge but now a cog wheel instead of a circle. This type of cap badge was also worn by the Vlaamsche Fabreikswacht and the V.W.B. (see below).

Officers   Other ranks

Prior to the introduction of the wolf-hook on an orange shield as the arm badge, the DM-ZB wore instead the V.N.V. delta in a circle emblem. On page 31 this is incorrectly attributed to the V.N.V. Staff and the illustration itself is not entirely correct. Above are two photographs (from the Dodkins Collection). The first is a white design on black and was worn by officers, the second is black on orange and was worn by other ranks.

The DM-MB emblem illustrated on page 29 is correct (it was worn above the left breast pocket) but it may be noted that this replaced a previous rather similar badge worn in the same place by the forerunner of the DM-MB, the ZB-GK (Zwarte Brigade Gemotoriserd Korps - Black Brigade Motorized Corps). This is illustrated below.

White design on black

Peaked cap for a non-commissioned member of the Black Brigade, 2nd design. The wolf-hook is not worn above the wreath, as in the first design, but placed inside it. In 1942 the Blauwvoet with a delta within a cog wheel in its claws was adopted by the Black Brigade and other militia bodies of the V.N.V. Officers wore the same type of cap as the above but the wreath, wolf-hook, and Blauwvoet emblem were all embroidered in silver wire. Officers had a silver chin strap, other ranks had a green chin strap. In all cases the piping was green.

BELGIUM. FLANDERS

The following collar patches for medical personnel of the Black Brigade were introduced in May 1944:

**Senior Doctor
(Opperarts)
Worn on left collar
(on right, the sector number)**

**Staff Doctor
(Stafarts)
Worn on both collars**

**Chief Inspector
(Hoofdinspecteur)
Worn on left collar
(on right the Sector numb**

All ranks in the DM-ZB wore a "wolf-hook" arm badge, but Brigadeleiders had in addition silver oak leaves added to this. (This was unique to this rank.)

The original designation of the uniformed militia of the V.N.V. was the Grey Brigade *(Grijze Brigade)*, a title which derived from the grey shirts of its members. In order to avoid a government ban on political militias, it had to masquerade under a variety of guises as, for example, Sports Brigade, Marching Brigade, Propaganda Brigade, etc. It was only after May 1940 that it was given the name Black Brigade (Zwarte Brigade, or Z.B.). A year later (10 May 1941) it was renamed the DM-ZB.

During its time as the Z.B. it had only a modest seven ranks: Soldaat, Groepsoverste, Luitenant, 1e Luitenant, Kapiteen, Commandant, and Algemeen Commandant. Uniform was all black with a black forage cap. Only officers had tunics (on the shoulder straps of which were silver bars denoting rank), collar patches were not, at this time, worn.

An orange brassard with the V.N.V. delta-in-a-circle emblem in blue on white was worn on the left upper arm.

The Z.B. remained a comparatively small force until the compulsory fusion with other political militias which created the combined force known as the DM-ZB. The DM-HB was raised as an auxiliary to it in July 1941.

V.N.V. Orange Brassard

V.N.V. POLITICAL LEADERS (pages 30-32)

The V.N.V. Political Leader's uniform is as described on page 30 except that the shirts were grey, not white. Piping round the cap was purple. The party was divided into *Afdelingen* (sections), *Gewesten* (districts), and *Gouwen* (the equivalent of the Nazi concept of *Gaue* - that is to say the Main Party Regions), there were also *Departmenten* (Main Offices of the Party). It is now possible to give the detailed scheme of ranks which was used by the Political Leadership Corps of the V.N.V. This underwent three changes of design, each an expansion of its predecessor, the last being introduced in July 1943 - after which time the V.N.V. went into rapid decline. The published dress regulations of the V.N.V. state that "special runes" will be worn on the left cuff of the tunic and greatcoat to denote different functions within the Party, but it would appear that these never materialized as no evidence of their actual existence has come to light.

Rank Insignia, 1st Type

- and Cel-leider. lder strap type (a)

Wijkleider. Shoulder strap type (b)

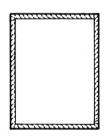

Afdelings-secretaris. Shoulder strap type (c)

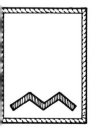

estsecretaris and Af- gsleider. Shoulder type (c)

Sectiehoofd. Shoulder strap (d). Districts- secretaris, type (c) shoulder strap.

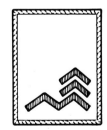

Dienstleider. Shoulder strap (d). Gewestleider, type (c)

285

Arrondissementleider.
Shoulder strap type (d)

Leider voor Inhood (Training, Finance, Propaganda, etc.). Shoulder strap type (d)

Gouwleider. Shou…
strap type (d)

All members of the Raad van Leidung (the Leadership Council of V.N.V.). Strap type (d)

All collar patches mauve, all (except three lowest ranks) piped in silver, all emblems on collar patches are silver.

Type (a) **Type (b)** **Type (c)** **Type (d)**

(a) Worn only by Blok- and Celleiders: mauve with black piping and single silver bar.
(b) Worn only by Wijkleiders: mauve with black piping and two silver bars. Ordinary members (Leden) had same type of shoulder strap as (a) and (b) but without silver bar.
(c) Worn by lower ranking officials: four parallel silver strands on a black underlay.
(d) Worn by senior officials: interwoven strands of silver (similar to German army Major) worn on a black underlay.

The above applies to the first design of ranks only. In the second design only the most senior ranks retained the type (d) strap. The following changes were introduced: Arrondissementleider: black shoulder strap with three silver bars. Gewesten Ass. to Arrondissement Secretaris: black shoulder straps with three mauve bars.

In the third design of V.N.V. Political Leaders ranks, shoulder straps were done away with for all grades.

Rank Insignia, 2nd Type

AFDELINGEN

Celleider

Blokleider

Wijkleider

Adfel. Ass.

Afdel. Ref.

Afdel. Sekr.

Afdelingsleider

GEWESTEN

Gew. Ass.

Gew. Ref.

Gew. Skr.

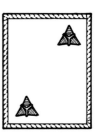

Gewestleider

GOUW and ARRONDISSEMENTEN

Gouw Ass.

Gouw Ref.

Gouw Skr.

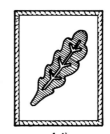

Adj.
Arrondissementleider

Arrondissement-
leider

Gouwleider

As before, all collar patches are mauve, all
surrounding piping (except for lowest ranks)
is silver , all rank emblems are silver.

287

Rank Insignia, 3rd Type

AFDELINGEN

Blokleider

Wijkleider

Kernleider

Afdel. Ass.

Afdel. Referent

Afdel. Sekr,
Beheerder Leider

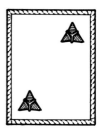
Afdelingsleider

GEWESTEN

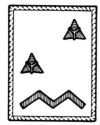
Gew. Assistent.

Gew. Referent

Gew. Sekr.,
Beheerder
Leider

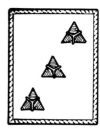
Gewestleider

GOUW and ARRONDISSEMENTEN

Gouw Assistent

Gouw Referent

Gouw Sekr.,
Beheerder Leider

Adj. Arrondissements-
leider

Arrondissementsleider   **Gouwleider**

DEPARTMENTEN

Dienstleider   **Hoofdienst en**   **Dept. Leider**   **Algemeen**
                    Arrond. Leider   **Leider**

Colors of patches and piping and emblems all as for two previous types.

Cap of the V.N.V. Political Leader. Silver wreath in center of which is the V.N.V. badge - a blue delta on white encircled by blue, then orange. Above the wreath is a white metal Blauwvoet (n.b. *without* the triangle-in-a-cogwheel). The cap is black, the piping purple, the chin strap silver.

Chin straps varied according to rank and were:
 Celleider to Afdelingssecretaris: mauve
 Afdelingsleider to Arrond. Sec.: silver and mauve
 Arrondissementsleider to Gouwleider: silver.

The cap badge set could be (as above) metal or, as in the illustration on page 30, silver wire.

The badge "Wie leven wil moet strijden" - illustrated on page 32 - seems to have been in one class only: gilt, and was not, as incorrectly stated, for military sports. It was awarded to those who had been subjected to attack by "terrorists" (i.e., the resistance). The other badge illustrated on the same page and called the Civil Badge of Merit should, properly, be referred to as the Fidelity Award (Trouwkenteken). It was given in two grades: silver for five year's service and gold for ten years - this being reckoned, of course, back to the creation of the V.N.V. before the way.

A further V.N.V. merit award was created in June 1944. This was known as the "Honor and Loyalty" (Eer en Trouw) badge and was intended to reward special acts of courage at home or at the front. For those killed in the course of military action or by the forces of the resistance in Belgium, the badge came mounted on a commemorative plaque. It is a bronze badge and is illustrated from an example in the Van Wiele Collection.

The V.N.V. Golden Party Badge

This is illustrated, slightly inaccurately, as a sketch on page 36. Above is a photo of an actual example (in the van Wiele collection). It is a blue delta outlined in gold on a white background within a blue circle narrowly outlined in gold, then an orange circle, with an outer edge of golden laurel leaves. This badge was awarded in bronze for 5 year's service, silver for 10 year's service, and in gold for 15 year's service.

N.S.J.V. (pages 33 to 44)

In 1933 the V.N.V. formed a youth section known then as the A.V.N.J. (Algemeen Verbond van Nationale Jeugd - General Union of National Youth). It was suppressed by a governmental regulation of 1937 banning para-military formations, but a new A.V.N.J. was reformed in 1938 under the leadership of Dr. Edgard (not Edgar) Lehembre. After the occupation of Belgium in May 1940, it was again reconstituted, this time as the A.V.N.J. *Blauwvoetvendels* (Stormy Petrel Companies). It was sub-divided into the D.B.V. for boys and the D.M.S. for girls. At this stage the uniform was the grey shirt (of the ZB), black shorts (or for girls a black skirt). The emblem of the youth movement was now a Blauwvoet with a delta in a circle in its claws. At this point in time there were only seven ranks. A Marineschaar (Naval Section) was formed in Antwerp and a Luchtvaarschaar (Flying, or Air, Section) in both Antwerp and Brussels. In June 1941 some twenty A.V.N.J. leaders attended a Hitler Youth training course in Weimar.

On 8 July 1941 all youth organizations in Flanders were required to merge with the A.V.N.J. or face disbandment. The A.V.N.J. thus acquired the important Jongdinaso and the less significant Rex Jeugd Vlaanderen as well as the out-and-out Nazi Vlaamsche Jeugd (see later) and a handful of minor and largely insignificant groupings (but *not* the youth of Devlag).

The new combined youth movement was rechristened the N.S.J.V. (Nationaal-Socialistische Jeugd Vlaanderen). At its optimum strength it may have amounted to around 8,000 boys and 6,000 girls. It adopted the "netherlandic" orange/white/blue flag as its own. Each Vendel (company) had on its flag a stylized Blauwvoet while each Schaar (squad) had a black pennent with an individual runic emblem.

Various concessions in respect of dress and insignia were made to Dinaso. For example, the grey shirt was replaced by the green shirt of the Jongdinaso. With this boys wore black shorts, a neckerchief (orange for the younger lads, black for their seniors), white or grey stockings, black shoes, and a black forage cap. A belt (with the Blauw-voet and delta emblem as the buckle) was worn with a cross strap. The foregoing was the summer uniform worn between Easter and 1 October. The winter dress was vir-tually identical to that of the Hitler Youth with orange piping round the collar and shoulder straps. On the left cuff (or upper arm) a Blauwvoet was worn with both types of uniform. The black cap was piped in orange. Officers wore green (later khaki) shirts, orange ties, and black breeches with black top boots. Their black tunics had black collar patches piped in orange (not red). Their peaked caps were also piped in orange with a cap badge as illustrated on page 37. Lower ranking officers had a black leather chin strap, higher officers silver. The most senior officers were allowed to wear white or green shirts with a black tie.

The rank structure is illustrated on pages 37/38 but is incomplete. The final scheme of ranks is illustrated below:

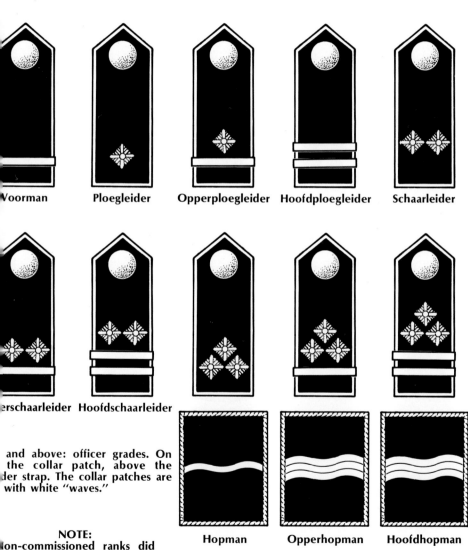

Voorman   Ploegleider   Opperploegleider   Hoofdploegleider   Schaarleider

erschaarleider Hoofdschaarleider

and above: officer grades. On the collar patch, above the der strap. The collar patches are with white "waves."

Hopman   Opperhopman   Hoofdhopman

NOTE:
Non-commissioned ranks did not have collar patches.

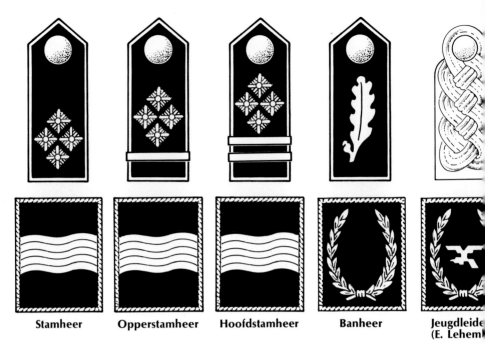

| Stamheer | Opperstamheer | Hoofdstamheer | Banheer | Jeugdleide (E. Lehem |

In addition to the above, NCOs wore colored lanyards as follows: Ploegleider, a short green lanyard; Opperploegleider, short red lanyard; Hoofdploegleider, a short white lanyard; Schaarleider, a long green lanyard; Opperschaarleider, a long red lanyard; Hoofdschaarleider, a long white lanyard.

The D.M.S. was sub-divided into three age groups: 10 to 14 years; 14 to 18 years; 18 to 25 years (this latter was known as *Adel en Schoonheid* - Nobility and Beauty). Girls wore a dark blue skirt, white or beige blouse, and a neckerchef which was, like that of the boys, orange for younger members, black for seniors. This had a metal toggle as illustrated below.

The D.M.S. "borrowed" its age group symbols (with the exception of one) from the Dinaso girls as follows:

| 10 to 14 years (orange) | 14 to 18 years (green) | 18 to 25 years (blue) |

Girls ranks were indicated by a scheme of blue circles (one, two, three, and four) combined with, below these, blue "bars" (one or two) to indicate the 15 grades. These were worn on the left, upper side of the blouse. In 1942 two new items of dress for girls were introduced. One was a short, waist-length blue tunic with a double row of three buttons down the front and a Blauwvoet on the left cuff. The other was a blue forage cap.

In 1943 the N.S.J.V. formed what might be seen as its equivalent of the H.J. Streifendienst. This was known as the N.S.J.V. Weerkommando (Defense Commando) or W.K. There were three W.K. companies (each of about 40 boys) in the three Flemish provinces - Brabant, Flanders, and Limburg. They carried out guard duties at games and rallies. Unlike the other members of the N.S.J.V., they were allowed to carry daggers and even, occasionally, revolvers. They wore the normal N.S.J.V. uniform with the addition of a cuff title, Joris van Severen (the murdered leader of Dinaso who had by now been "adopted" as a hero-martyr by the V.N.V. as well).

Cuff title of the N.S.J.V. Weerkommando
(orange-white on black)

The N.S.J.V. Landdienst (page 42) was taken over by the Hitler Youth in November 1943 and thereafter wore H.J. uniform. The service was disbanded in March 1944. In September-October of that year, most of the former Landdienst youths were absorbed into the H.J. Battalion "Langemarck." An official N.S.J.V. decree of November 1943 states that a *Landdienstdraagteken* (Landdienst portable emblem) will be worn 2 cm above the left breast pocket. This is described as a silver bordered Landdienst emblem (i.e., the sword piercing an Odalsrune as on the fanfare trumpet banner shown on page 43) but no evidence for the actual existence of such a badge has come to light.

Corrections: the badge of the Vlaamsche Jeugd illustrated on page 43 is for female leaders (see later), the date of introduction of this badge (1943) must be incorrect since the V.J. had ceased to exist by that date. The flag illustrated on the same page is an N.S.J.V. Vendel flag. The N.S.J.V. flag proper was, as stated above, simply the orange/white/blue flag of the "netherlandic region" (that is to say, Holland/Flanders).

Five merit, or commemorative, awards were issued by the N.S.J.V. They were:
(i) The Loyalty Award *(Trouwkenteken)*. This is a round badge with a *Blauwvoet* in a circle which has at its base an oakleaf sprig. It was given in bronze to all those who had been members of the A.V.N.J. or Jongdinaso before the war and who had continued to belong to the youth movement, or in silver to those who had completed more than five year's duty.
(ii) Merit badge *(Vaardigheidsteeken)*. Instituted in the spring of 1944, this badge is illustrated on page 40, but no actual example of it has come to light.
(iii) Sports Badge of Honor. This is also illustrated on page 40 and was certainly both manufactured and awarded.
(iv) Tollenaere Commemorative Medal *(R. Tollenaereherdenkingsmedaille)*. Although this is described as a "medal," it is in fact, a pin-back badge with a portrait of the fallen hero, Raymond Tollenaere. It must not, of course, be confused with the more prestigious Tollenaere Commemorative Badge illustrated on page 13, which was given only to those who had belonged to the Grey Brigade before the war.
(v) Staf de Clercq Commemorative medal *(Staf de Clercqherdenkingsmedaille)*. Again this is a pin-back badge, not a "medal" and was issued to commemorate the death of the V.N.V.'s first leader in October 1942.

The *Nationaal-Socialistische Jongvliegerkorps* (the Nat. Soc. Young Fliers Corps) issued a *Jongvlieger Vaardigheidskenteken* (Young Fliers Merit Badge) in February 1944 in three types: iron (for 15 and 16 year olds), in bronze (for 17 year olds), and in "silver" (for 18 year olds). The design is shown on page 39.

In addition to these Belgian-instituted badges, young lads of the N.S.J.V. who attended Hitler Youth camps in Germany were eligible for the H.J. Leistungsabzeichen and the H.J. Marksmanship badges, which could be worn with N.S.J.V. uniforms.

Correction: The Jongdinaso badge illustrated on page 40 was *not* issued as a commemorative item. This mistake arose out of confusion with no. (i) above, which it closely resembles.

Fidelity Badge	**Tollenaere** **Commemorative "medal"**	**Staf de Clercq** **Commemorative "medal"**

Flemish Labor Service (V.A.v.V.)

The Flemish Labor Service was originally called the National Labor Service *(Nationale Arbeidsdienst,* or N.A.D.). The title Volunteer Labor Service for Flanders *(Vrijwillige Arbeidsdienst voor Vlaanderen,* or V.A.v.V.) was only adopted in November 1940 when the service was split into its Flemish and Walloon components.

In April 1944, when the V.A.v.V. was taken over by the German Labor Service, it was rechristened simply Labor Service Flanders *(Arbeids-Dienst Vlaanderen,* or A.D.V.).

A girls' branch of the V.A.v.V. known as the V.A.v.V.v.J. (V.A.v.V. *Vrouwelijke Jeugd* - Female Youth) was established in October 1941 under the leaderhsip of Celina van de Weyer. It was open to girls between the ages of 17 and 25 who could sign on for a six month engagement. Before the liberation of Belgium, 13 camps had been established each with around 40 girls (and leaders). The girls' uniform was a brown, three-quarter tunic, brown skirt, and brown hat, green shirt, white stockings, and black shoes. Normal working dress was a blue cotton overall. In cold weather a brown coat with pockets was worn. The V.A.v.V. emblem was worn as a brooch at the throat and on the left cuff of the tunic and left breast of the coat. Ranks were as follows:

Kameraadschapsleidster: one green stripe round left cuff
Kandidate Meisjesleidster: two green stripes round the left cuff
Hulpmeisjesleidster: green border to collar
Meisjesleidster: intertwined silver/green piping round collar
Oppermeisjesleidster: silver piping round collar
Hoofdmeisjesleidster: gold piping round collar.

From March 1942 onwards, trainees for leadership had to attend courses run by the R.A.D. in Germany. At the time of the liberation of Belgium (September 1944) the female V.A.v.V. was taken over by the R.A.D. It consisted of, at that point in time, around eight or nine hundred girls. They were then issued with R.A.D. uniforms and rank insignia.

In December 1944 René van Thillo, the V.A.v.V. leader, was awarded the Order of the German Eagle.

A Sports Badge *(Sportbrevet)* for the V.A.v.V. was instituted in July 1943 in two classes - bronze and silver. Although an illustration of this badge appeared in the

Sketch of the proposed Sports Badge of the V.A.v.V. as it appeared in the Belgian press.

Belgian press at the time, there is no evidence to suggest that it was ever awarded or manufactured.

Corrections: The cap band is brown, not green (page 45). The bell heather on the cuff, and other, badges is not green but white (page 48). The rank bar on a Voorman's shoulder strap is orange, not brown, while the bar(s) for Ploegleider and Senior Ploegleider are white, not orange. Arbeidsman and Voorman both have an orange chevron on the collar patch, not a plain collar patch (page 48).

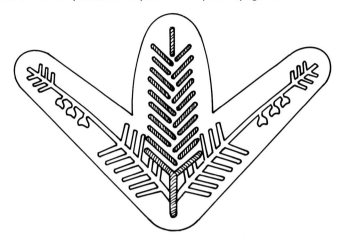

V.A.v.V. cap badge. Ear of barley is orange colored, the bell heather is white, the background is brown. Worn on front of forage cap.

Cuff band worn on lower left arm by V.A.v.V. As above, the barley ear is orange, the bell heather white, the "waves" are light blue. Background is brown. The actual size (from one end of waves to the other) is 9 inches. Sometimes the badge, without the waves, was worn on a circular background on left cuff.

Flemish Labor Service. (V.A.v.V.), Female Ranks

Kameraadschapsleidster
(green band round left cuff)

Kandidatemeisjesleidster
(two green bands round left cuff)

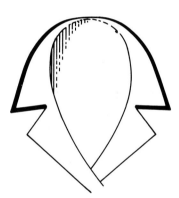

Hulpmeisjesleidster
(green piping round collar)

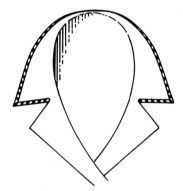

Meisjesleidster
(green/silver piping round collar)

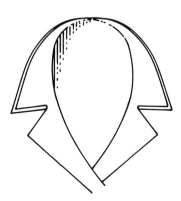

Oppermeisjesleidster: silver piping round collar
Hoofdmeisjesleidster: gold piping round collar

Flemish General S.S. (Pages 51-55)

The Vlaanderen Korps was intended to be for those who were either too young, too old, or not up to the physical requirements of the S.S. Vlaanderen. Members of the Vlaanderen Korps were not entitled to wear the peaked cap or the arm diamond with the S.S. runes. The photo on page 54 is, therefore, of the Vlaanderen Korps. The belt buckle illustrated on page 53 is that of the Vlaanderen Korps. The buckle for the S.S. Vlaanderen (later Germaansche S.S. in Vlaanderen) is slightly different (as shown below).

More can now be said about the short-lived youth branch of the Flemish General S.S. This was formed at roughly the same time as its parent body and by the same pair of individuals, Ward Hermans and René Lagrou. It was intended that this would be the direct Flemish equivalent of the Hitler Youth, thus it was named simply Flemish Youth (Vlaamsche Jeugd). It was a faithful facsimile of the H.J., indeed, the sole difference in uniform between the two was that the Flemings had a Sigrune in place of a swastika as the principal emblem of their organization. The uniform of the V.J. is illustrated on pages 80 and 81 but wrongly attributed to the youth of DeVlag - an error caused by the fact that DeVlag maintained close connections with the Flemish General S.S. The DeVlag leader, van de Wiele, held an honorary commission in its ranks. Uniforms were supplied by the Hitler Youth. Apart from the brassard, the only significant difference between the V.J. and H.J. uniform was the officers cap badge which was a silver sigrune on the band with, above this, a yellow shield with the black lion of Flanders.

The V.J. proper was for youths between the ages of 14 and 18 years. Younger boys (10 to 14 years) belonged to the J.V. - Jongvolk - the equivalent of the German D.J. There was a girls section, the V.J.M. (Vlaamsche Jeugd Meisjes) for females between the ages of 14 and 18; their younger sisters (10 to 14 years old) could join the J.M. (Jong Meisjes). Girls consisted of a white blouse and dark blue skirt, on the left upper arm they wore the same brassard as the boys (illustrated on page 81). Female officers wore, above the left breast pocket, the badge illustrated at the top of page 43. The date of institution quoted under this illustration must be incorrect since the V.J. had ceased to exist by 1943.

On 8 July 1941 the V.J. was obliged to merge with the N.S.J.V. At this time it had a membership of around eight hundred which would seem to indicate that much of its organizational structure existed only on paper. It comprised, in theory, five Ban (Antwerp, East Flanders, West Flanders, Brabant, and Limburg) and each Ban was supposed to have a strength of 810 boys.

N.S.K.K. (pages 62-63)

The first motor transport auxiliary to be formed in Flanders after the occupation was the Z.K.K. (Zivil Kraftfahr Korps) Civil Motortransport Corps. At first it reflected its civilian nature, but after the German invasion of Russia a year later, the Z.K.K. was given ex-Belgian army uniforms dyed black with, on each collar, a small silver motor wheel. On the left upper arm a brassard with "Im Dienste der Deutschen Wehrmacht" (In the Service of the German Armed Forces) was worn. A belt with a German army buckle was issued. On active duty behind the front a rifle or revolver could be carried to ward off possible attack by Partisans.

Volunteers for the N.S.K.K. from the DM-MB (the Motor Section of the Black Brigade) continued at first to wear their political militia uniform, but were later issued

297

with French army uniforms dyed black, later still with Luftwaffe uniform, dyed black, and finally with standard blue-grey Luftwaffe uniforms with black N.S.K.K. insignia. At first a black wolf-hook on an orange shield was worn as the Flemings' distinguishing feature. According to the regulations, this should have been worn on the left arm, but it was, in practice, as frequently worn on the right. Later the black lion of Flanders on a yellow shield was authorized. There is some doubt as to whether the version of this shown on page 62 was one of the types worn. The lion shield is known to have existed in a number of variants but normally these were without any wording at the top, also the fact that FLANDERN is in German spelling is an unusual feature and would suggest that this perhaps belongs to that series of "nationality" badges produced by the BeVo firm with the name of the country in German. None of these was ever actually worn. There is still some question of the positive identification of the Einsatz-Regiment. 1 Komp. Flandern (page 63) arm shield. No photo of this actually being worn has been found.

For each year of service, a silver "bar" could be worn below the arm shield (examples of these bars can be clearly seen in the photo of Belgian N.S.K.K. men on pages 1 and 32, and of French N.S.K.K. on page 163 of volume 1. This type of service distinction appears to have applied only to non-Germans).

N.S.K.K. Motorgruppe Luftwaffe was formed in May 1942 and consisted of two brigades each of three regiments (sub-divided into two *Abteilungen)*. Most of the Flemish N.S.K.K. volunteers were in the 4th and 6th regiments of the 2nd Brigade. In May 1943 there were around 6,000 Belgian volunteers in the N.S.K.K. and of these 3,-267 were Flemings.

DeVlag raised a *Motorkorps* of its own, but this was absorbed into the N.S.K.K. Motorgruppe Luftwaffe in April 1943. All the Flemish volunteers had green piping except the DeVlag men who had black.

INTERNAL SECURITY FORCES (pages 67-76)
(i) *Vlaamsche Wacht (V.W.)*

This was formed in June 1941 and its uniform underwent no less than five changes in the course of its existence. At first Belgian army khaki with Belgian army ranks on the collar was worn. There were at this stage only officers, no NCOs or other ranks! In July 1941 the khaki uniforms were dyed dark blue and ranks in the form of one, two, three, or four gold "rings" were worn round the cuff by the different grades of non-commissioned officers. Commssioned officers had one, two, or three stars (according to rank) on a black collar patch piped in yellow. At this juncture officers did not wear shoulder straps; these were added in mid-1943.

Towards the end of 1943 the V.W.'s special rank insignia was replaced by the standard German Army/Luftwaffe scheme and the number of commissioned grades was expanded from three to four and the non-commissioned from four to six. The distinctive unit badge (a Roman numeral in a wreath of oak leaves) was still retained above the right breast pocket, but now, in addition, all ranks wore on the lower left arm the black lion of Flanders on a yellow shield.

In June 1944 the V.W. was formally incorporated into the German Wehrmacht. During the following months its dark blue uniform was replaced by German field grey. The fifth and final amendment to its uniform was that unit badge above the right breast pocket was done away with (the lion of Flanders was still worn on the cuff) while the collar patch was now German army type and all gradings were on field grey and not, as previously, on dark blue. In all, 1,687 men of the V.W. were taken over by the Wehrmacht.

Prior to this take-over, the organizational structure of the V.W. was as follows:
Four main units *(Afdelingen)*
    Afd. I: Ghent (four companies)
    Afd. II: Antwerp (six companies)
    Afd. III: Brugges (three companies)
    Afd. IV: Brussels (two Railway Guard companies and one Canal Guard company).

The Railway and Canal Guard companies did not have an *Afdeling* number. The badge they wore above the right breast pocket, unlike that of the other unit,s was simply the open oakleaf wreath without a Roman numeral inside. The same applied to their cap badge.

There were, in addition to the above, two Training companies. In February 1943 the three companies which made up Afd. III (Brugges) were granted the honor of names:

1st Company: Van Severen
2nd Company: Tollenaere
3rd Company: Staf de Clercq.
It is not known if they were given cuff titles with these names (but this is unlikely). Each *Afdeling* was under the command of a Major (the highest V.W. rank).

On the eve of the liberation of Belgium (September 1944), the total strength of the V.W. was 2,604 men. As mentioned above, more than half were incorporated into the Wehrmacht, mainly into its 406th *Landesschützen Division*. Others went into the Luftwaffe Flak Brigade, the N.S.K.K. or various "alarm" units; some 700 ended up in the Waffen S.S.

Men of Afd. II saw some minor action during the allied airborne landings at Arnhem and later rather heavier fighting in the battle for Antwerp (their home city and a stronghold of Flemish nationalism).

In December 1943 a V.W. Sports badge *(Sportkenteken)* was instituted, but it appears never to have got beyond the theoretical stage as no evidence can be found for its actual existence (even the projected design is not known).

VLAAMSCHE WACHT. 2nd and 3rd DESIGN OF RANKS
JULY 1941 TO END of 1943

Non-Commissioned Officers:

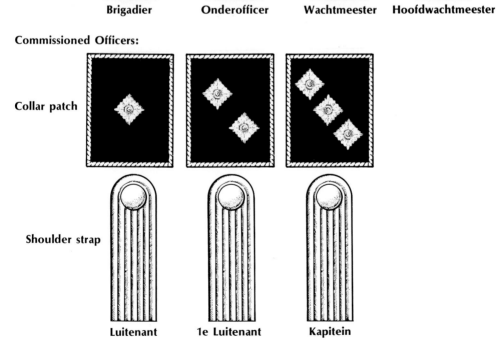

For the second design of ranks (July 1941 to mid-1942) officers did not have shoulder straps. The shoulder straps (without stars) were added as the third change of rank.

VLAAMSCHE WACHT. 4th DESIGN OF RANKS
END of 1943 to JUNE 1944

These were worn with the dark blue uniform which had on the left cuff a yellow shield with the black lion of Flanders.

| Brigadier | 1e Brigadier | Onderofficier | Wachtmeester | Opperwachtmee |

(Silver tress on shoulder straps and around collar as for German senior NCOs)

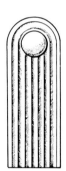

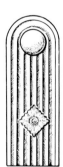

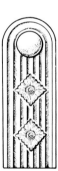

| Hoofdwacht-meester | Luitenent | 1e Luitenant | Kapitein | Majoor |

(also wore two silver bands round cuffs)

(ii) *Vlaamsche Fabriekswacht (V.F.W.)*

The Flemish Factory Guard was formed in May 1941 as part of the Black Brigade and wore the same uniform with the addition of the V.F.W. cuff title illustrated on page 67.

(iii) *Vlaamsche Wacht Brigade (V.W.B.)*

The V.F.W. was, in June 1943, enlarged to become the Flemish Guard Brigade (V.W.B.). It remained part of the Z.B. and continued to wear its all-black uniform with green shoulder straps and green collar patches. On the left cuff three different emblems were worn in turn: at first a delta in a cog wheel and an upward pointing sword, then a black wolf hook on a yellow shield, lastly the black lion of Flanders on a yellow shield.

At a maximum strength it had four battalions sub-divided into 14 companies. In June 1943 its recorded strength was 3,362 officers and men. The V.W.B. was armed with old French Lebel rifles (it did not receive the more up-to-date German 98K rifle until 1944), or, for officers and senior NCOs, revolvers. On duty guards wore black German steel helmets with, on the left side, the Luftwaffe eagle, since the V.W.B. was

300

under the command of Luftgau Belgien-Nord Frankreich (Belgium-Northern France). It served in its homeland and also within the Luftgau region of northern France.

As stated above, both the V.F.W. and the V.W.B. wore basically the uniform of the DM-ZB, and when there was a change in the cap badge of the DM-ZB, it was reflected in that of the other V.N.V. militia units. From 1942 the cap badge consisted of a wolf hook within an oakleaf wreath on the band and, on the peak, a Blauwvoet with a delta in a cog wheel in its claws. It would appear, however, that for a brief period the V.F.W. wore in place of the wolf hook, the black lion of Flanders on a yellow shield. On the left collar the DM-ZB and the V.W.B. wore a set of ranks based almost exactly on those of the German S.S. (although the Flemings contrived to add two new grades of their own!). Different designations were given to these ranks in the DM-ZB and the V.W.B. (both are given in the chart of ranks of the Black Brigade earlier in this chapter). Shoulder ranks corresponded to German Waffen S.S./Army ranks.

Corrections: a number of errors have been made with regard to the identification of the photographs on pages 66 to 74. The *Schaarleiter* shown on page 66 could be a member of either the Black Brigade, Fabriekswacht, or V.W.B. (since, as detailed above, all these had the same uniform). The file of men shown on page 68 are not Vlaamsche Fabriekswacht, but Garde Wallonne (note the characteristic unit badge worn above the right breast pocket by both the Vlaamsche Wacht and the Garde Walloone. It is the French type steel helmet which confirms these as the latter. The Flemings had Dutch helmets.) The same correction applies to the photo upper left, page 71. These men are also certainly Garde Wallonne. The badge shown on page 68 is not that of the V.F.W. but was the lapel emblem of the Technical Branch of the V.N.V.

The badge illustrated on page 70 and described as "civil lapel badge of the V.F.W." is, in fact, for long service (see photo right). It was given in bronze for two year's service and in silver for four year's. It was worn on the left breast pocket. The photo is not the scale; its actual size is smaller.

The ranks illustrated on page 72 are, of course, incomplete. The military band shown on page 74 belongs to the V.W.B., not the Vlaamsche Wacht. The occasion was the funeral of Staf de Clercq. Despite the similarity in names between the Vlaamsche Wacht and the Vlaamsche Wacht Brigade, they were two separate entities and retained their individual identity and uniforms until the end. Both carried out much the same tasks and worked for the same masters; the principal difference was that the V.W.B. was part of the organizational structure of the V.N.V. whereas the Vlaamsche Wacht was not. The author apologizes for his failure to make clear the distinction in the original chapter on Flanders!

(iv) Boerenwacht

This was formed first on 26 June 1941 as a voluntary police auxiliary but made obligatory on 4 August of the same year for men between the ages of 35 and 50. At first only a green brassard with B.W. in yellow was worn, but later a dark brown uniform in the style of the Belgian Army was introduced. The full scheme of ranks is shown below:

(v) S.S. Guard Unit "Sint Truiden"

Shortly after the occupation of Belgium in May 1940, a group of some 60 Flemings formed a semi-official guard unit which adopted the decidedly unorthodox garb of Luftwaffe uniform with S.S. collar patches. The commanding "officer" of this formation was a German Luftwaffe NCO. It took upon itself the designation of *S.S. Wacht*

Sint Truiden (S.S. Guard Unit "Sint Truiden" - the name deriving from a district of Brussels).

The following year it was incorporated into the General (or Germanic) S.S. Flanders and adopted the black uniform of that corps. At the end of 1941 it was divided into two separate guard platoons and placed under the aegis of the Works Department *(Bauleitung)* of the Luftwaffe. Its personnel were armed with rifles or revolvers and accorded the undramatic task of guarding Luftwaffe constructions sites in Belgium. Age limits for membership of this unit were 17 to 40 years.

Ranks of the Boerenwacht

NCO ranks worn on both cuffs.

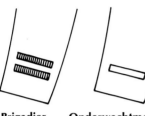 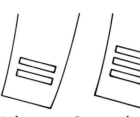 

Brigadier two red bars	**Onderwachtmeester** silver bar	**Wachtmeester** two silver bars	**Opperwachtmeester** three silver bars

1e Operwachtme‹
silver star on co‹

Commissioned ranks (both collars)

Onderveldmeester one gold star	**Veldmeester** two gold stars	**Opperveldmeester** three gold stars	**1e Opperveldme‹** three gold sta‹ and gold ba‹

Onderhoofdman gold star and gold bar	**Hoofdman** two gold stars and gold bar	**Opperhofdman** two gold stars and two gold bars	**1e Opperhofdm‹** two curved gold

CHILDREN IN ARMS (pages 79-84)

The Hitler Youth Flanders (Hitler Jugend Vlaanderen, or H.J.V.) was founded on 15 October 1943. Some 300 boys from the Flemish School at Antwerp (opened the previous September for the sons of national-socialist parents) enrolled at once. They were followed, on 14 November, by almost the entire complement of the youth of DeVlag.

The organizational structure of the H.J.V. was exactly parallel to that of the H.J. itself. The boys were sub-divided into two age groups:

H.J.-J.V. (Jongvolk: 10 to 14 year olds
H.J.V.:   14 to 18 year olds

The girls were likewise:

J.M (Jong Meisjes): 10 to 14 years
M.B. (Meisjesbond): 14 to 18 years

In April 1944 the youth branch of DeVlag in French-speaking Wallonie was absorbed into the H.J.V. In October 1944 a Youth Battalion of the 27th S.S. Volunteer Grenadier Division "Langemarck" was created.

BELGIUM, FLANDERS
(Information not previously included)

The civilian firm of Reitz (part of the Vanderelst industrial complex) in Antwerp made uniforms for the German forces and employed its own Werkschutz (Factory Guard) which, being located in the very heartland of Flemish nationalism (the city of Antwerp) not unnaturally also included Flemish volunteers. Their uniform was the normal Werkschutz dark grey but they had their own individual factory belt buckle (illustrated here).

J. R. Angolia

Another privately raised guard company was the Wachgruppe Nordland (also known as the Wachtkorps Nordland). This comprised some four to five hundred Flemings employed mainly on guard duty at Luftwaffe repair installations in Antwerp, Brussels, and other parts of Belgium. They had to sign on for a minimum of one year's service, and were given a four-week initial training which included the use of small arms. On duty they wore a black uniform with, on both collars, a silver wire W.N. (illustrated) on a black patch, piped in red.

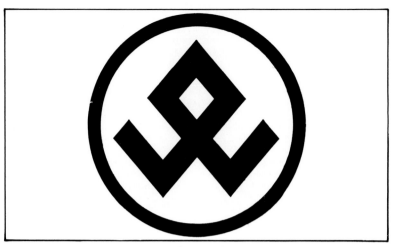

Brassard worn by members of the Volksverweering - a black Odalsrune in a black circle on a white background.

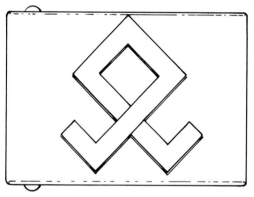

Belt buckle of Volksverweering. Rather poorly cast in bronze (drawn from an actual example in the Van Wiele collection).

BELGIUM. WALLONIE

FORMATIONS DE COMBAT OF REX (Page 88)

The uniform of the Rexist Formations de Combat (F.C.) was all black (not dark blue). The red Burgundian cross was worn on the right (not the left) breast pocket. The cap badge which is illustrated on page 88 for Political Leaders of Rex was also worn by NCOs and officers of the F.C. It can be metal or in an embroidered version as shown below.

Brian Ambrose Collection

This embroidered version is in white cotton for NCOs, silver wire for junior officers, and gold wire for top ranks. The Burgundian cross is, in each case, red.

Members of the General Staff of the F.C. had a special two-piece cap badge set which is illustrated (in both its versions), below.

Cap badge of officers of the General Staff of the F.C. Yellow cotton eagle with red Burgundian cross with, below this, a red Burgundian cross whose "flames" are gold thread.

(the above is drawn from an example in the Van Wiele Collection)

Al alternative version of the upper part of the General Staff officer's cap badge set (also in the Van Wiele Collection).

FORMATIONS DE COMBAT OF REX RANKS

Chef de Piquet

Chef de Fanion

Chef d'Enseigne

Commandant de Flamme

Commandant de Bannière

Commandant de Groupe

Commandant d'Etendard

Commandant de Brigade

The rank insignia of the F.C. is illustrated above and was as follows:
Chef de Piquet: a red "flame"
Chef de Fanion: two red flames
Chef d'Enseigne: three red flames.
The above were the non-commissioned ranks. Officer ranks were:
Commandant de Flamme: one gold flame
Commandant de Bannière: two gold flames
Commandant de Groupe: three gold flames.
The above were roughly equivalent to 2nd Lieutenant, 1st Lieutenant, and Captain.
the flames are in gilt metal. Higher ranks were:
Commandant d'Etendard: one gold flames and two gold briquets
Commandant de Brigade: two gold flames and two gold briquets

Commandants Fédéraux (Federal Commandants) had two gold briquets and a Burgundian cross à *deux flammes* (not illustrated).

The word *briquet* can be translated as a flint or a tinderbox (presumable the flint from which the "flame" was struck!).

The all-black uniform of the F.C. consisted of: for the two lowest ranks a black "shirt" (a sort of "battle dress" blouse), black breeches and black boots, black forage cap (even the piping was black), black tie, black belt without a cross strap. Chefs de Fanions and Chefs d'Enseignes were allowed to wear a black tunic (Belgian army officer type, dyed), peaked cap (again with black piping), black belt without cross strap. Officers wore a similar tunic with a belt with a cross strap. All ranks had the red Burgundian cross on the right breast pocket with the exception of probationers who had not yet been enrolled as full F.C. members. Buttons for all ranks were gold with the lion of Belgium. All F.C. flags were black with a red Burgundian cross. The individual unit number in red Arabic numerals appeared in the upper left quarter of the flag followed by the number of the *fanion* to which it belonged in red Roman numerals (e.g., 2/II indicated Piquet 2 of Fanion II). The flags of Banniere and Groupe units had red borders, those of Etendard and Brigade-sized formations had gold borders.

Serments de la Jeunesse
(pages 92-101)

rm badge of boys in 12 to 16 years age roup (red on black)

Arm badge of boys in the age group below 12 years (white on black)

Arm badge for commissioned ranks (white dagger, yellow Burgundian cross, on red within brown circle.

Up to the end of 1940 members of the Serments de la Jeunesse of the Rexist party wore the arm badges shown above to indicate (a) age group, and (b) officer status. These were discontinued when in January 1941 the ranks shown on page 96 were introduced.

307

AGRA (pages 102-103)

Membership lapel badge

"Honor Badge" of Agra

The membership lapel badge of Agra is a yellow mobile swastika on an orange circle which is outlined in yellow. The "Honor Badge" of Agra is this same badge in the center of a grey metal cross (as illustrated above from an example in the Van Wiele Collection).

Labor Service (page 105)

Arm badge

The emblem of the Service des Volontaires du Travail is mentioned on page 105 and illustrated on page 127, but shown here is a more accurate representation. It is a black crossed pick and spade on a yellow circle with a red border (red/yellow/black are the national colors of Belgium). It was worn on the right upper arm as shown in the accompanying photograph (Van Wiele Collection).

GREAT BRITAIN (pages 130-136)

I am indebted to Mr. Adrian Weale of London for the following additional information on the British "Frekorps," the official designation of which was, in fact, British Free Corps (S.S.). The name was, apparently, suggested by Alfred Minchin after he had read in "Signal" about the Freikorps Danmark. Official correspondence, however, sometimes referred to it as the Britishe Frei-corps (note the English spelling of the last work, not Korps). A cuff title with the English words BRITISH FREE CORPS may have existed. Some doubt must exist as to the authenticity of the cuff title BRITISCHES FREIKORPS.

When the B.F.C. men objected to wearing the Union Jack shield below the Nazi emblem, the British device was transferred to the upper right arm (not, as wrongly stated on page 134, to above the S.S. eagle on the left sleeve). This point is made quite clear in a letter dated 13 June 1944 from *S.S. Standartenführer* Dr. Brandt (adjutant to *S.S. Obergruppenführer* Berger, chief of foreign recruitment of the Waffen S.S.), which concludes, "*den englischen Landesschild auf dem rechten Armel und nicht unter den Hoheitsadler tragen zu dürfen.*"

The three successive commanders of the B.F.C. were:
January 1944 to November 1944: *S.S. Hauptsturmführer* Hans Werner Roepke
November 1944 to February 1945: *S.S. Hauptsturmführer* Dr. Walter Kühlich
February 1945 to end of war in Europe: *S.S. Hauptsturmführer* Dr. Alexander Dolezalek

HOLLAND (pages 138-141)

As mentioned on pages 138/39, there were two political parties in Holland calling themselves the N.S.N.A.P. The integration of Major Kruyt's N.S.N.A.P. with Mussert's N.S.B. shortly after the start of the occupation left the part of E.H. Ridder van Rappard as the sole N.S.N.A.P. still in business. It seems to have been van Rappard's policy to make his followers into virtual facsimiles of their German counterparts. His N.S.H.J. had its name changed to simply Dutch Hitler Youth *(Nederlandsche Hitlerjougd,* or N.H.J.)* in August 1941 and thereafter wore the uniform of the German H.J. differentiated only by having green instead of black shoulder straps and by a blue band added to the central white part of the brassard (thus making up the Dutch colors - red/white/blue). The girls section was, like the German counterpart, called the B.D.M. and wore its uniform with, above the left breast pocket, a red/white/blue "bar" measuring 7 cm long by 3 cm wide.

**Brassard of the Dutch Hitler Youth
(N.H.J. of van Rappard)**

The Storm Troop *(Storm Afdeeling)* of the van Rappard N.S.N.A.P. wore an almost identical uniform to that of the German S.A. except that ties were black instead of (as in the German S.A.) brown. Collar patches were green. Collar and collar patch were piped with red/white/blue cord. Collar patches had, in the German manner, rank insignia on the left and unit numeral on the right. There were eleven S.A. *Stormen* in the Netherlands (one in each of the main towns). The brassard was like that of the German S.A. but had the addition of 3 cm wide edges of red/white/blue. The van Rappard S.A. men did not have a kepi or other headgear.

The "Political Leaders" of the N.S.N.A.P. wore the same uniform as the S.A. but had rank on both sides (again on green collar patches). There was no piping except for the national leadership *(landelyke leiding)*. The Women's Section *(Vrouwenschap)* wore the same as the B.D.M. but with the addition of a black tunic.

The flag of the N.S.N.A.P. was simply the swastika flag of Germany with, in the left upper quarter, horizontal red/white/blue. The Party greeting was "heil Hitler" and the Party song, the German "Horse Wessel Lied."

HOLLAND (pages 160-161)

An interesting photo showing the cuff title "Vendel Peter Ton" (see page 161) being worn by W.A. men and also sewn to their battle flag (see page 160); here the flag has in the corner the arms of The Hague.

The cuff title "OVERSTE MUSSERT" (shown on page 156) was not for the Mussert Bodyguard, and the Mussert is not the N.S.B. Leader. It was Anton Mussert's brother *Overste* (Lt. Col.) Mussert who, although not a member of the N.S.B., was murdered "on suspicion by some of his fellow army officers in May 1940 during the height of the invasion panic. This cuff title was awarded, like the Peter Ton one above, as a name for a distinguished Vendel of the W.A.

HOLLAND (page 215)

The collar patch for Director General of the Police (shown on page 215) should be gold not silver. When this rank was in silver it was for the grade below this, namely the Chief of Staff of the National Police.

Some additional information on the Landwacht (pages 218-221) may be of interest. Early in September 1944 the liberating allied armies were in the south of Holland and it looked very much as though the whole of the country would soon be cleared of the Germans (as it turned out, this was not to be so and the rest of the Netherlands had to wait until May 1945 before being freed). However, so great was the panic among N.S.B. supporters that some 65,000 attempted to flee to Germany. The Germans said they would provide 25 special trains for this evacuation, but there was a catch. Only the wives and children could go, the men would have to join the Landwacht. Thus, by October 1944 the Landwacht was able to increase its strength to 5,700 with a further 2,-000 in the Hulp-Landwacht.

Mussert tried to expel from the party those who had fled during the September panic. He succeeded in getting rid of Rost van Tonningen in this way (he joined the Landstorm Nederland). The leader of the Dutch (Germanic) S.S., "Henk" Feldmeyer, was killed in action on 22 February 1945.

One Dutch unit not inluded in Vol. 2 was the S.S. Bau-Einsatz Ost (S.S. Construction Unit East). Dutchmen in this formation wore field grey with plain black collar patches. On the left upper arm, in place of the S.S. eagle, they wore the badge here illustrated - the word NEDERLAND within a wreath of oak leaves (white cotton on black). As their headgear they wore a forage cap with the S.S. eagle and swastika above a death's head. They were employed on the construction of military bunkers, airfields, etc., mainly in the Caucasus. They were sent as S.S. Frontarbeiter to Russia under the command of the S.S. Wirtschaftshauptamt in arrangement with the firm of Furnier Beton A.G./Berlin representing Dutch building constructors.

ITALY (pages 240-245)

Flag of the Italian S.S. The flag party are in Italian uniform with black S.S. collar patches.

In a recently published book, *"Uniformi e distintivi dell'esercito italiano, 1933'1945"* by Paolo Marzetti, the badge illustrated is attributed to Italian Waffen S.S. troops. This is somewhat similar to the collar patch badge shown on page 244. It has been suggested that these badges may have derived from that of the *Frecce Rosse* (Red Arrows) group of the Italian army, the "arrows" being a commemorative device in honor of the fact that many of its members had fought with the Italian volunteers on Franco's side during the Spanish Civil War.

Standschützen Collar Patches:

Right collar patch with Battalion and Company numerals

Gruppenführer

Zugführer

Kompanieführer

Bataillionführer

Signor Marco Pennisi of Vincenzi (Italy) adds the following to the information on "Police and Local Security Units" (in Northern Italy) contained in Vol. 2 (pages 247/8).

Although the Standschützen wore a diversity of uniforms and collar insignia, the correct system of ranks was as follows (on lime-green patches of the same dimensions as those of the S.S.):

Gruppenführer (Squad leader): 1 star
Zugführer (roughly Sgt-Major): 2 stars
Kompanieführer (roughly 1st Lt.): 3 stars
Bataillionführer (roughly Major): 4 stars.

This is the same type of ranking as in the Volkssturm in the Reich. The nomenclature is also the same, the only differences being that in the Volkssturm the collar patches were black and rank was worn on both collars, while in the Standschützen they were green and rank appeared only on the left collar. The right collar patch featured the battalion number (in Latin numerals) and the company number (in Arabic), the two being separated by an oblique bar.

In addition to the German/Italian formations listed in the above-mentioned section of Vol. 2, the following security units were also known to have existed:

(i) *Corpo di Sicurezza Trentino,* or CST (Security Corps of Trento - a town in the South Tirol). This had a strength of some 1,000 men.

(ii) *Hilfspolizei ("Hipo")* Companies *(Kompanien),* Battalions *(Bataillonen)* and Regiments. These auxiliary police units were formed from Italians (still in Italian uniform) distinguished only by an armlet with the German word "POLIZEI."

(iii) *Landschutzen Bataillonen.* There were five of these in the Istria region, one in each of the main towns: Trieste, Udine, Gorizia, Fiume, and Pola (these last two are now part of Yugoslavia, but were then Italian). Each battalion had around 1,000 men.

(iv) *Battaglione Lavoratori "Novara."* (The Novara Workers Battalion) formed from Italian O.T. workers and others in the autumn of 1943, but disbanded in December of the same year and its personnel dispersed among existing German/Italian S.S. and Police security formations or sent to man the Flak defences of northern Italy and southern Germany.

SPAIN (page 267)

Alain Taugourdeau

On page 267 the upper two photographs show an arm shield in the Spanish colors with an Iron Cross and the Falangist arrows in the center. The author suggested that this was possibly a version worn only by veterans on their return to Spain, but he has recently been given a photograph (above) which clearly shows this version of the shield being worn on German uniform. As the man further from the camera appears to wear the more usual type of arm shield (without the Iron Cross and arrows) it would appear that both types were worn concurrently.

On page 270 it was suggested that there was some confusion over who commanded the Spanish S.S. Volunteer Battalion. Two names were mentioned: Miguel Sanchez and Miguel Ezquerra. In fact, this was one and the same person, his full name being Miguel Ezquerra Sanchez. He took his father's name, Ezquerra, and to this added (in formal usage only, according to Spanish custom) his mother)s name, Sanchez. The

Germans, obviously ignorant of Spanish practice in this regard, listed his as Miguel E. Sanchez (a form of name no Spaniard would use).

SWEDEN (page 272)

Post-war research has failed to establish the precise number of Swedes who served in the German forces, but it was probably in the region of 130, of whom perhaps 30 fell in action. There was certainly no "Swedish Legion" (although the Germans would have wished to create one) and no all-Swedish unit. The nearest approach to this was the 3rd Company of Reconnaissance *Abteilung* 11 (sometimes referred to as the *Swedenzug* "Sweden Company") of the S.S. "Nordland" Division. Swedes were scattered throughout the other sections of this division as well as being found in the supposedly all-Dutch 23rd S.S. Volunteer Panzer-Grenadier Division "Nederland" and the multi-national "Wiking" Division. At least eleven Swedes passed through the S.S. Officer Training School at Bad Tolz.

Officially, Sweden did not permit recruiting by belligerents within her neutral frontiers, and this was successfully upheld until the start of the campaign against the Soviet Union in June 1941; thereafter German pressure and Swedish anti-communist sentiment caused the government to turn a blind eye to clandestine recruitment by the German Legation in Stockholm and the German *Auslands Organisation*. Volunteers proceeded via occupied Norway to Germany. A supposedly "top secret" questionnaire was circulated among senior officers of the Swedish army seeking to discover how many would be prepared to serve actively in the German armed forces should this be made legal. The response was decidedly negative. Neither the Swedes nor the Germans sought to pursue the matter!

The Swedish government, however, took a less hard line with regard to enlistment by their nationals in the Finnish army. This occurred on a sufficient scale to allow for the creation of an all-Swedish battalion (the Hangö Battalion) within the 13th Infantry Regiment of the Finnish army. This saw action against the Soviets on the Svir Front. There was even an official "Finland Volunteers" department within the Swedish High Command.

Almost all the Swedish volunteers who served with the German forces did so in the Waffen S.S. (enlistments continued right up to February 1945). There are only two recorded instances of Swedes serving in other branches of Hitler's armed services. One was in the 3rd Panzer Division of the army, the other in the 8th Field Division of the Luftwaffe. Swedes (of the "Nordland" Division) served and died in the final defense of Berlin at the end of the war in Europe.

No Swede won a Knight's Cross, although one *(S.S. Obersturmführer* Hans-Gösta Pehrsson, company commander of the *Swedenzug)* was awarded the rare honor of an *Ehrenblattspange* (Roll of Honor Clasp) of the army in addition to the Iron Cross 1st and 2nd Class, the Wound Badge, and the Close Combat Clasp in Silver.